Pro Microsoft Speech Server 2007

Developing Speech Enabled Applications with .NET

Michael D. Dunn

Apress®

Pro Microsoft Speech Server 2007: Developing Speech Enabled Applications with .NET

Copyright © 2007 by Michael D. Dunn

ISBN-13: 978-1-59059-902-0

ISBN-10: 1-59059-902-0

Printed and bound in the United States of America 9 8 7 6 5 4 3 2 1

Trademarked names may appear in this book. Rather than use a trademark symbol with every occurrence of a trademarked name, we use the names only in an editorial fashion and to the benefit of the trademark owner, with no intention of infringement of the trademark.

Java™ and all Java-based marks are trademarks or registered trademarks of Sun Microsystems, Inc., in the US and other countries. Apress, Inc., is not affiliated with Sun Microsystems, Inc., and this book was written without endorsement from Sun Microsystems, Inc.

Lead Editor: Jonathan Hassell
Technical Reviewer: Jason Bock
Editorial Board: Steve Anglin, Ewan Buckingham, Gary Cornell, Jonathan Gennick, Jason Gilmore,
    Jonathan Hassell, Chris Mills, Matthew Moodie, Jeffrey Pepper, Ben Renow-Clarke,
    Dominic Shakeshaft, Matt Wade, Tom Welsh
Project Manager: Beth Christmas
Copy Edit Manager: Nicole Flores
Copy Editor: Marilyn Smith
Assistant Production Director: Kari Brooks-Copony
Production Editor: Katie Stence
Compositor: Susan Glinert
Proofreader: Linda Seifert
Indexer: Brenda Miller
Artist: April Milne
Cover Designer: Kurt Krames
Manufacturing Director: Tom Debolski

Distributed to the book trade worldwide by Springer-Verlag New York, Inc., 233 Spring Street, 6th Floor, New York, NY 10013. Phone 1-800-SPRINGER, fax 201-348-4505, e-mail orders-ny@springer-sbm.com, or visit http://www.springeronline.com.

For information on translations, please contact Apress directly at 2855 Telegraph Avenue, Suite 600, Berkeley, CA 94705. Phone 510-549-5930, fax 510-549-5939, e-mail info@apress.com, or visit http://www.apress.com.

Contents at a Glance

Contents

About the Author

 **MICHAEL DUNN** is a consultant for Magenic (www.magenic.com), a Microsoft-centric consulting firm based in Minneapolis. He is a Microsoft MVP for Microsoft Office Communications Server and a frequent speaker at user groups and conferences across the United States. In his free time, he can be found answering questions about Office Communications Server 2007 in the various MSDN newsgroups or blogging on GotSpeech.NET (www.gotspeech.net).

About the Technical Reviewer

JASON BOCK is a senior consultant for Magenic Technologies (www.magenic.com). He has worked on a number of business applications using a diverse set of substrates and languages such as C#, .NET, and Java. He is the author of *Applied .NET Attributes, CIL Programming: Under the Hood of .NET, .NET Security,* and *Visual Basic 6 Win32 API Tutorial.* He has written numerous articles on software development issues and has presented at a number of conferences and user groups. Jason holds a Master's degree in Electrical Engineering from Marquette University. Visit his web site at www.jasonbock.net.

Acknowledgments

First, I have to thank wife, Jaclyn, and my sons, Jadyn and Ashton, for allowing me to take the time to write this book. They have allowed me to miss family dinners and events so that I could concentrate on writing.

I'd also like to thank all of my coworkers at Magenic for being very supportive of my authoring of this book. I'd like to especially thank Frank Shink, my Consulting Manager, and Shari Brandt, Magenic's Marketing Director, for their continuing support and giving me the extra encouragement when I needed it most.

A big thank you goes out to the entire Apress team, all of whom have really impressed me with their professionalism and dedication to making this a great book. Thank you!

Finally I'd like to thank my father, Donald, just for always being there.

Introduction

This book covers the basic skills you will need to implement a solid interactive voice response (IVR) application using Office Communications Server 2007 Speech Server. You'll also find some general information about speech application development, such as voice user interface (VUI) design, which also applies to earlier Speech Server versions as well as other IVR platforms.

Here's a quick chapter-by-chapter summary of what you'll find in this book:

- *Getting Started with Microsoft OCS 2007 Speech Server*: The first chapter explains how to install Speech Server and use the Administrator Console.

- *Building Grammar*: Chapter 2 explores the different methods available for creating grammar for your applications and helps you decide which method to use to best suit your particular application's needs.

- *Building Prompts*: Chapter 3 covers VUI design concepts and how to create prompts for your application. You will learn the different techniques for getting responses from your application's users.

- *Creating SALT Applications*: In Chapter 4, you will learn how to create IVR applications using SALT and the SALT-based ASP.NET controls.

- *Creating VoiceXML Applications*: In Chapter 5, you will learn how to create VoiceXML applications. Although SALT and VoiceXML are rival standards, they are now both supported in Speech Server. You will be able to see the differences and similarities between the two standards.

- *Creating Voice Response Workflow Applications*: Chapter 6 covers a new method for creating IVR applications, called Voice Response Workflow, which is based on .NET Framework 3.0 Windows Workflow Foundation. Voice Response Workflow offers a highly time-efficient way to create IVR applications.

- *Creating Unified Communications and Messaging Applications*: In Chapter 7. You will learn how to create a unified messaging (UM) application using the Exchange 2007 Web Services API.

- *Speech Application Analysis and Tuning*: Chapter 8 wraps up the Speech Server coverage with logging and analysis. Microsoft has created a lot of new tools that allow you to easily review your logs, including logged audio, and to analyze how your application's grammar and prompts are performing.

- *Creating Speech Applications for Windows Vista*: The last chapter shows you how to create speech recognition applications using Windows Vista Speech Application Interface (SAPI) 5.3. This API is very similar to the Speech Server API and uses the same standards for grammar and prompts as used by Speech Server.

To follow the examples in this book, you will need Office Communications Server 2007 Speech Server beta or higher, along with Microsoft Visual Studio 2005 and all of the prerequisites described in Chapter 1. If you are planning to use any of the logging and reporting tools covered in this book, you will need SQL Server 2005 Express or higher installed.

I am always personally available if you have any questions on the content of this book or questions about Speech Server itself. You can reach me via my blog at www.gotspeech.net or via email at michaeldu@magenic.com.

■■■

Getting Started with Microsoft OCS 2007 Speech Server

Microsoft Office Communications Server (OCS) 2007 Speech Server is an optional component of OCS 2007, the successor of Live Communications Server. The Speech Server component is the successor of Microsoft Speech Server 2004, a stand-alone product. The Speech Server component can be installed separately from OCS 2007, from the OCS installation media. In this book, I will first cover how to create telephony applications using Speech Server separately, and then explain why the merging of these two products makes sense.

This chapter begins with an overview of Speech Server, including the new features of this version and how it works. Then you will learn how to install and configure Speech Server.

OCS 2007 Speech Server Overview

Speech Server is an interactive voice response (IVR) platform that integrates with Visual Studio 2005.

Speech Server provides tools for developing applications that run over a telephone, or *telephony applications*. For example, telephony applications let you check your bank balance via a telephone or get an automated call from your doctor's office reminding you of your next appointment. Speech Server is to a telephony application what a web server such as Internet Information Services (IIS) is to a web application.

Speech Server applications can have the following capabilities:

- Speech recognition allows users to respond to application prompts.

- Touch-Tone capabilities, called dual-tone multi-frequency (DTMF), let users respond to application prompts via the telephone keypad.

- Text-to-speech (TTS) capabilities allow applications to read and speak written text to users.

New Features of OCS 2007 Speech Server

As I noted at the beginning of this chapter, the Speech Server component of OCS 2007 is the successor to Microsoft Speech Server 2004. The new version offers a lot of additional features, including Voice over Internet Protocol (VoIP) support, new project types, and more tools.

VoIP Support

One of the more exciting new features of Speech Server is its native support for VoIP. VoIP basically allows users to place and receive calls over the Internet. Speech Server can accept VoIP calls without any additional software or hardware.

Project Types

Microsoft Speech Server 2004 supported only Speech Application Language Tags (SALT). The new version supports three types of projects:

- *SALT*: A World Wide Web Consortium (W3C) standard language for speech over the Web and telephone. It runs on top of ASP.NET pages.

- *VoiceXML*: VoiceXML follows the same web-based paradigm as its rival standard, SALT, also running on top of ASP.NET pages. You can now convert your current VoiceXML-based IVR application to Speech Server without a lot of coding changes.

- *Voice Response Workflow*: If you do not want to follow the web paradigm, you have a new alternative: Voice Response Workflow applications. This project type is based on Windows Workflow Foundation (WF). Unlike SALT and VoiceXML, Voice Response Workflow allows you to see your application's call flow.

If you are creating new IVR applications, Voice Response Workflow is highly recommended over SALT or VoiceXML, as all IVR applications generally follow a workflow. If you want to incorporate a SALT or VoiceXML page within a Voice Response Workflow application, you can do this with the SALT and VoiceXML interpreter controls, as you'll learn in Chapter 6.

New Tools

Several new tools are available with OCS 2007 Speech Server:

Conversational Grammar Builder and Grammar Design Advisor: The Conversational Grammar Builder allows you to easily and rapidly build grammar in a natural conversational flow. You still have the options of building your grammar either by writing your own Grammar XML (GRXML) or the Visual Studio Grammar Editor. Debugging support for your grammar has also been added, along with the Grammar Design Advisor, which provides warnings about possible incorrect grammar when you are compiling. Chapter 2 discusses grammar and grammar building.

Lexicon Editor: The Lexicon Editor allows you to add or change the pronunciation of words for the Conversational Grammar Builder, which affects how the Speech Recognizer Engine recognizes audio input from the user. This editor is discussed in Chapter 2.

Pronunciation Editor: Like the Lexicon Editor, the Pronunciation Editor allows you to add or change the pronunciation of words. However, this editor applies only to the Grammar Editor's grammar. The Pronunciation Editor is also covered in Chapter 2.

Analysis and tuning: The new analysis and tuning tools allow you to view details about your speech application, such as user responses that did not have a matching grammar. This will help you in making decisions for improving your speech application. Chapter 8 covers analyzing and tuning applications.

Business Intelligence Tools: If you have high call volume, you might want to consider installing the Business Intelligence Tools. These tools allow you to create SQL Server Integration Services (SSIS) packages in SQL Server 2005, for activities such as creating an online analytical processing (OLAP) cube. These tools are installed separately from Speech Server. You can install them from the Business Intelligence Tools directory of the OCS 2007 installation media.

How Speech Server Works

Speech Server has two main components: Speech Engine Services and ASP.NET. While IIS isn't technically a part of Speech Server, it plays a vital role in its architecture. Figure 1-1 shows a conceptual overview of how Speech Server works with other servers and with Visual Studio.

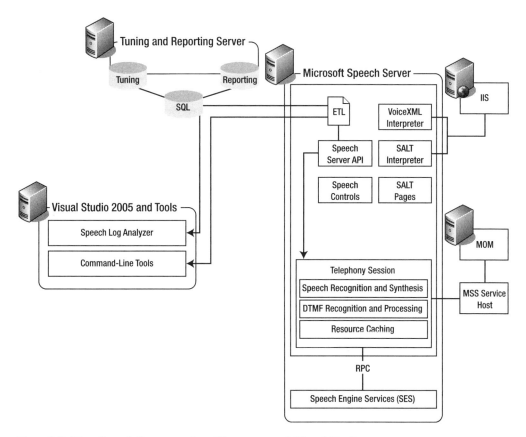

Figure 1-1. *How Speech Server works with servers and Visual Studio*

Speech Recognition and Speech Synthesis

Speech Engine Services (SES) has two main components: the Speech Recognizer Engine and the Speech Synthesis Engine.

The Speech Recognizer Engine produces an XML document in Semantic Markup Language (SML). This SML document contains the words or phrases the Speech Recognizer Engine recognizes and a numerical value for how confident it is that the user has said the word or phrase, based on the application's defined grammar. SML is discussed in Chapter 2.

The Speech Synthesis Engine, also known as the TTS engine, produces audio based on an XML document in Speech Synthesis Markup Language (SSML). The SSML document contains the text that the Speech Synthesis Engine will say. Before the Speech Synthesis Engine speaks, it checks the Prompt Engine. If the Prompt Engine contains the phrase or word that the Speech Synthesis Engine should say, it will play the associated prerecorded prompt instead of using the TTS engine. SSML is discussed in Chapter 3.

Client Connections

As noted earlier, Speech Server supports VoIP for telephone calls over the Internet. The underlying protocol that makes native VoIP support for Speech Server possible is Session Initiation Protocol (SIP).

For communications, first a client, such as Office Communicator, registers with an SIP server—in this case, OCS 2007—giving the SIP server certain data, such as its location, IP address, and the protocol it supports. When a user wants to place a call to another registered user, an INVITE message is sent to the registered user, based on the data that client gave the SIP server when it registered. Once the client accepts the INVITE, the two clients can communicate. The reason for the INVITE is that a client can be registered at multiple locations, such as a mobile device and a computer. The first location to accept the INVITE will receive subsequent messages.

If your network does not currently support VoIP, you will need to use the more traditional setup (as was the case with Speech Server 2004): a telephony card and the associated Telephone Interface Manager (TIM) software. Speech Server provides backward compatibility via the Telephony Interface Service (TIS), which serves as an interface between your TIM and the telephony application proxy (TAP). The TAP acts very much like a SIP redirect server, as it interprets requests to and from the TIS and other SIP peers, and routes them to the appropriate server.

Figure 1-2 shows a conceptual overview of how Speech Server works with client connections.

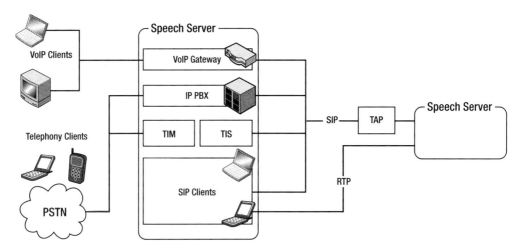

Figure 1-2. *How Speech Server works with client connections*

TELEPHONY APPLICATION ACRONYMS

The following are common acronyms you'll come across when working with telephony applications:

- *DTMF*: Dual-tone multi-frequency. Refers to Touch-Tone on a standard telephone.

- *IVR*: Interactive voice response. An automated telephone system with speech recognition capabilities.

- *PBX*: Private branch exchange. Allows for private companies to control their telephone lines inside their buildings, instead of having private telephone numbers for each extension.

- *PSTN*: Public switched telephone network. Provides access to outside telephone lines.

- *RTP*: Real-time Transport Protocol. A common protocol that allows real-time video and audio over User Datagram Protocol (UDP) transport.

- *SALT*: Speech Application Language Tags. A World Wide Web Consortium (W3C) standard language for generating speech over the Web and telephone.

- *SIP*: Session Initiation Protocol. A protocol to initiate VoIP and instant messaging (IM) sessions.

- *TIM*: Telephony Interface Manager. Provides an interface between a telephony board and Microsoft Speech Server.

- *TTS*: Text-to-speech. An automated component that turns text into speech, essentially reading text.

- *VoIP*: Voice over Internet Protocol. A protocol to carry telephone calls over an IP network, such as the Internet.

- *VUI*: Voice user interface. Describes an IVR application's presentation layer, similar to a graphic user interface (GUI) for a visual application.

Speech Server Installation

Speech Server requires certain hardware and software to run properly. Before proceeding with the installation, make sure that your system meets these requirements. If this is your first time using Speech Server, you should do an installation in a development environment before installing it in a production environment.

■**Caution** OCS 2007 Speech Server cannot run on the same machine as Microsoft Speech Server 2004. You must first uninstall Microsoft Speech Server 2004.

Installation Requirements

Speech Server can run under the following Microsoft operating systems:

- Windows XP Professional Service Pack (SP) 2

- Windows Vista Business, Enterprise, and Ultimate

- Microsoft Windows Server 2003 Standard Edition and Enterprise Edition

---

■**Caution**   The Telephony Interface Manager Connector component is supported only on the server versions of Windows. It will not run on the client versions, such as Windows XP.

The system on which you install Speech Server determines which edition you are installing. For example, if you install it on a client operating system such as Windows XP, you are essentially installing a developer version, which is limited to two simultaneous connections.

Hardware Requirements

Speech Server has different hardware requirements depending on which edition you have installed, as shown in Table 1-1.

Table 1-1. *Microsoft Speech Server Hardware Requirements*

Hardware	Developer Edition	Server Edition
Processor	One 2.5GHz or faster	Two 2.5GHz or faster
Memory	1GB	4GB
Hard drive	3.5GB available for installation; 5GB minimum	3.5GB available for installation; 20GB minimum
Network interface card	Required	Required
Telephony board	Not required (only one per server supported)	Required for systems without VoIP (one per server supported)
Microphone	High-quality universal serial bus (USB) microphone (recommended)	High-quality universal serial bus (USB) (recommended)
Sound card	Recommended	Recommended

For a list of supported TDM and VoIP hardware, visit the Microsoft Speech Server web site, www.microsoft.com/speech/partners/default.mspx.

Software Requirements

The following are the software prerequisites for Speech Server, listed in the recommended order in which they should be installed:

- IIS

- Microsoft Message Queuing (MSMQ)

- Microsoft .NET Framework 3.0

- Visual Studio 2005 with SP1

- Visual Studio Extensions for Windows Workflow Foundation

■**Note** If you are installing Speech Server in your production environment, you do not need to install Visual Studio 2005 or the Visual Studio Extensions for Windows Workflow Foundation.

Installing Speech Server Components

The first step to installing Speech Server is running the setup.exe file from the installation media. After choosing Install, you must enter your user information and product key, and then accept the terms of the End User License Agreement (EULA) to continue the installation.

■**Tip** You should read the product release notes before installing any application. This file may contain directions or warnings pertaining to your particular setup.

Next, select the components you wish to install, as shown in Figure 1-3. If you are installing the 32-bit version, you can also select to install the Telephony Interface Manager Connector component, if a telephony board and the TIM are already installed on your system. Note that if you are using a VoIP-based setup, you do not need to install the Telephony Interface Manager Connector component.

Production machines must have the Server Components installed, and the Administrative Tools are recommended as well. You do not need to install the Development Tools or the Documentation on production machines. This book focuses on the development areas, including the Data Processing Utilities.

After you select and confirm the components, the Installation Wizard will install Speech Server.

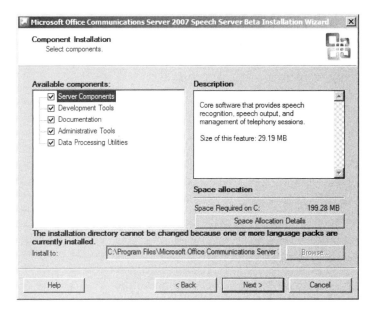

Figure 1-3. *Choosing Speech Server components to install*

When the component installation is complete, you will need to install a language pack. The language packs can be found on your installation media, in the language pack directory. Currently, the following language packs are available:

- English (United States)
- English (United Kingdom)
- German
- French
- Spanish

These language packs provide the necessary support for the language(s) your applications will be speaking. You must install the English (United States) language pack. If your application will support multiple languages, you will need to install all applicable language packs.

Configuring Speech Server

After installation, you may need to configure some components depending on your setup:

- If you have multiple servers, you may want to set up deployment groups. This will allow you to manage settings for every server in one spot.
- If you are using VoIP, you will need to set up the SIP peers before Speech Server will accept any calls from your VoIP gateway.

You perform most Speech Server configuration and management tasks through the Administrator Console. To open the Administrator Console, select Start ➤ Programs ➤ Microsoft Office Communications Server 2007 Speech Server. The Administrator Console is divided into two panes: the left pane lists nodes for Servers, Applications, and SIP Peers, and the right pane shows a details view of the selected node.

Setting Up Deployment Groups

Deployment groups allow you to easily manage multiple servers at the same time, so you don't need to adjust settings for each individual server. You can also copy settings from a server to the other servers in the same group.

Adding a Deployment Group

You can set up deployment groups through the Administrator Console, as follows:

1. Select Start ➤ Programs ➤ Microsoft Office Communications Server 2007 Speech Server to open the Administrator Console.

2. To create a new group, right-click the topmost node and choose New Group. You will be prompted to enter the name of the group you wish to add.

3. To add servers to the deployment group, right-click the Servers node in your deployment group and choose Add Server. You will be prompted to enter the servers' names, as shown in Figure 1-4.

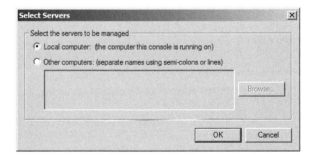

Figure 1-4. *Adding servers to a deployment group*

Copying Server Settings

After you have added multiple servers to the same deployment group, you can copy server settings to all of these servers. This is useful when you have a distributed deployment model for your production environment, as you do not need to manually change the settings for each group.

To copy the server settings to the group, select the Servers node in the Administrator Console, and then click the Copy Server Settings to Group link, as shown in Figure 1-5. You will be prompted for which settings you want to copy. As shown in Figure 1-6, you can copy the properties, application settings, and the trusted SIP peers.

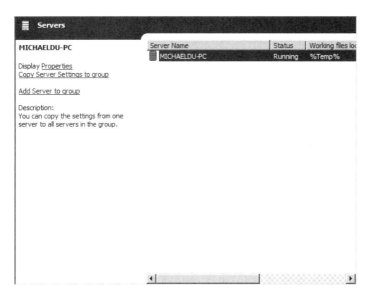

Figure 1-5. *Viewing your servers*

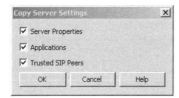

Figure 1-6. *Copying server settings*

Setting Up SIP Peers

For Speech Server to accept or place phone calls, you need to first set up a SIP peer. SIP peer configuration is done through the Administrator Console.

Adding a New SIP Peer

To create a new SIP peer, open the Administrator Console, right-click the SIP Peers node, and choose New ➤ SIP Peer, as shown in Figure 1-7. You will be prompted to enter information about the SIP peer, as shown in Figure 1-8.

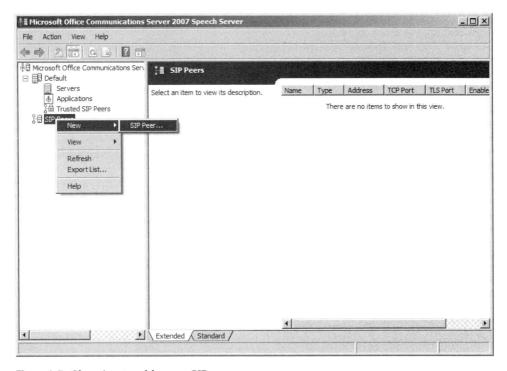

Figure 1-7. *Choosing to add a new SIP peer*

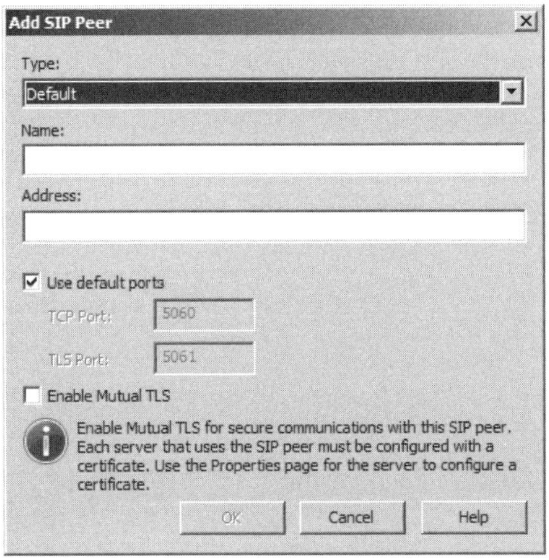

Figure 1-8. *The Add SIP Peer dialog box*

The Add SIP dialog box has three fields:

- *Type*: The drop-down list has the choices Default and TIS. Default describes VoIP gateways, IP PBXs, and SIP clients. TIS describes your traditional telephony card and TIM.

- *Name*: Enter a name that is descriptive enough for you to recognize it from a list of other SIP peers.

- *Address*: Enter either the host name or IP address of the SIP peer.

You also have the option of changing the default ports and enabling Mutual Transport Layer Security (TLS) for secure communications.

After you click OK, the SIP peer will be added to the details view (the right pane) of the SIP Peers node.

Adding a Trusted SIP Peer

If your application will be making outbound calls or transfers through this SIP peer, you will need to identify it as a trusted SIP peer. The SIP peer must be added, as described in the previous section, before it can be set up as a trusted SIP peer.

To add a trusted SIP peer, right-click the Trusted SIP Peers node in the Administrator Console and choose New ➤ Trusted SIP Peer. You will be prompted to choose which SIP peer to trust. You can enable and disable outbound and transfer calls after selecting the SIP peer, as shown in Figure 1-9.

■**Note** You can change only the Allow Transfers and Allow Outbound Calls options in the Add Trusted SIP Peer dialog box. Any other properties must be changed from the SIP Peers node, rather than from the Trusted SIP Peers node.

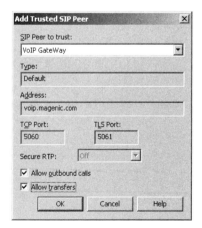

Figure 1-9. *Adding a trusted SIP peer*

You can optionally enable Secure RTP (SRTP) for standard SIP peers. SRTP is not available for TIS type peers. After you click OK, the SIP peer will be listed in the details view of the Trusted SIP Peers node.

Installing Applications in a Production Environment

If you are migrating applications from Microsoft Speech Server 2004, you will need to install your applications on the Speech Server Administrator Console before they will run in a production environment. And, of course, once you have developed and deployed your application, you will need to install it in your production environment via the Administrator Console. Development and deployment are discussed in the following chapters. This section covers only the installation of your application on the server.

Adding a New Application

To add a new application, open the Administrator Console (select Start ➤ Programs ➤ Microsoft Office Communications Server 2007 Speech Server), right-click the Applications node, and choose New Application. You will be prompted to enter information about your application, as shown in Figure 1-10.

Figure 1-10. *Creating a new application*

The Create New Application dialog box has the following fields:

- *Application Name*: Enter a name that is descriptive enough to be picked out of a list, so that you can find your application easily.

- *Application Type*: The drop-down list contains three choices: Voice Response Workflow Application, SALT, and VoiceXML. This represents your application's programming model.

■**Note** If your application is a Voice Response Workflow type, the application must be deployed to the IIS instance on which Speech Server is installed. SALT and VoiceXML applications may be deployed on remote machines.

- *URL*: Enter the URL where your application is hosted.

- *Deployment Location*: Enter the directory where the source of your application is located.

- *Manifest*: Optionally, enter the relative path to the manifest XML file for your application that contains the grammars and prompts to preload.

- *Message Queue*: For outbound calling applications, this should reference the queue in MSMQ that is to be used for outbound calling. The next section explains how to configure your application for outbound calling.

After you click OK, your application will be added to the Applications node in the Administrator Console.

Setting Call Answering Precedence

Speech Server allows you to set call answering precedence, which lets applications with the same phone number determine which application the user is trying to call.

When you select the Applications node in the Administrator Console, you will see the list of installed applications in the details view, along with Set Call Answering Precedence link. Click the link to open the Call Answering Precedence dialog box.

Figure 1-11 shows an example of setting call answering precedence. In the example, the Employee Application has precedence over the Customer Application, simply because it is at the top of the list. The Customer Application uses the wildcard, *, in its phone number. This means all calls to any number will go to the Customer Application. However, since the Employee Application has precedence over the Customer Application, it is evaluated first. Therefore, if the number called is 555-1212, it will go to the Employee Application and calls to any other number will be forwarded to the Customer Application.

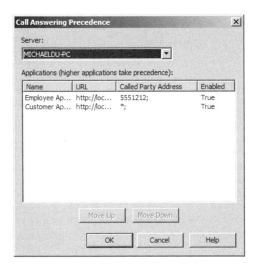

Figure 1-11. *Setting call answering precedence*

Setting Up Outbound Calling for an Application

To allow your application to place outbound calls, you need to first enable outbound calling on the Speech Server application by entering the name of the queue in the Message Queue field of the Create New Application dialog box, as described in the previous section. Then you need to do the following:

- Create a message queue in MSMQ.

- Change security to allow Speech Server access to the queue.

Creating a New Message Queue

To create the message queue, from the Windows Control Panel, open Administrative Tools, and then Computer Management. Under the Services and Applications node, you will find the Message Queuing node. Expand that node, as shown in Figure 1-12.

Right-click Private Queues and click New ➤ Private Queue. You will be prompted for the name of the new queue, as shown in Figure 1-13. Enter the same name as you supplied in the Message Queue field of the Create New Application dialog box, as described in the previous section. (Speech Server does not currently support transactional queuing, so leave the Transactional option unchecked.)

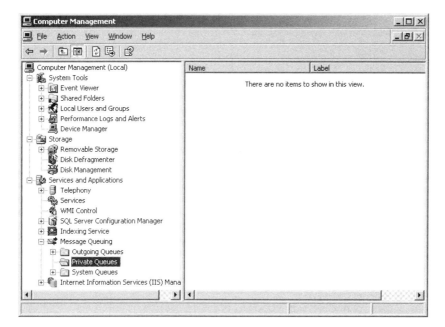

Figure 1-12. *Navigating to Message Queuing*

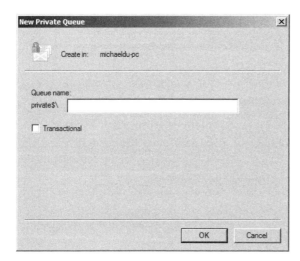

Figure 1-13. *Creating a new queue*

■**Note** To avoid any problems, double-check to make sure the new queue has the same name as the queue for the application it will be serving. This is the name you entered in the Message Queue field when you set up your new application (see Figure 1-10).

Setting Up Queue Security

After creating the queue, you need to set up security for the queue so that Speech Server can access it. Right-click the newly created queue and choose Properties. In the Properties dialog box, choose the Security tab, as shown in Figure 1-14.

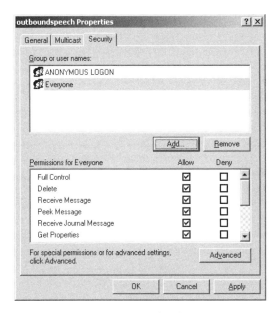

Figure 1-14. *Setting security for the message queue*

Click the Add button, and type **Network Service** in the Names to Select field. After you click OK, Network Service will be listed in the Groups or User Names list. Select Network Service and check the Allow boxes for Peek Message and Receive Message in the Permissions list. Clicking OK completes your queue setup.

Conclusion

This chapter provided an overview of OCS 2007 Speech Server, including the new features available in this version and a summary of how it works. Then you learned the basics of installing and configuring Speech Server. Installation is very important to get correct the first time, as it can be time-consuming to go back and fix a Speech Server installation.

The following chapters will walk you through each step of creating an IVR application. One of the first steps in your IVR application development should be building grammar, and that is the topic of the next chapter.

CHAPTER 2

■■■

Building Grammar

For an application to recognize speech, it needs to know which words and phrases to expect. Building grammar involves compiling lists of predicted user responses to specific prompts. Creating grammar doesn't necessarily have to be the very first step in creating an IVR application, but it certainly should be done early in the development process.

Grammar is stored in a W3C-compliant format called Speech Recognition Grammar Specification (SRGS), specifically in an XML format known as Grammar XML (GRXML). The uncompiled format is stored with a `.grxml` file extension, and the compiled format is stored with a `.cfg` file extension. When speech from grammar is recognized, it produces the results in an XML format called Semantic Markup Language (SML).

When developing an IVR application, building grammar is the most time-consuming piece. It will take more time than writing the application itself. Fortunately, Speech Server offers a couple GUI tools to ease the process and save you some time: the Conversational Grammar Builder and the Grammar Editor. Both tools support keyword grammar, but only the Grammar Builder supports conversational grammar. Speech Server also provides several other utilities to aid in grammar building, including the Semantic Script Builder, Lexicon Editor, and Pronunciation Editor. In this chapter, you'll learn how to use each of these tools, as well as how to build grammar manually, by writing your own GRXML, and dynamically, based on existing data in a database.

Using the Conversational Grammar Builder

Let's suppose that your client, ABC Company, wants an IVR application to direct users to the Sales or the Support department, depending on their needs. ABC Company sells three products: widgets, gadgets, and sprockets. The Sales department can deal with all products; the Support department is divided into three groups that handle each product individually. The application will first ask the user, "Which department would you like to speak to: Sales or Support?" Then it will ask the user, "Which product are you calling about?" You need to build grammar to support answers to these questions. The Support department is sometimes called the *help desk*, and the sprocket product is sometimes referred to as a *gear*, so the application should also listen for these alternatives.

The Conversational Grammar Builder allows you to build simple grammars quickly and easily. It supports both keyword grammar and conversational grammar. First, you'll see how to build keyword grammar for the sample application, and then you'll work through another version using conversational grammar.

Building Keyword Grammar

Keyword grammars are single words or short phrases that the application will recognize. With the Conversational Grammar Builder, they are easy to construct.

To start building your grammar, first add a Conversational Grammar file to your Visual Studio project. Right-click the project in the Solution Explorer, choose Add New Item, and select Conversational Grammar File from the Templates list, as shown in Figure 2-1.

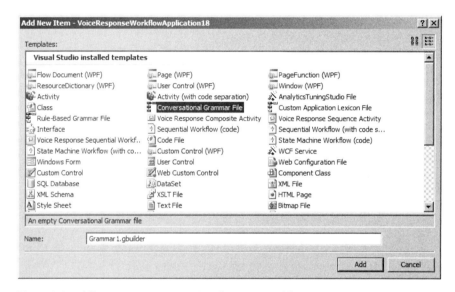

Figure 2-1. *Adding a new Conversational Grammar file*

When you open the Conversational Grammar file in Visual Studio, it appears in the Conversational Grammar Builder, as shown in Figure 2-2. The Conversational Grammar Builder has two main areas: Keywords and Answers. Keywords are the words or phrases that you want the application to recognize. Answers are the possible responses that the user might say to trigger recognition.

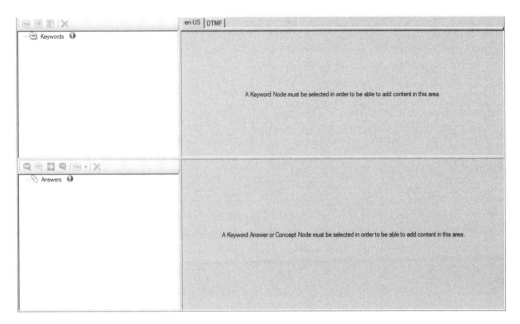

Figure 2-2. *The Conversational Grammar Builder*

Setting Up Keywords

To begin, you need to set up the application's keywords to the Keywords pane. This involves the following steps:

- Create keyword containers. A keyword container should be created for each of your application's prompts.

- Add keywords to the keyword containers. A keyword represents a group of phrases, and should be named according to how you want the results returned.

- Add keyword phrases to the keywords. The keyword phrases represent each individual word a user can say to return the keyword.

For this example, you want to ask the user "Which department would you like: Sales or Support?" and then ask the user "What product are you calling about?" So, you need to create two keyword containers to represent each prompt.

To add a keyword container, right-click the Keyword node and choose Add Keyword Container, as shown in Figure 2-3. Add one container named **Department** and another named **Product**.

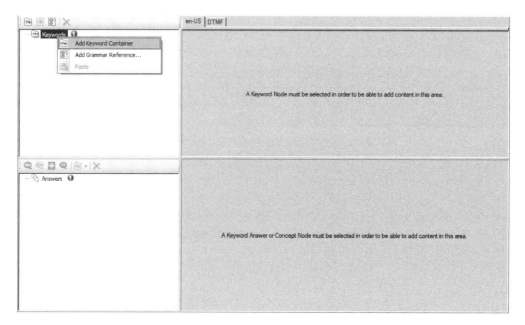

Figure 2-3. *Creating a keyword container*

Next, you need to create keywords for each of the keyword containers. The keywords are actually just another grouping for the possible individual answers a user could give, rather than the actual words users can say.

To add a keyword, right-click the keyword container name and choose Add Keyword, as shown in Figure 2-4. For the Department keyword container, add keywords for the two possible departments: **Sales** and **Support**. For the Product keyword container, add keywords for each of the three products: **Widget**, **Gadget**, and **Sprocket**.

Now it's time to add keyword phrases for each of your keywords. Keyword phrases are any specific words you want the application to recognize for a keyword. They represent the individual answers that the user can say for a given prompt. You can add synonyms for words to handle alternative answers to prompts.

To add keyword phrases, select the keyword you added, right-click in the details pane (the right pane), and choose Add Keyword Phrase, as shown in Figure 2-5. In the Department container, for the Sales keyword, add the phrase **Sales**. For Support, add two phrases: **Support** and **Help Desk**. In the Product container, add the product names as keyword phrases under their respective keywords: **Widget**, **Gadget**, and **Sprocket**. Additionally, for the Sprocket keyword, add the phrase **Gear**. Table 2-1 summarizes the setup you should now have in the Keywords section of the Conversational Grammar Builder.

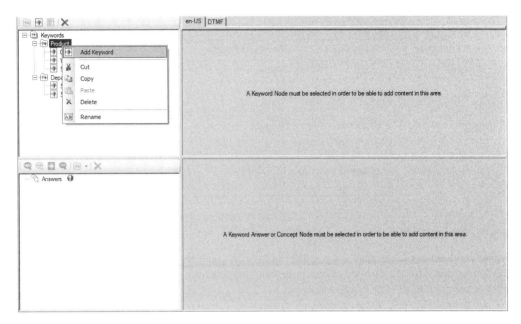

Figure 2-4. *Creating keywords*

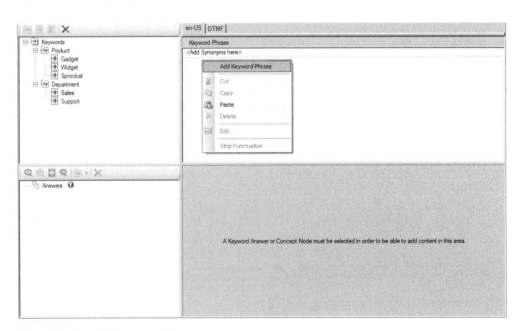

Figure 2-5. *Creating keyword phrases*

Table 2-1. *Keywords Structure for the Example*

Keyword Container	Keyword	Keyword Phrase
Department	Sales	Sales
	Support	Support Help Desk
Product	Widget	Widget
	Gadget	Gadget
	Sprocket	Sprocket Gear

Setting Up Answers

Now that you have created all the possible keywords, you need to set up the answers in the Answers pane. The answers will contain the exact phrases the user can say to trigger recognition. This involves the following steps:

- Create keyword answers. A keyword answer container should be created for each of your keyword containers.

- Add keyword references to the answer nodes. A keyword reference associates the answer node with its corresponding keyword node.

- Add answer phrases to the answer nodes. The answer phrases represent the user responses the application will recognize.

- Parse the response for each answer node. This will allow the user to say the name of any keyword in the keyword list for that node, and the grammar will recognize it.

You need to create a keyword answer container for each prompt. To add a new keyword answer container, right-click the Answers node and choose Add Keyword Answer, as shown in Figure 2-6. Add an answer named **ProductAnswer** and another named **DepartmentAnswer**.

You add references so that you need to type a phrase only one time for the container, instead of one time for each keyword. For example, after adding a reference to the Department container, you can just add the response, "I'm calling about a widget" to the DepartmentAnswer node. Because the keyword Widget belongs to the referenced keyword container, it can be replaced automatically by any other keyword in that container. That means the responses "I'm calling about a sprocket" and "I'm calling about a gadget" are automatically covered as well.

To add a keyword reference, right-click the answer node, choose Add Keyword Reference, and then choose the corresponding keyword container, as shown in Figure 2-7. For the example, add a reference to the Product keyword container for the ProductAnswer node, and a reference to the Department keyword container for the DepartmentAnswer node.

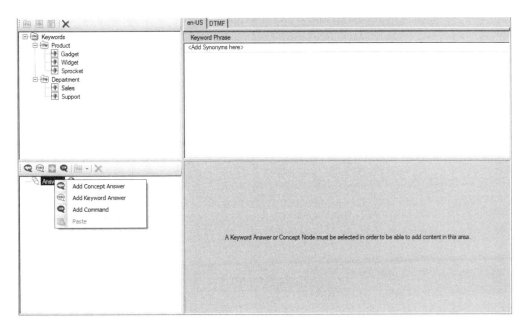

Figure 2-6. *Adding keyword answers*

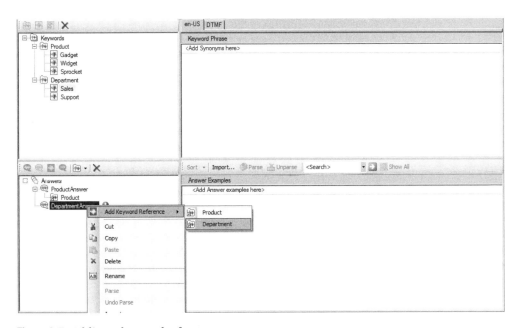

Figure 2-7. *Adding a keyword reference*

To add answer phrases, right-click in the Answer Examples pane and choose Add Answer Phrase. Add the following answer phrases for the ProductAnswer node:

- Widget

- I'm calling about a Widget

- A Widget

Then add the following answer phrases to the DepartmentAnswer node, as shown in Figure 2-8:

- I would like to talk to Sales

- Sales

- Transfer me to Sales

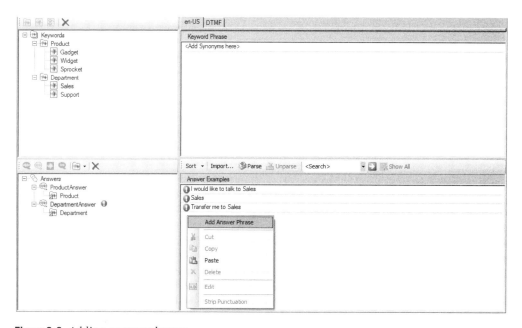

Figure 2-8. *Adding answer phrases*

Finally, you need to parse the answers for each answer node. This will work with your references to allow the user to say the name of any department in your keyword list and the grammar will recognize it. For example, a user could say "Support" in place of "Sales" in the answer phrase, because Sales and Support belong to the same keyword container, which was referenced by the DepartmentAnswer answer.

To parse the answers, select each answer node and click the Parse button on the toolbar above the Answer Examples pane.

Now that you've seen how to build a simple keyword grammar, let's take a look at building conversational grammar.

Building Conversational Grammar

The Conversational Grammar Builder also allows Speech Server to support natural language, also known as How May I Help You (HMIHY) grammar and conversational grammar. Natural language lets users answer an open-ended question without limiting how they can respond. For example, your application can ask a question like, "What can I help you with today?" and direct users based on their response. If the user were to answer, "I need my bank account balance" or "How much money is in my account?" the application would recognize that as a request for an account balance and would direct the user to that area of the application.

■**Note** While natural language can be beneficial, it takes substantial work to create all the appropriate grammar. Not all applications will benefit significantly from natural language, and you should take this into account when designing your IVR application.

Natural language is great when users may not know what they should do. For example, in the sample application introduced in the previous section, ABC Company customers may not know whether they should speak to the Sales department or the Support department. Natural language allows your application to ask, "How may I help you" and the user can respond, "I would like to buy a widget." The application would then direct the user to the Sales department.

To build conversational grammar with the Conversational Grammar Builder, you use *concept answers*, which tell the application how to proceed based on the user's response. Let's revisit the ABC Company application and build a conversational grammar for it this time.

Adding Keywords

To start building the natural language for this application, add a keyword container named **Product** with three keywords representing each product—**Widget**, **Gadget**, and **Sprocket**—just as you did in the previous example. For each keyword, add the product name as the keyword phrases, plus the additional phrase **Gear** for the Sprocket keyword (see Table 2-1).

This example has the single Product keyword container. Do not create a Department keyword container, as you did in the previous example.

Creating a Concept Answer

Rather than creating keywords to figure out which department the user wants, you will use a concept answer to determine the correct department based on the user's response. For example, if the user says "I would like to buy a gadget," you can reasonably assume that the user needs to talk to the Sales department, not the Support department. This involves the following steps:

- Create a concept answer.

- Add concepts to the concept answer.

- Add answer phrases to the concepts.

- Add keyword references to the concepts.

- Parse the responses.

To add a concept answer, right-click the Answer node and choose Add Concept Answer, as shown in Figure 2-9. Name the concept answer **Department**.

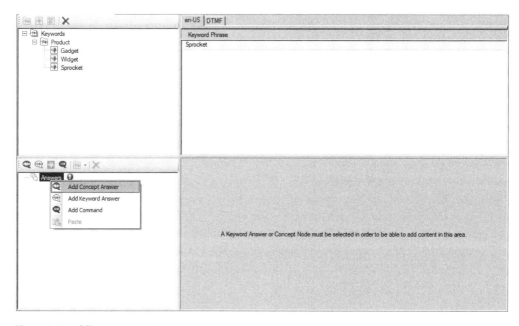

Figure 2-9. *Adding a concept answer*

Next, you need to add concepts to the concept answer to represent the two possible departments that the user could need to reach. To add a concept, right-click the Department node and choose Add Concept, as shown in Figure 2-10. Create one concept named **Sales** and another named **Support**.

Now you need to add the answer phrases for each concept. These represent what the user can say to trigger the concept as the recognition result. Right-click in the Answer Examples pane and choose Add Answer Phrase to add these phrases.

For the Sales concept, add the following answer phrases:

- I would like to buy a gadget

- Um looking for a gadget

- I'd like a gadget

- Purchase a gadget

- Sales

- Sales department please

- I'd like to talk to sales please

- Can I speak with a sales rep?

- I want to speak to the Sales department

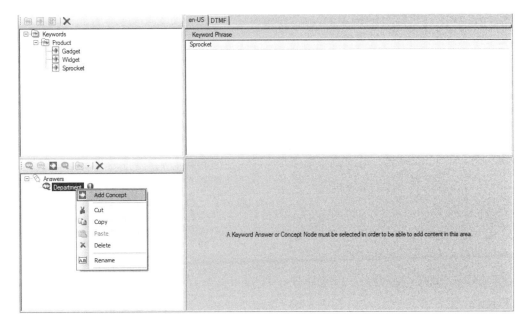

Figure 2-10. *Adding a concept*

For the Support concept, add these answer phrases:

- My gadget is broken

- I need help with my gadget

- I need to repair my gadget

- I purchased a gadget and it is no longer working

- Support

- I need the Support department

- Can I speak with a technician?

- Um support please

Finally, you need to reference the keyword container, Product, for both concepts you just created (right-click the concept node and choose Add Keyword Reference), and then parse the responses (click the Parse button on the toolbar). While it looks like the grammar is recognizing only the keyword Gadget, once you parse the responses, your grammar is actually recognizing all the keywords that belong in the keyword container you referenced. For example, just as the answer phrase "I would like to buy a gadget" directs the user to the Sales department, so does "I would like to buy a widget." Similarly, the user would be directed to the Support department if he said, "My widget is broken."

Supporting Multiple Languages

As long as you have the appropriate language packs installed (as explained in Chapter 1), the Conversational Grammar Builder makes it easy to add support for multiple languages. Simply select Grammar ➤ Add Speech Language Tab from the menu bar, as shown in Figure 2-11.

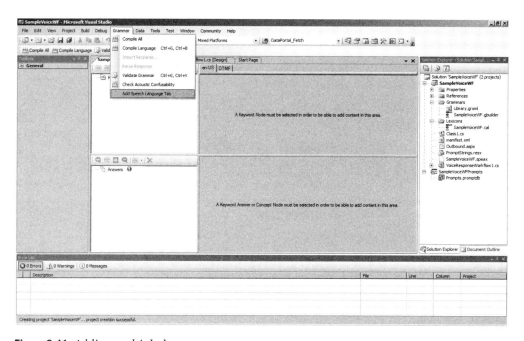

Figure 2-11. *Adding multiple-language support*

You will be prompted for which language you would like to add, as shown in Figure 2-12. This list is based on the language packs you have installed.

Figure 2-12. *Selecting a language to add*

After selecting your language, a separate tab will be added to your grammar in the Conversational Grammar Builder. On that tab, you can add keywords and answers in the language you chose, as described in the preceding sections. To add multiple languages, simply add keywords and responses for each language.

Building DTMF Grammar

Instead of having users answer prompts by speaking, your application could allow them to respond by pushing a button on their telephone. This is useful when you are prompting the user for sensitive information, such as a personal identification number (PIN). For this type of application, you build DTMF grammar.

To develop DTMF grammar using the Conversational Grammar Builder, click the DTMF tab at the top of the right pane, as shown in Figure 2-13. You can assign any keyword node values 0 through 9, *, and #. These values correspond to the buttons on a standard Touch-Tone telephone.

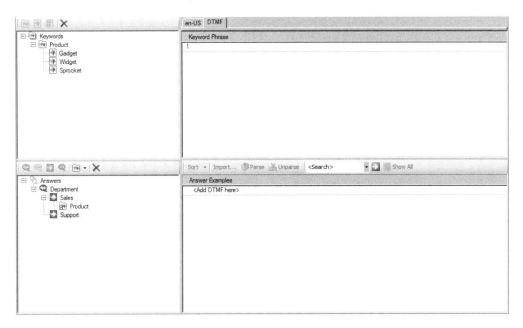

Figure 2-13. *Building DTMF grammar*

For example, to build DTMF grammar for the ABC Company example, rather than support speech recognition, you could assign the keyword phrase 1 to the Sales keyword and the keyword phrase 2 to the Support keyword. This would allow your application to prompt the user "If you would like the Sales department, press 1. If you would like the Support department, press 2."

Using the Lexicon Editor

If you have an unusual word or would like to change the acceptable user pronunciation of an existing word, you can define the pronunciation using the Lexicon Editor, which works with Conversational Grammar Builder grammars. (The corresponding tool for Grammar Editor grammars is the Pronunciation Editor, described later in this chapter.) A good example where you might use this is for the word *tomato*. Some people pronounce it "ta-may-toe," and others may say "ta-ma-toe."

To use the Lexicon Editor, first add a new Customer Application Lexicon file to your project using the Add New Item dialog box, as shown in Figure 2-14.

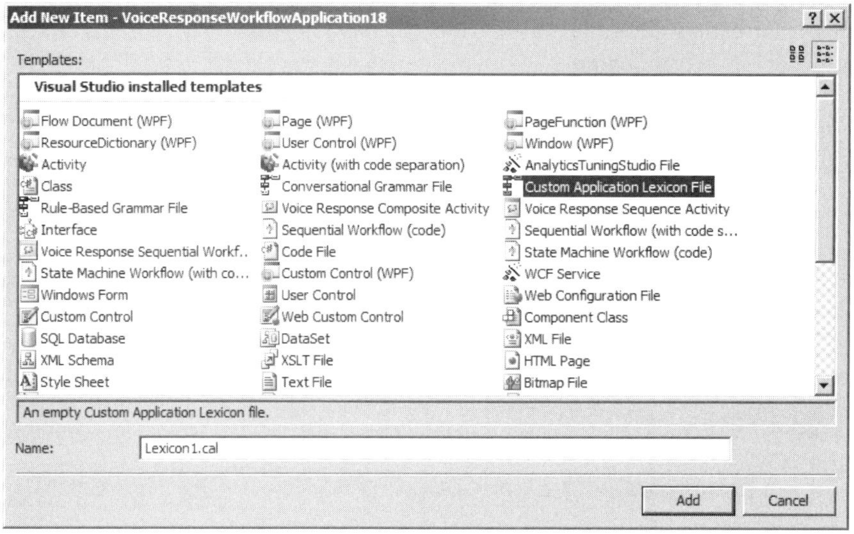

Figure 2-14. *Adding a Custom Application Lexicon file*

Your new file will open in the Lexicon Editor. First, you should look up the word and get the default pronunciation. Enter the word in the text box beneath Default Pronunciations Lookup and click the Lookup button. Figure 2-15 shows the result for *tomato*.

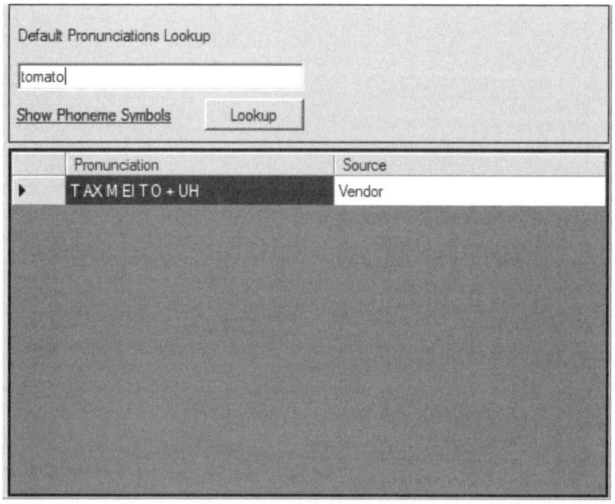

Figure 2-15. *Looking up default pronunciation*

The pronunciations are defined using the Universal Phone Set. In this case, the default pronunciation of tomato is T AX M EI T O + UH, which sounds like "ta-may-toe."

Tip The Universal Phone Set white paper is available from Microsoft's web site, `download.microsoft.com/download/speechSDK/Patch/1/NT5XP/EN-US/UPSWhitePaper(3.2).doc`. This white paper includes phoneme tables, which show the forms used for pronunciation.

In the editor section, you can add the word tomato and define another pronunciation: T AX M AH T O + UH, which sounds like "ta-ma toe," as shown in Figure 2-16. Click the Build button, and your application will now recognize the new pronunciation for the word tomato.

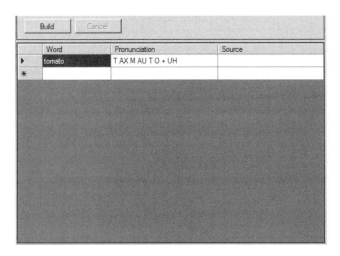

Figure 2-16. *Adding a custom pronunciation*

So far, you've learned how to use the Conversational Grammar Builder to create grammars for your applications. It is easy to use and may suit all your needs. However, if your application has more complex grammar requirements, you can use Speech Server's other grammar-building tool: the Grammar Editor.

Using the Grammar Editor

The Grammar Editor works differently from the Conversational Grammar Builder, in that it actually produces the XML-formatted SRGS grammar, GRXML. The editor provides a GUI with drag-and-drop capabilities, so you do not need to know GRXML syntax to use it. (If you prefer to write the GRXML yourself, you can do that, as I'll explain after the discussion of the Grammar Editor.)

Building Rule-Based Grammar

To demonstrate using the Grammar Editor, let's expand ABC Company's product line. In this example, the application should prompt the user for the department, Sales or Support, and then prompt the user for the product of interest. ABC Company now has six products: widget, gadget, sprocket, gizmo, thingamajig, and doodad. A doodad is also referred to as a *doohickey*, and a sprocket is also referred to as a *gear*.

To start building the grammar, in Visual Studio, right-click the project in the Solution Explorer, choose Add New Item, and select Rule-Based Grammar File, as shown in Figure 2-17.

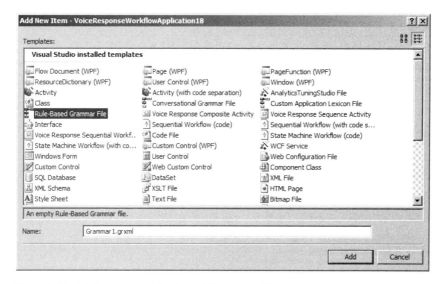

Figure 2-17. *Adding a new Rule-Based Grammar file*

After you added a new Rule-Based Grammar file to your project, you need to add rules to the file. Each rule represents the information for which you are prompting the user. For this example, you need to create a rule for selecting a department and a rule for selecting a product.

Adding a Department Rule

To create a rule, right-click the topmost node of the Grammar Explorer and choose New Rule, as shown in Figure 2-18. After you create a new rule, the name of rule is immediately editable. Name your new rule **Department**.

Double-click the Department rule that you just created to open the Grammar Editor. In the Grammar Editor, you add list elements, phrase elements, and script tags to define your rule. A list element represents a choice, and phrase elements in the list element represent the possible choices. A script tag holds the value from your list that was spoken by the user.

To add a list element, drag the List component from the Grammar toolbox, shown in Figure 2-19, and drop it on the Grammar Editor document. Add one list element to your Department rule.

Figure 2-18. *Adding a new grammar rule*

Figure 2-19. *Grammar toolbox in Visual Studio*

▓**Tip** Visual Studio also has a Rule Editor toolbar. You can enable the toolbar by right-clicking the Visual Studio toolbar and choosing Rule Editor. This offers you an alternative to dragging and dropping from the Grammar toolbox.

To add phrase elements, right-click the list element and choose Add Child Element, as shown in Figure 2-20. Add two phrase elements to your rule. Type the word **Sales** into one of the phrase elements, and the word **Support** into the other phrase element.

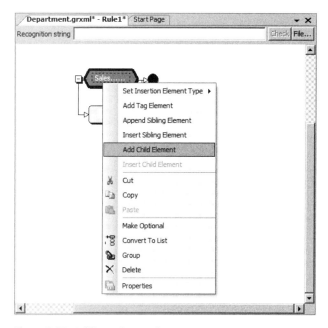

Figure 2-20. *Adding phrase elements*

Finally, drag a Script Tag component from the Grammar toolbox to the right side of the list element. Adding values for script tags is discussed in the "Editing Script Elements with the Semantic Script Builder" section later in this chapter.

Adding a Product Rule

Next, create a new rule named **Products**. In the Products rule, add a list element, and then give it a phrase element for each of the products:

- Gadget

- Widget

- Sprocket

- Thingamajig

- Doodad

- Gizmo

Since two products have multiple names, you need to convert the Sprocket and Doodad phrase elements to list elements, by right-clicking the list element and choosing Make Optional from the menu. Next, you need to add a phrase element for each to include the keyword **Gear** and **Doohickey**, respectively. Your rule should look like this:

- Gadget

- Widget

- Sprocket
  - Gear
- Thingamajig
- Doodad
  - Doohickey
- Gizmo

Next, add a script tag to each of the products. In the next section, you'll edit these script tags so that they collect the name of the product. Your grammar document should now look like Figure 2-21.

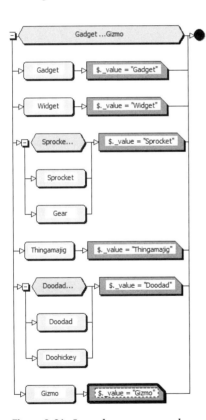

Figure 2-21. *Sample grammar rule*

ELEMENTS AVAILABLE IN THE GRAMMAR EDITOR

In the Visual Studio Grammar Editor toolbox, you'll find the following components:

- *Phrase*: Represents the phrase that the user will speak and that you want your application to recognize.

- *List*: A list of phrase elements, which will perform the same action when spoken.

- *RuleRef*: Allows you to reference other grammars and rules.

- *Group*: Helps maintain readability; does not affect the grammar itself.

- *Wildcard*: Allows you to ignore this part of the response.

- *Halt*: Stops the recognition and returns that the recognition has failed. This is useful when debugging or testing.

- *Skip*: Allows the grammar to be an optional grammar.

- *Script Tag*: Sets the return value of the recognition item.

Editing Script Elements with the Semantic Script Builder

Just as the Grammar Editor is nothing more than a GUI for creating GRXML, the Semantic Script Builder (also known as the Semantic Editor) is really just a GUI to edit the script elements of a GRXML document.

You can access the Semantic Editor by highlighting a script tag element in your grammar document and choosing Grammar ➤ Semantic Editor from the menu bar, or by clicking the ellipsis button on the script tag. This editor has two tabs: Assignment and Script. On the Assignment tab, you can set how to return the semantic items. On the Script tab, you can write your own script.

Assigning a Semantic Result

In the ABC Company example, you added a script tag for each product. Now you need to add a property named Product to each of those tags and set it as a constant value that reflects the name of the product. You can do this via the Semantic Script Builder.

In the Grammar Editor, click the ellipsis button on the script tag for the Gizmo product to open the Semantic Script Builder. On the Assignment tab, check the first check box, Return Result in a Sub-property of This Rule. In the Name of Property field, type **Product**. (After a property name has been entered, it will be available in the Name of Property drop-down list.) Then select the Constant option, and in the Enter Value field below it, type the name of the product, **Gizmo**, as shown in Figure 2-22. Repeat this procedure for each of the product script tags.

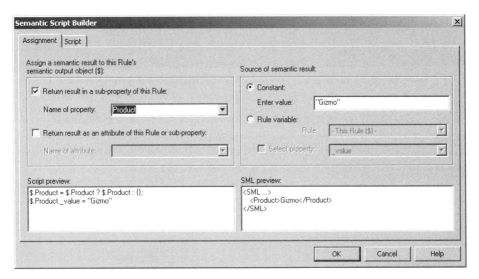

Figure 2-22. *Assigning a constant value to a semantic result with the Semantic Script Builder*

In this example, you created a script tag for each product and assigned it a constant value. If you just wanted to get the value of what the user said, you could add just one script tag for the entire document and place it to the right of the main list element. You could then open the Semantic Script Builder for that script tag, choose the Rule Variable option, and select Recognized Text from the Rule drop-down list. This would return exactly what the user said. However, this isn't ideal for the sample application, because some of your items have multiple names; for example, *sprocket* is also called *gear*. By adding a constant, even if the user says "gear," it will return "sprocket."

If you wanted to collect the color of the product users were calling about, you could create a Color grammar list, with three options: Red, Yellow, or Blue. This list could be a part of the same rule and marked as optional (right-click the list element and select Make Optional) in the Grammar Editor. You could return the color as an attribute to the subproperty, Product. To do this, in the Semantic Script Builder, you would check the Return Result as Sub-property of This Rule option and choose Product. Then you would check the Return Result As An attribute of This Rule or Sub-property option, and type in **Color** as the name of the attribute. The SML results would look something like the following:

```
<SML ...>
    <Product Color="Yellow">Gizmo</Product>
</SML>
```

Writing Your Own Script

If you need to do more complex operations, such as add conditions or do mathematical calculations, you can write your own script via the Script tab of the Semantic Script Builder, as shown in Figure 2-23.

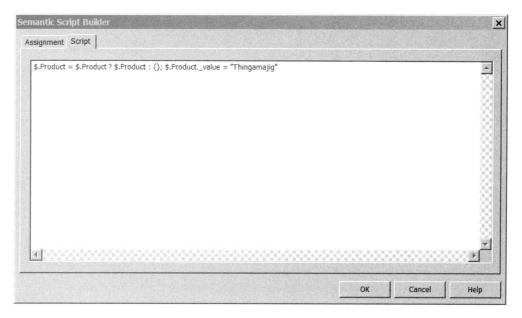

Figure 2-23. *Adding a script via the Semantic Script Builder*

For example, suppose you want the SML results to contain a separate node for the whole product description and want the results to look like <FullProduct>Yellow Gadget</FullProduct>. This requires a string operation on the color and the product name. To do this, you would add a separate script tag to the right of the Product list element, and then add the following code to the script tag via the Script tab of the Semantic Script Builder:

```
$.FullProduct = $.Product.Color + "   " + $Product._value
```

If you had referenced rules, you could access the values of the previous referenced rule. For example, suppose you have two grammar rules, one named Product and another named ProductColor. The Product rule contains a list of all products, and the ProductColor rule contains a list of all colors, with an additional ColorCode node. You could reference the ProductColor rule in your Product rule grammar before the Product rule is applied, and access the results of the ProductColor rule in the Product rule. To do this, you would add a script tag at the end of the grammar, with the following script code:

```
$.FullProduct = $$.Color + " " + $.Product._value + " " + $$.ColorCode.
```

Figure 2-24 shows this example in the Grammar Editor.

This would produce SML results that look like the following:

```
<SML text="Yellow Gadget" utteranceConfidence="1.000" confidence="1.000">
        <Product confidence="1.000">Gadget</Product>
        <FullProduct confidence="1.000">Yellow Gadget 1</FullProduct>
</SML>
```

The SML results are discussed in more detail in the "Testing Your Grammar" section later in this chapter.

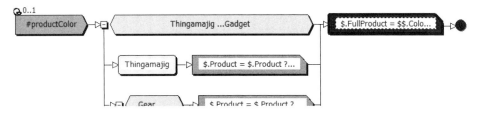

Figure 2-24. *Sample grammar using scripts*

Using Mixed-Initiative Dialog for Multiple Responses

By using *mixed-initiative dialog* in your application, you can allow users to answer multiple prompts at one time. Mixed initiative and the other common design patterns for voice user interfaces (VUIs) are discussed in Chapter 3. Here, we will look at an example of how to build the grammar for this type of design.

In the sample ABC Company application, you are prompting the user twice: "Which department would you like?" and "Which product are you calling about?" Suppose that the user answered the first prompt, "I would like to talk to the Support department about my widget." The current system would still prompt the user, "Which product are you calling about?" Mixed-initiative dialog allows you to collect the answer and then decide if the user has already given you an answer to a future prompt.

To construct this mixed-initiative dialog, you first need to create a new Rule-Based Grammar file and add a new rule. In the Grammar Editor, add two ruleref elements to your rule: one referencing the Department grammar file and the other referencing the Product grammar file from the previous example. Add a script tag element to each ruleref element. The script tag needs to get the value from that rule and put that value into a property of the current document. Also add wildcard elements to support the user saying something like, "I would like the Support department because my widget is broken."

Figure 2-25 shows the rule design in the Grammar Editor. The grammar contains two identical groups on both ends. Both of the groups contain the Product ruleref and both groups are marked optional. The Product ruleref element is used twice because you want to allow the user to say the product in the beginning or end of a response. For example, the user could say "I'd like the Widget Support department." This allows users to specify just the department they would like, without saying the product; you can prompt the user later for the product. This grammar restricts the users, as they must say the department; they cannot just say the product.

Figure 2-25. *Mixed-initiative dialog example*

Using the Pronunciation Editor

If you have an unusual word or would like to change the pronunciation of an existing word, you can define the accepted user pronunciation using the Pronunciation Editor, which works with grammar built in the Grammar Editor. (For grammar built with the Conversational Grammar Builder, use the Lexicon Editor, as described earlier in this chapter.)

To open the Pronunciation Editor, highlight a phrase element in the Grammar Editor and choose Grammar ➤ Pronunciation Editor, as shown in Figure 2-26.

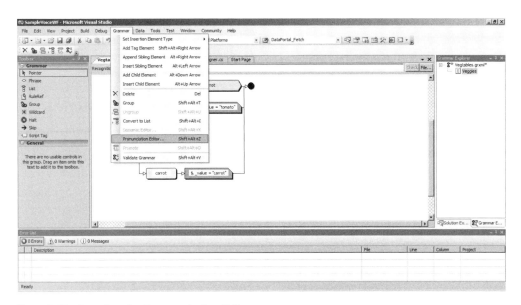

Figure 2-26. *Opening the Pronunciation Editor*

Using the same example as earlier in the chapter, suppose you want to add two pronunciations for the word *tomato*: "ta-may-toe" and "ta-ma-toe." First, in the Grammar Editor, add a list element with two phrase elements, both with the word **tomato**. Select one of the tomato phrase elements and open the Pronunciation Editor. Then click the Add Custom Pronunciation button and add the custom pronunciation, as shown in Figure 2-27. See the "Using the Lexicon Editor" section earlier in this chapter for information about how the pronunciations are defined.

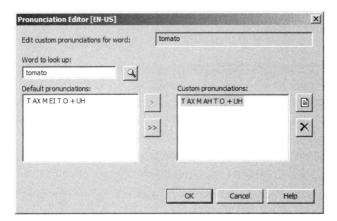

Figure 2-27. *Adding a custom pronunciation with the Pronunciation Editor*

Now, in the Grammar Editor, you can see that a custom pronunciation was defined for this word, indicated by Æ, as shown in Figure 2-28.

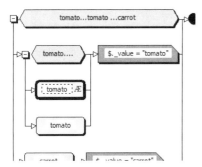

Figure 2-28. *Custom pronunciation indicated in the Grammar Editor*

Testing Your Grammar

You can test your grammar by typing a phrase into the Recognition String text box at the top of the Grammar Editor window, shown in Figure 2-29. After typing in the keyword or phrase, click the Check button to the right of the text box.

Figure 2-29. *Enter a phrase to test your grammar.*

If your string wasn't recognized, the Output window will display an error message, as shown in Figure 2-30.

If the word or phrase was recognized, you will see your results in the Output window, as shown in Figure 2-31.

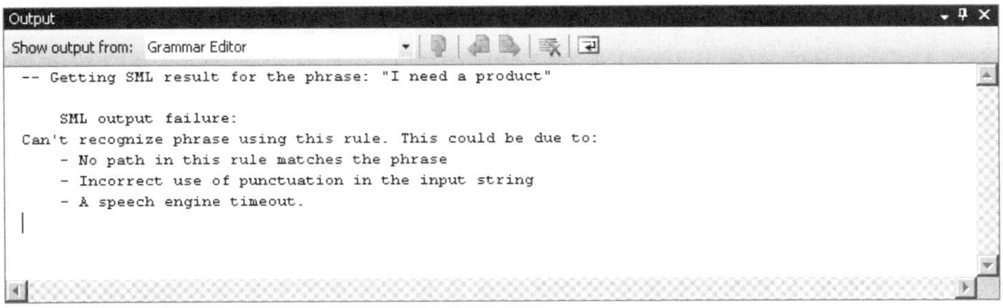

Figure 2-30. *Output showing the recognition string wasn't recognized*

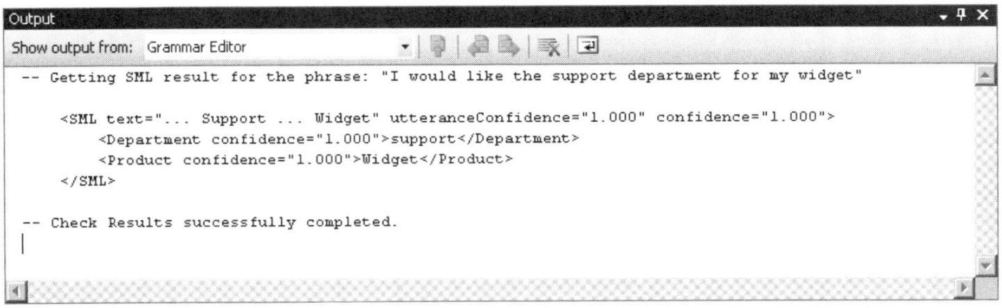

Figure 2-31. *Output showing the recognition string was recognized*

The SML results contain three main attributes: utteranceConfidence, text, and confidence. The utteranceConfidence attribute represents the percentage of how confident the Speech Recognizer Engine heard and recognized what the user said. The text attribute will contain exactly what the user said. The recognizer automatically sets the utteranceConfidence and the text value, and automatically assigns the confidence value equal to the value of the utteranceConfidence value.

When you're using the Recognition String text box, if the word or phrase is recognized, the Speech Recognizer Engine will always return an utteranceConfidence value of 1, indicating that it is 100% confident that you "said" something that matched the grammar. This is because you typed the answer. In an actual application, you will get something smaller than 1, depending on how clearly the user is speaking and the quality of the user's hardware.

Compiling Grammar

You have the option of compiling your grammar. The benefit of compiling is that it reduces the physical size of the file, which allows Speech Engine Services (SES) to download the grammar faster.

You can compile your grammar via the command-line prompt, using the SRGSGC.exe compiler, which is in the SDK directory of Speech Server. The following is the command-line syntax for compiling your grammar:

```
SRGSGC.exe /O C:\Input.grxml C:\Output.cfg
```

Using the Grammar Editor and the Conversational Grammar Builder Together

Grammar developed using the Grammar Editor is easy to maintain. The Conversational Grammar Builder allows you to develop grammar easily. To take advantage of both tools, you can design the keyword grammar using the Grammar Editor and use it in the Conversational Grammar Builder.

To use the grammar you built using the Grammar Editor (or by writing your own GRXML, as described later in this chapter), in the Conversational Grammar Builder, right-click the Keyword node and choose Add Grammar Reference.

For example, in the ABC Company Conversational Grammar Builder example, you can remove the keyword grammar and reference the grammar you built using the Grammar Editor. To do this, right-click the Keyword node, select Add Grammar Reference, and browse to the location of your .grxml or .cfg files. Choose the Department and the Product rules attached to the grammar document, and they will be added in the Conversational Grammar Builder, as shown in Figure 2-32.

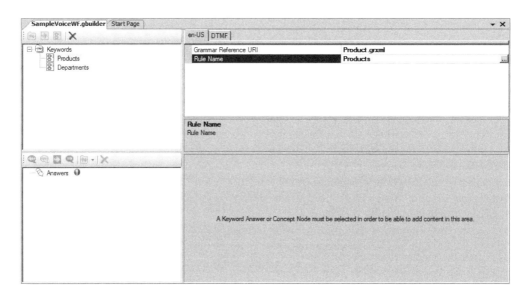

Figure 2-32. *Referencing Rule-Based Grammar files*

■**Note** The limitation to referencing Grammar Editor files in the Conversational Grammar Builder is that you cannot have mixed-initiative dialog.

Writing Your Own GRXML

Rather than using the Grammar Editor, you may prefer to write your own GRXML files. You can create a GRXML file in a text editor like Notepad or the Visual Studio 2005 XML editor by entering the GRXML tags and saving the file with a .grxml extension.

The following GRXML tags are available:

- `<grammar>`

- `<rule>`

- `<one-of>`

- `<item>`

- `<ruleref>`

- `<token>`

- `<example>`

- `<tag>`

GRXML documents do not need to be complex. The following is a simple grammar from this chapter's previous examples.

```
<grammar xml:lang="EN-US" version="1.0" mode="voice">
    <rule id="Department" scope="public">
        <one-of>
                <item>Support</item>
                <item>Sales</item>
        </one-of>
         <tag>$.Department = $recognized.text</tag>
    </rule>
</grammar>
```

■**Tip** You can create grammar using the Grammar Editor and then open the grammar using an XML editor to access the GRXML directly.

The `<grammar>` tag must be the topmost container in the `.grxml` document. The `<grammar>` tag should contain the following attributes:

- The `language` attribute contains the standard abbreviation for the spoken language that the grammar supports. For example, if your application supports US English, the value of the `language` attribute should be `en-US`.

- The `version` attribute is the version number of SRGS that your grammar supports; currently the highest supported version is 1.0.

- The `root` attribute is the name of the root rule for your grammar. The root rule must be contained in the same grammar document as the `<grammar>` tag referencing it.

- The `mode` attribute defines what type of application the grammar supports. This can be either `voice` or `dtmf`.

The following is an example of a valid `<grammar>` tag:

```
<grammar xml:lang="en-US" version="1.0" root="Department" mode="voice">
```

A GRXML document can contain multiple rules. The `<rules>` tag must contain an `id` attribute, which uniquely identifies the rule from other rules in the document. You can optionally add the `scope` attribute. Here is an example:

```
<rule id="Department" scope="public">
```

The `scope` attribute with a `public` value can be accessed by any other `.grxml` file. A `scope` attribute with a `private` value means that no other `.grxml` file can reference this rule.

The `<one-of>` tag allows you to build a list of alternative choices for the user. The `<one-of>` list must contain child `<item>` tags. For example, to ask the user, "Which department would you like: Sales or Support?" create the following `<one-of>` element:

```
<one-of>
  <item>Support</item>
  <item>Sales</item>
</one-of>
```

The `<item>` element contains rule expressions. It can consist of a word or phrase that represents what the user will say. It may also contain a `<tag>` element, a `<ruleref>` element, or another `<item>` element, which may contain a combination of supported elements. The following example shows nested `<item>` elements in a `<one-of>` element.

```
<one-of>
  <item>
    <item>Support</item>
    <tag>$.value="Support"</tag>
  </item>
  <item>
    <item>Sales</item>
    <tag>$.value="Sales"</tag>
  </item>
</one-of>
```

The `<ruleref>` element allows you to reference another rule, either in the same document or in another document. The `<ruleref>` element has an `URI` attribute and a `type` attribute. The URI attribute specifies the location of another `.grxml` document and its rule. The `type` attribute defines the type of grammar that the referenced rule supports. Here is an example:

```
<ruleref uri="Product.grxml#Product" type="application/srgs+xml"/>
```

The `<tag>` element's purpose is to generate semantic values. It also allows you to format the SML results. When you add a `<tag>` element to an `<item>` element, it adds an attribute to your SML results. Here is an example:

```
<item>Sales<tag>$.department={}; $.department._value="Sales";</tag></item>
```

This `<tag>` element would produce a `department` attribute in your SML results, such as the following:

```
<SML confidence="1.0" text = "Sales" utteranceConfidence=3"1.0">
     <department confidence="1.0">Sales</department>
</SML>
```

Your application could then access the result via the following code:

```
RecognitionResult.Semantics["Products"].Value
```

■**Tip** For more information about GRXML, visit the W3C web site for SRGS standards, `www.w3.org/TR/speech-grammar/`.

Creating Dynamic Grammar

Another way to build grammar is dynamically, based on existing data in a database. In this chapter's ABC Company example, if the products were stored in a database, you could dynamically create the grammar from product data in the database. One way to do this is to use the Data Source property of a speech control, such as the Menu control. Alternatively, you could create a method or grammar class for your specific data-driven grammar.

Using a Control's Data Source Property

A few of the speech controls have a Data Source property. You can set this property, and the grammar will be created automatically based on the data from the data source. For example, the Menu control allows you to prompt users with a list of options and ask which option they would like.

Here, we will look at the use of speech controls only in the context of creating grammar dynamically. The use of speech controls in applications is covered in the upcoming chapters about the types of Speech Server application.

The following is a sample Voice Response Workflow application with a Menu control. In the `TurnStarting` event of the Menu control, you set the data source to a generic list, which could get its values from a database. (The use of the Menu controls in Voice Response Workflow applications is covered in more depth in Chapter 6.)

```
    private void menuActivity1_TurnStarting(object sender,
TurnStartingEventArgs e)
    {
        //Simulate getting data.
        List<string> products = GetProducts();
```

```
        //Clear the prompt
        this.menuActivity1.MainPrompt.ClearContent();
        this.menuActivity1.MainPrompt.AppendText("Please say the
 product you would like, ");
        for(int index=0;index < products.Count;index++)
        {
            this.menuActivity1.MainPrompt.AppendText(products[index] + ", ");
        }
        this.menuActivity1.DataSource = products;
        this.menuActivity1.DataBind();
    }
    private List<string> GetProducts()
    {
        List<string> products = new List<string>();
        //Fill list from database
        return products;
    }
```

Using a Method or Class to Create a Grammar

If you want to create grammar that will work with any control, you could create a method to return a SrgsDocument type. When building a SrgsDocument type, you should approach it the same way as if you were designing it using the Grammar Editor:

- Create a SrgsDocument object. This is equivalent to the physical .grxml document.

- Create a SrgsRule object. This is equivalent to the rule in the Grammar Editor.

- Create a SrgsOneOf object. This represents a list element in the Grammar Editor.

- Create a SrgsItem object. This represents a phrase element in the Grammar Editor.

In this example, you have the following method to return a SrgsDocument type based on data stored in a generic list.

```
    private SrgsDocument CreateGrammar(List<string> productList)
    {
        SrgsDocument productGrammar = new SrgsDocument();
        productGrammar.Mode = SrgsGrammarMode.Voice;
        SrgsRule productRule = new SrgsRule("Products");
        SrgsOneOf products = new SrgsOneOf();

        foreach (string product in productList)
        {
            SrgsItem item = new SrgsItem(productList[0]);
            products.Add(item);
        }
```

```
        productRule.Add(products);
        productGrammar.Rules.Add(productRule);
        productGrammar.Root = productRule;

        return productGrammar;
    }
```

Alternatively, you could create a grammar class for your specific data-driven grammar. This class should inherit from the `Microsoft.SpeechServer.Recognition.Grammar` class. The following code is an example of how you might define this class.

```
    internal class ProductGrammar : Grammar
    {
        public event EventHandler<SemanticUpdateEventArgs<string>>
ProductRecognized;

        public ProductGrammar()
            : base(CreateSrgsDocument())
        {
            base.Recognized += ProductGrammar_Recognized;
        }

        private static SrgsDocument CreateSrgsDocument()
        {
            SrgsDocument grammar = new SrgsDocument();
            grammar.Mode = SrgsGrammarMode.Voice;

            SrgsRule rule = new SrgsRule("Products");

            SrgsOneOf choice = new SrgsOneOf();

            List<string> products = GetProducts();
            for (int index = 0; index < products.Count;index++)
            {
                SrgsItem item = new SrgsItem(products[index]);
                choice.Add(item);
            }

            rule.Add(choice);
            grammar.Rules.Add(rule);
            grammar.Root = rule;

            return grammar;
        }
```

```
        private List<string> GetProducts()
        {
            List<string> products = new List<string>();
            // Fill list from database
            return products;
        }
        private void ProductGrammar_Recognized(object sender,
RecognizedEventArgs e)
        {
            if (ProductRecognized != null)
            {
                ProductRecognized(this, new SemanticUpdateEventArgs<string>
(e.Result.Text, e.Result.Confidence, e.Result.Text));
            }
        }

    }
```

■**Caution** Data-driven grammar can add response time. If you create grammar this way, you may want to use data caching and other options to improve data response times.

Accessing Recognition Results

Once you have completed the grammar, you need to know which word or phrase the user said. Generally, you can do this on the Closed or Confirmation event of the control that contains the grammar.

In the ABC Company grammar example, the product grammar has a semantic item named Product. You can access the result of the grammar by using the RecognitionResult property of the control to which your grammar is attached. RecognitionResult has a Semantics property. You could access your results by providing the key to the Semantic collection. The key is the name of the rule in your grammar. For example, if your grammar were attached to a QuestionAnswer control, you could access the results with the following code:

```
questionAnswerActivity.RecognitionResult.Semantics["Products"].Value
```

or

```
questionAnswerActivity.RecognitionResult.Text
```

This difference between the two is that the Products item might have multiple values for which you would want to get a common value. This is the case in the ABC Company example. If the user said "Gear," the RecognitionResult.Text would return Gear, while RecognitionResult. Semantics ["Products"].Value would return Sprocket.

You can also access the confidence result value using the following line of code:

```
questionAnswerActivity.RecognitionResult.Confidence
```

This number represents how confident the Speech Recognizer Engine is that the user said what it recognized. This is useful if you want to play confirmation prompts based on this result.

Another useful class when dealing with grammar is the `Microsoft.SpeechServer.Dialog.SemanticItem<T>` class. The `SemanticItem` object raises a `Changed` event whenever the value is changed. The `SemanticItem` also keeps track of its state. The states are `Confirmed`, `Unconfirmed`, and `Empty`. The following sample code shows how to use the previous `ProductGrammar` class to assign the grammar to a speech control and use the `SemanticItem`.

```
private SemanticItem<string> _product;
protected override void Initialize(IServiceProvider provider)
{
    base.Initialize(provider);

    _product = new SemanticItem<string>(this, "product");
}

private void chooseProduct_TurnStarting(object sender,
TurnStartingEventArgs e)
{
    _product.Clear();

    //Create Prompts Here

    //Add SemanticItem to Answers
    chooseProduct.Answers.Clear();
    chooseProduct.Answers.Add(_product);

    //Create Grammar and get Semantic Item Data
    ProductGrammar productGrammar = new ProductGrammar();
    chooseProduct.Grammars.Add(productGrammar);
    productGrammar.productRecognized += _product.Update;
}
```

This will update your semantic item every time the user says a product name that is recognized. You then can use this item throughout your application to get the value of the semantic item.

Conclusion

This chapter has covered the different methods for creating grammar for your application. The examples are primarily based on creating a Voice Response Workflow application. Each type of Speech Server application will be covered in detail in upcoming chapters.

The next chapter discusses how to create prompts for your application. The order in which you develop grammar and prompts does not matter. You may find it easier to create the prompts and then build the grammar. However, both should be created early in the application development process.

CHAPTER 3

Building Prompts

Prompts are what your application will say to the user. Prompts can be a question, statement, or instruction for the user. You have two main options for how you want users to hear your prompts: prerecorded prompts or speech synthesis, generated by the TTS engine. Prerecorded prompts are recommended over speech synthesis, as they sound more natural than the robotic voice of the TTS engine.

Voice user interface (VUI) design is probably 80% of developing an IVR application. If your prompts are not clear to users, they will not be able to give valid responses. This will have an adverse effect on the users' experience.

In this chapter, you will learn how to build prompts with Speech Server. But before you start to create prompts, you should have an understanding of the design guidelines and common design patterns for VUIs.

VUI Design Guidelines

Prompts are the main component to a VUI, since they are what the users will hear. Designing a VUI is significantly different from designing a GUI. Generally, the user will hear your prompt only one time, so your prompts should be clear and concise so that the users will give correct predicted responses.

People have come up with many ideas and theories as to how a VUI should sound, such as why prerecorded prompts are preferred to TTS and whether users respond better to a female or male voice. Although there is no official standard for VUI design, some initiatives exist, such as the gethuman standard (www.gethuman.com). Here, we will take a look at the gethuman standard, and then review general guidelines for four main areas of VUI design: menus, navigation, confirmation prompts, and error handling.

An Initiative Standard for VUI Design

The gethuman standard tries to address problems with corporate IVR design and the frustration of users not being able to talk to live person. The main gethuman standard guidelines are summarized as follows:

- Callers should be able to dial 0 or to say "operator" to indicate they wish to speak to a human.

- The system should give callers an accurate estimated wait time, based on call traffic statistics at the time of the call. A revised update should be provided periodically during hold time.

- Callers should never be asked to repeat any information (name, full account number, description of issue, and so on) provided during a call.

- When a human is not available, callers should be offered the option to be called back. If 24-hour service is not available, callers should be able to leave a message, including a request for a callback the following business day.

- Speech applications should provide DTMF fallback.

- Callers should not be forced to listen to long, verbose prompts.

- Callers should be able to interrupt prompts (by pressing a key and/or speaking) and say their input before the prompt has finished, whenever doing so will enable them to complete their task more efficiently.

- The system should not disconnect for user errors, including when there are no perceived key presses (as the caller might be on a rotary phone). Instead, queue for a human operator and/or offer the choice to be called back.

- The default language should be based on consumer demographics for each organization. Primary language should be assumed, with the option for the caller to change the language. (For example, English should generally be assumed for the United States, with a specified key for Spanish.)

- All operators/representatives of the organization should be able to communicate clearly with the caller (for example, accents should not hinder communication, and representatives should have excellent diction and enunciation.)

The gethuman standard also includes seven "gold standards," which you should incorporate to go above and beyond the minimum requirements. These are summarized as follows:

- While holding, callers should be allowed to disable hold music, and the system should remember their selection for future calls.

- Callers should be able to disable any ads or promotions that are played.

- Where appropriate, callers should be able to identify themselves via caller ID and a securely defined PIN, rather than be required to enter long account numbers.

- The application should remember callers' language preference for future calls, and default to their preferred language based on their caller ID.

- Organizations should support and publicize separate toll-free phone numbers for each individual language.

- The system should allow callers to access audio transcriptions of their calls via a web site.

- The system should call back callers at the time that they specified.

The guidelines presented in the following sections will help you design your VUI to meet the goals of the gethuman standard.

Menu Design

Menus should let the users know what they can say to interact with the application. Here are six guidelines for designing your IVR menu system:

- Limit choices and depth to three or four options.
- Use simple one- or two-word options.
- Allow barge-ins.
- Avoid the "For . . . say" method in speech applications.
- Avoid mixing DTMF with speech.
- Provide navigational landmarks.

The following sections discuss these guidelines in more detail.

Limit Choices

Menu choices and depth should not exceed three or four options, so users can keep track of where they are in the application. If your menu structure is very complex, users can become lost.

For example, suppose you called an airline and heard, "Please say one of the following: Flight Status, Book Flight, Change Reservation, Delete Reservation, Update Account Information, or Upgrade Flight Options." You could easily forget what the first option was by the time you heard the last option. It would be better to hear, "Please say one of the following: Reservation, Flight Status, or Account Information," and have the remaining options offered on submenus. For example, the Reservation main menu item could have a submenu that asks, "Please say one of the following: New Reservation or Existing Reservation." The Existing Reservation menu might have another submenu that will say, "You have a reservation for November 11 at 9:30 a.m. departing from Minneapolis and arriving in Phoenix. Do you want to change this reservation?"

However, you should be careful not to take this to the other extreme and have too many submenus. Limit the system to three to four submenus.

■**Note** If your application must be complex, you may want to think about using natural language. This would allow your application to ask users an open-ended question, such as "How may I help you?" However, as discussed in Chapter 2, this approach has some pitfalls and isn't recommended for all applications.

Use Simple One- or Two-Word Options

Like more than three or four options on a menu, complex, multiple-word options make it difficult for users to remember all the choices. Use very short options with simple words that your users can easily understand and remember.

Allow Barge-Ins

Allowing *barge-ins* means that users can say their input before the prompt has finished speaking. Experienced users will be able to get to the part of your application that they need more quickly. New users will find it helpful to say the selection they want as they hear it. By allowing barge-ins, your users will complete their calls more quickly, saving them time and saving you resources— shorter call times mean fewer resources you need to provide.

Avoid the "For . . . Say" Method

The "For . . . say" method refers to prompts such as "For Sales, say Sales" and "For Support, say Support." Although this method is acceptable for DTMF applications, speech applications don't need to have such a long prompt. It is more acceptable to simply say "Please say one of the following. . ." or "Would you like Sales or Support?"

Avoid Mixing DTMF with Speech

Prompts like "For Sales, say Sales or press 1," and For Support, say Support or press 2 now" are examples of mixing DTMF with speech (as well as the "For . . . say" method discussed in the previous section). You should provide a DTMF fallback only if speech recognition fails. You can do this by designing your application so that it first says the prompt requesting a voice response, and then if it does not recognize the voice response, it generates a prompt requesting a DTMF response. Here is an example: "I didn't understand what you said. If you would like Sales, press 1. If you would like Support, press 2."

Provide Navigational Landmarks

You should use navigational landmarks whenever you are dealing with systems that are many menus deep. This provides users with an audio cue as to where they are in the application. For example, your main menu prompt may say, "Main menu. Please say Balance, Transfer, or Inquiry." If the user says "Balance," the application may respond, "Account balance. Your account has a balance of $453.45."

Using navigational landmarks allows the advanced users of your application to work more efficiently. As they hear the landmark, such as "Main menu," they could state an option, such as "Balance," immediately, without listening to the rest of the prompt.

Navigation Design

The following are two main guidelines for designing your IVR application's navigation system:

- Provide global commands.

- Allow the user to return to a previous menu without starting over.

Include global commands, such as those to repeat a prompt or return to a previous menu, and let the user know what the global commands are after the greeting of your application. The most common global commands are listed in Table 3-1.

Table 3-1. *Common Global Commands*

Command	Action
Repeat	Repeat the last prompt the user has not given a response to
Help	Provide direction to the users based on where they are in your application
Main Menu	Take users back to the beginning
Previous	Take users back to the previous menu
Operator	Forward users to a live person

The Previous global command reflects another best practice: you should allow users to go back to a previous menu after they have completed a menu item without having to start over. For example, if you have a reservation application and the user has just completed a reservation, you might prompt the user, "Do you wish to make another reservation?" This allows the user to stay in her current workflow without starting over from the beginning.

Confirmation Prompts

Confirmation prompts can help the user and the application guarantee that they both have the correct information. Confirmation prompts are important, but they also can be overwhelming to the user. Take the following conversation for example:

IVR: What size pizza would you like?

User: Large

IVR: Did you say large?

User: Yes

IVR: What kind of topping would you like?

User: Pepperoni

IVR: Did you say pepperoni?

User: Yes

In some cases, confirming everything with the user is necessary, such as in a banking application that allows bank transfers over the phone. If you are required to confirm each answer with the user, you can do it passively, in this style:

IVR: What size pizza would you like?

User: Large

IVR: OK, got it. A large pizza.

User: Yes

IVR: What kind of topping would you like?

User: Pepperoni

IVR: OK, got it. A large pepperoni pizza.

User: Yes

Alternatively, you could confirm the entire order at one time, as in this example:

IVR: What size pizza would you like?

User: Large

IVR: OK got it. What kind of topping would you like?

User: Pepperoni

IVR: So you want a large pepperoni pizza?

User: Yes

You could also write your confirmation prompts to play only when the confidence value is under a certain score. This would eliminate needless confirmation requests when you are fairly confident that the user said what you heard. Playing prompts based on conditions like minimum confidence scores is discussed in the following chapters about the different IVR application types.

Error Handling

Errors will occur when the user says something that the grammar doesn't recognize. The system should prompt the user in an informative way, instead of blaming the user. For example, this type of error handling will not give the user a good experience:

IVR: What size pizza would you like?

User: Enormous

IVR: I'm sorry. You didn't say a correct response.

User: Big

IVR: I'm sorry. You didn't say a correct response.

Instead, allow the user to recover easily, like this:

IVR: What size pizza would you like?

User: Enormous

IVR: I didn't recognize what you said. Would you like a small, medium, or large pizza?

User: Large

However, you can avoid this type of situation entirely by either changing the grammar to recognize more keywords, such as Big and Enormous for a large size, or by changing the starting prompt to include which words are acceptable, such as "What size pizza would you like: small, medium, or large?"

Now that we've looked at some guidelines for your application's prompts, let's consider the prompt styles you can use for VUI design.

VUI Design Patterns

Your prompts guide the flow of your application, or its design pattern. Three design patterns are commonly used for a VUI:

- System initiative

- User initiative

- Mixed initiative

Each design pattern is discussed in the following sections.

System Initiative

In a system-initiative model, the system directs the flow of the dialog by asking specific questions. This is probably the most common design used today. It avoids recognition problems because the users are always told what they can say.

The two most commonly used system-initiative techniques are form-filling dialog and menu dialog.

Form-Filling Dialog

Form-filling dialog is useful when the user has information you want, and the user does not know how to accomplish the application's task. The user is essentially just answering questions that your application asks, and your application stores the user's answers. For example, if you are writing an IVR application for a flight reservation system, you might want the following dialog to take place:

IVR: Where are you flying from?

User: Minneapolis

IVR: What date are you leaving?

User: November 17

IVR: Where are you flying to?

User: Phoenix

IVR: When are you returning?

User: November 20

IVR: Here is what I heard: you want to fly from Minneapolis to Phoenix on November 17 and return to Minneapolis on November 20. Is that correct?

Figure 3-1 illustrates the form-filling dialog technique.

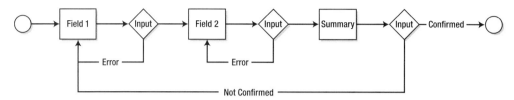

Figure 3-1. *Form-filling dialog pattern*

Menu Dialog

With the menu dialog technique, the application presents the user with a series of choices, and the user must select one. Here is an example:

> IVR: What size pizza would you like: small, medium, or large?

> User: Medium

> IVR: What toppings would you like: cheese, pepperoni, onions, or olives?

> User: Pepperoni

> IVR: So you would like a medium pepperoni pizza?

Figure 3-2 illustrates the menu dialog technique.

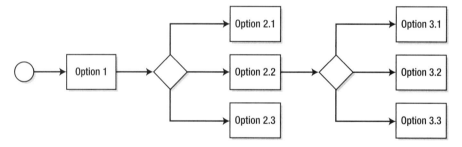

Figure 3-2. *Menu dialog pattern*

User Initiative

In a user-initiative system, the user drives the flow of the dialog. The system confirms what the user said only when it recognizes speech. In theory, this may sound like a great model—just accept anything the user says. However, using this model, the users must either know what they can say or they need to figure it out by trial and error. Take the following conversation for example:

> User: What time does flight 120 to Phoenix arrive?

> IVR: Flight 120 to Phoenix.

User: When does it arrive?

IVR: Excuse me, I didn't understand you.

User: Arrival time?

IVR: Arriving at 9:38 p.m.

This approach will cost you in terms of resources and development time. Users will be on the line longer, taking up valuable server resources and defeating the goal of allowing users to perform functions in the shortest amount of time.

You can expect to spend more time on development, as you are trying to predict a wider range of user responses in the grammar. If you do not handle the majority of user responses, users will decide that your application is broken, which will drive users to your live agents, minimizing your investment in your telephony application. Of course, developers make mistakes, and it is very easy to overlook something that users might say. So if you must go with a user-initiative type application, be prepared to spend more time developing and testing the application than you would with either of the other design patterns.

Mixed Initiative

The mixed-initiative pattern allows users to supply multiple pieces of information at one time, in any order. The application will then prompt the users for any missing information and ask them to confirm their selection. Basically, the application can be a user-initiative system, and then become a system-initiative system when it needs to be. Here is an example:

IVR: How may I help you?

User: I would like a flight from Minneapolis to Phoenix.

IVR: When would you like to depart?

User: On November 17

IVR: When are you returning?

User: On November 20

IVR: Here is what I heard: you want to fly from Minneapolis to Phoenix on November 17 and return to Minneapolis on November 20. Is that correct?

The user could give the same information, but in a different order:

IVR: How may I help you?

User: I would like a flight.

IVR: Where are you departing from?

User: From Minneapolis on November 17.

IVR: Where are you going?

User: Phoenix

IVR: When are you returning?

User: November 20

IVR: Here is what I heard: you want to fly from Minneapolis to Phoenix on November 17 and return to Minneapolis on November 20. Is that correct?

Figure 3-3 illustrates the mixed-initiative technique.

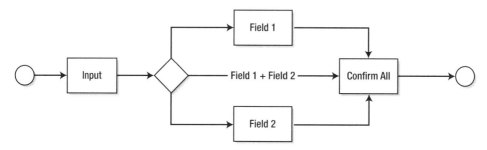

Figure 3-3. *Mixed-initiative dialog pattern*

The mixed-initiative system can work well if you put the necessary thought and work into it. The key to making mixed-initiative dialog work is wording the initial question well enough to cover most users. This is in accordance with the standard 80/20 rule: design for 80% of your users, not the 20% exception. The goal of the mixed-initiative pattern is to minimize prompts. If the users are not providing multiple answers, your mixed-initiative dialog will prompt them again for missing answers, meaning you probably wasted a lot of time on developing the extra grammars and code for mixed initiative.

With the design concepts covered, it's now time to get to work building your prompts using the Speech Server tools.

Working with Prerecorded Prompts

As noted at the beginning of this chapter, using prerecorded prompts is recommended, as they sound more natural than the robotic TTS voice. Speech Server has a tool named the Prompt Editor, which allows you to create and edit prerecorded prompts. The first step is to add a Prompt project to your solution. (For TTS prompts, you do not need to a Prompt project; TTS prompts are discussed later in the chapter.)

Creating a Prompt Project

Prompts have their own project type in Visual Studio. To create a Prompt project, click File ➤ New ➤ New Project ➤ Other Project Types, and then choose Prompt Project in the New Project dialog box, as shown in Figure 3-4.

In the newly created Prompt project, you need to add a prompt database. Right-click the project in the Solution Explorer, choose Add ➤ New Item, and then select Prompt Database, as shown in Figure 3-5. A Prompt project can have multiple prompt databases.

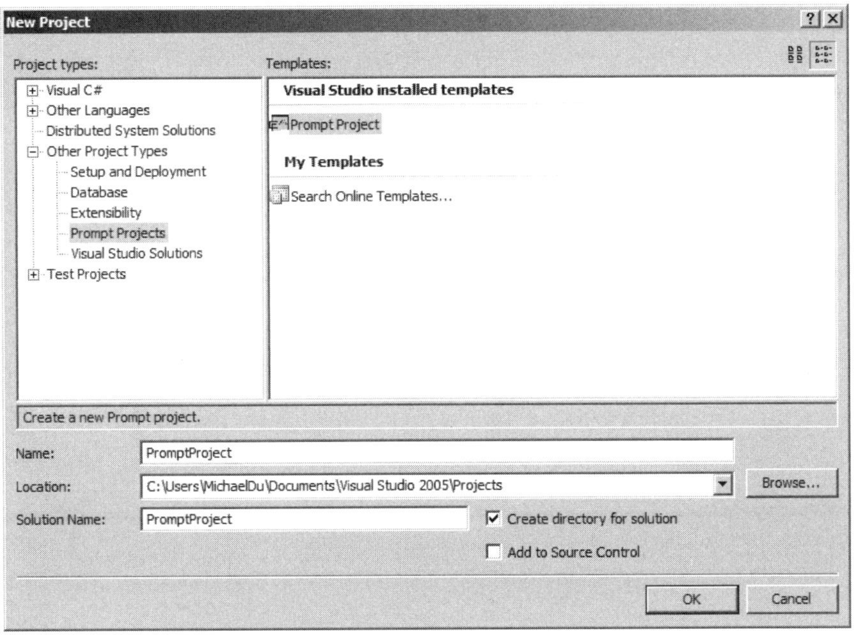

Figure 3-4. *Creating a new Prompt project*

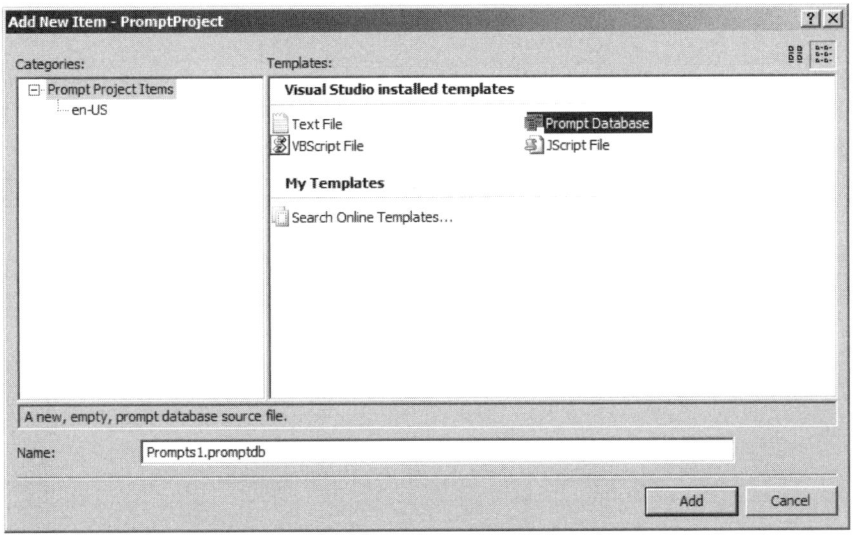

Figure 3-5. *Adding a prompt database to a Prompt project*

Speech Server also includes some prebuilt prompt databases with language-specific prompts, for which you just need to record the prompts. These prompts contain general information and formatting, such as date, address, phone numbers, and credit cards. To add one of the prebuilt prompt databases, from the Add New Item dialog box, select the installed language for which you want to create prompts in the Categories list, and then select the prompt type in the Templates list, as shown in Figure 3-6.

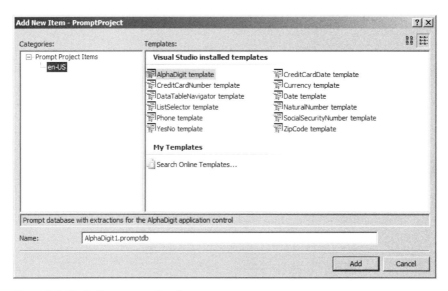

Figure 3-6. *Prebuilt prompt databases*

If you want to have multiple-language prompts, you can either create a new Prompt project or just add a new prompt database to an existing project, as explained in the "Modifying Prompt Project Settings" section later in this chapter.

To add new prompts to the prompt database, double-click the prompt database file in the Solution Explorer. The Prompt Editor will open, as shown in Figure 3-7. This is where you create, record, and edit your prompts.

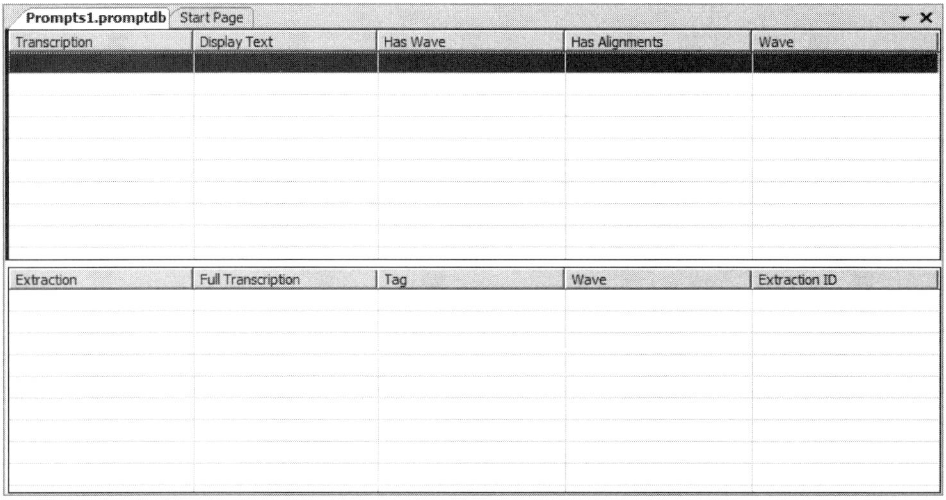

Figure 3-7. *The Prompt Editor*

Creating and Recording Transcriptions

The Prompt Editor is divided into two sections: one for transcriptions and one for extractions. *Transcriptions* are the words or phrases of the audio recording that the user will hear. *Extractions* are the individual words or phrases in transcriptions, extracted for the purpose of reusing those words or phrases to create completely new prompts.

Adding Transcriptions

Suppose you want to ask the user, "Which department would you like: Sales or Support?" and have a confirmation prompt like, "I heard you say Sales. Is that correct?" You need to create the following prompts:

- Which department would you like: Sales or Support?

- [I heard you say] Sales

- [Is that correct]

- [Sales]

- [Support]

The brackets are included to support extraction. They indicate that the word or phrase could be used in other prompts, such as "I heard you say Support."

You enter each prompt as a transcription in the Prompt Editor, as shown in Figure 3-8.

Transcription	Display Text	Has Wave	Has Alignments	Wave
Which department would …	Which department would …	✖	✖	Rec0000.wav
[I heard you say] Sales	I heard you say Sales	✖	✖	Rec0001.wav
[Is that correct]	Is that correct	✖	✖	Rec0002.wav
[Sales]	Sales	✖	✖	Rec0003.wav
[Support]	Support	✖	✖	Rec0004.wav

Figure 3-8. *Adding transcriptions*

To add a transcription, double-click in the text box in the Transcription column, and then type the text of your prompt, including brackets for extractions as desired. If you type punctuation characters (such as commas and question marks), they will not appear in the Transcription column, but they will be visible in the Display Text column, which is filled in automatically. The Display Text column does not affect how the application will sound; it simply shows the spoken phrase with punctuation and without extraction brackets. You are free to change the Display Text entry to whatever you like.

Recording Transcriptions

After you have entered the prompts in text format, you need to record the prompts. Click the row of the phrase you want to record and select Prompt ➤ Record from the menu, or simply click the Record button on the Prompt Editor toolbar. Clicking either one of these will open the Recording Tool at the bottom of the Prompt Editor window, as shown in Figure 3-9.

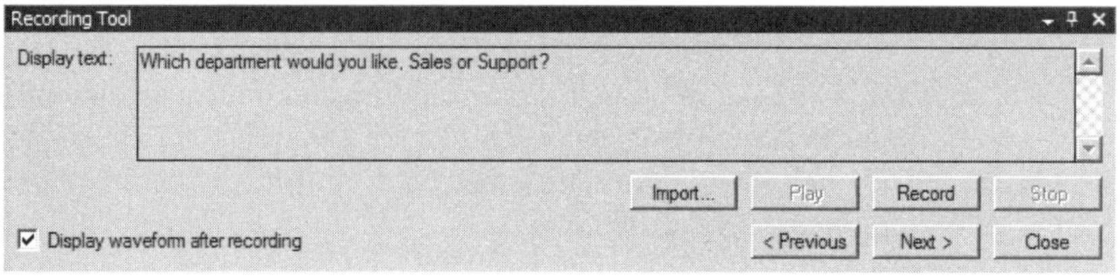

Figure 3-9. *Recording prompts*

If you want to use a different recording tool, you can export the prompt text so that you have the exact phrases that need to be recorded. For example, this might be required if you hired a professional voice artist who uses his own software for recording, You can export the prompt text by clicking the Export Script button on the Prompt Editor toolbar and choosing the location you want to save the text files. After recording your prompts in another tool, you can import multiple recordings at one time. To do this, select the rows of the prompts for which you are going to import recordings, right-click, and select Import Wave, as shown in Figure 3-10. You will be prompted to select the directory that contains the wave files. The Prompt Editor will then match the wave file to the prompt based on the name of the wave file.

■**Caution** Use 22.05kHz or 44.1kHz wave files. Avoid using 8kHz files, because they may result in prompts with extremely lower-quality sound.

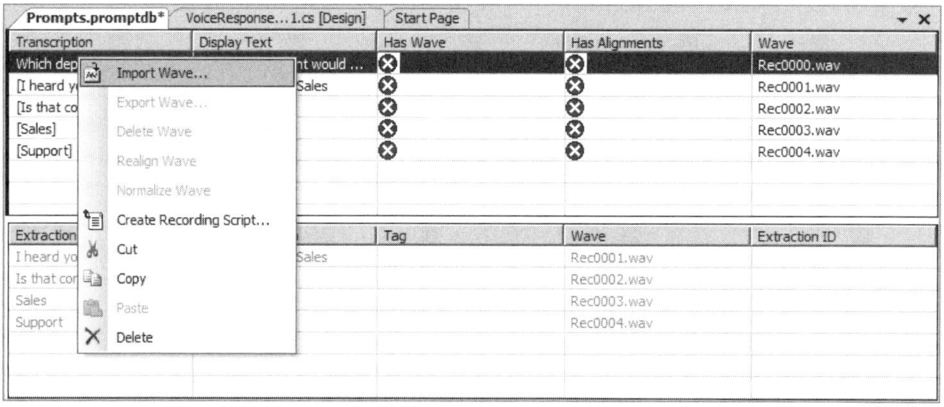

Figure 3-10. *Importing a wave file*

Working with Extractions

Extractions allow you to put two or more individual recordings together to form one prompt phrase. This way, you can reuse words and phrases for different purposes.

Extractions are created automatically for anything in between the square brackets. In the previous example, adding the transcriptions [I heard you say] Sales, [Sales], and [Support] creates three extractions: I heard you say, Sales, and Support. With these extractions, you could create a variety of phrases. For example, the application could say "I heard you say Sales" or "I heard you say Support."

You can further define extractions by adding tags to denote their context. You can also add an ID value that your application can use to call a specific extraction.

Adding Tags

You may want to record the same word or phrase multiple times but use the extraction in a different context, and you may need to specify how to say something based on the context. For example, you may want to use the Sales extraction in a different context other than referring to a department. To do this, you can add a *tag* to the word or phrase to identify its purpose—that it is a department, in this example.

You can add a tag in two ways:

- Add the tag directly to the transcription text by entering it within curly brackets ({}) brackets, before the closing extraction bracket, as in [Sales {department}]. To add multiple tags, use the semicolon to separate the tags, as in [Sales {department; name}].

- Add the tag directly to the Tag column of the Extraction section. Separate multiple tags with semicolons.

After you add a tag, it will appear in the Tag column of the Extraction section, as shown in Figure 3-11. In this example, the application can request the Sales prompt or Support prompt with the department tag.

Extraction	Full Transcription △	Tag	Wave	Extraction ID
I heard you say	I heard you say Sales		Rec0001.wav	
Is that correct	Is that correct		Rec0002.wav	
Sales	Sales	department	Rec0003.wav	
Support	Support	department	Rec0004.wav	

Figure 3-11. *Adding extraction tags*

Adding Extraction IDs

You can also assign an ID to an extraction, so that you can have your application play the prompt specified by the ID value, instead of by the extraction text and/or the tag.

To add an ID, you can simply type it directly in the Extraction ID column of the Extraction section. Alternatively, enter it within the transcription text within angle (<>) brackets before the closing bracket of the extraction. For example, [Sales {department; name} <1>] assigns an ID of 1. Figure 3-12 shows an example of assigning IDs to the Sales and Support extractions.

Extraction	Full Transcription	Tag △	Wave	Extraction ID
I heard you say	I heard you say Sales		Rec0001.wav	
Is that correct	Is that correct		Rec0002.wav	
Support	Support	department	Rec0004.wav	
Sales	Sales	department;name	Rec0003.wav	

Figure 3-12. *Adding extraction IDs*

Tuning Prompt Alignments

You can align each individual word in a prompt phrase to the specific section of the recording that says that word. Speech Server attempts to do so automatically, but you may want to check that it is accurate and make changes accordingly. This is especially useful to make sure that your prompts with extractions will not sound choppy.

Open the .wav file for alignment by double-clicking the Has Alignments column in the transcription section of the Prompt Editor. The recording will open in the spectrum view, as shown in Figure 3-13.

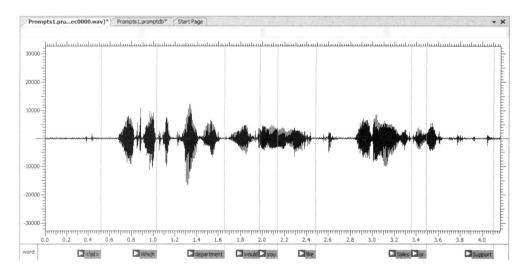

Figure 3-13. *Tuning alignment*

You can see each word of the phrase at the bottom of the view. To play each word individually and make sure it sounds correct when it is played separately from the whole phrase, click the play icon next to the word. If the individual word is being cut off, adjust the alignment by dragging the start and end alignment bar next to the word you want to align.

While doing tune alignment, you may want to increase or reduce the silence in between your words or phrases. For example, the prompt "Please say [Support] or [Sales]," has the words *Support* and *Sales* as extractions. You might want to include all or part of the silence between the word *or* and *Sales*, or you might want to include part or all the silence after the word *Support*. You can adjust the tune alignment bar accordingly. If you want more silence between words, you can right-click in the spectrum view, and copy and paste the silent segment from the front end of the recording to in between the words where additional silence is needed, as shown in Figure 3-14.

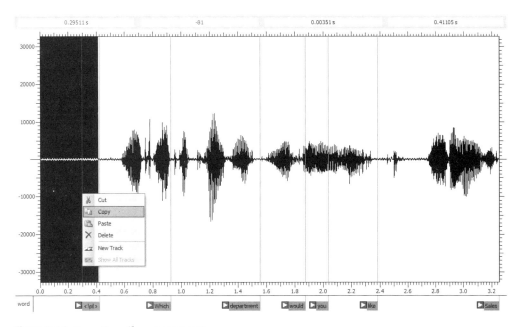

Figure 3-14. *Inserting silence segments*

Modifying Prompt Project Settings

You can change the Prompt project settings by right-clicking the Prompt project in the Solution Explorer and choosing Properties. This will open the project Property Pages dialog box, as shown in Figure 3-15.

As noted earlier in the chapter, if your application will support multiple languages, you need to add a prompt database for each language to the prompt project. Next, you need to set the language via the Language drop-down list of the Prompt project Property Pages dialog box. This list will contain only the languages for which you have a language pack installed. Then you will need to add and record the same prompts for each corresponding language. In the following chapters, I will show you how you can implement support for using multiple prompt databases.

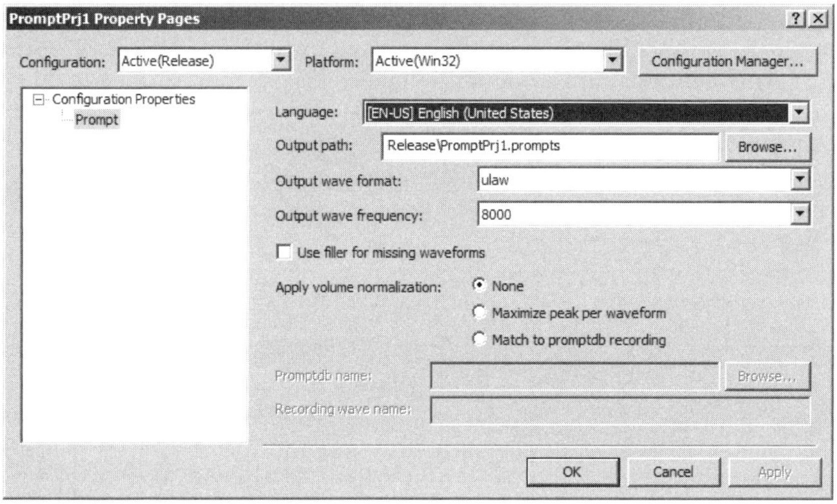

Figure 3-15. *Prompt project properties*

The Output Wave Format drop-down list offers two choices: alaw and ulaw. These represent the two telephony encoding standards defined by the International Telecommunications Union (ITU). The u-law format is the standard used in the United States and Japan, and a-law is used in the rest of the world. When communicating between two different standards—for example, United States to Spain or Spain to the United States—the burden of doing the audio conversion is placed on the u-law caller or recipient. This conversion is done automatically, but can sometimes result in poor sounding audio. To minimize this effect, you should set the format for the majority of your callers in the project Property Pages dialog box.

Using PEML

The Prompt Engine Markup Language (PEML) allows you to specify how the Prompt Engine should handle and modify certain prerecorded prompts. Although the examples in this book use the alternatives in managed code, rather than PEML, as you gain more experience with developing applications with Speech Server, you may want to use PEML. This section presents an overview of the PEML syntax and structure.

At the top of the PEML structure is the root element `<peml:prompt_output>`. All PEML elements must be enclosed by this element. Speech Server supports six PEML elements:

- `<peml:database>`

- `<peml:id>`

- `<peml:div>`

- `<peml:tts>`

- `<peml:withtag>`

- `<peml:rule>`

The `<peml:database>` element has two attributes: fname and idset. The fname attribute is required and should contain the URL for the location of the prompt database that you want to load. You can load multiple databases by adding multiple `<peml:database>` elements. For example, if you had two prompt databases—one for main prompts and the other for credit card prompts—you could specify both prompt databases as follows:

```
<peml:prompt_output>
    <peml:database fname="http://www.apress.com/main.prompts" />
    <peml:database fname="http://www.apress.com/creditcard.prompts" />
</peml:prompt_output>
```

The idset attribute tells the prompt engine that all IDs begin with a specific prefix, as in this example:

```
<peml:prompt_output>
    <peml:database fname="http://www.apress.com/main.prompts" idset="main"/>
    <peml:database fname="http://www.apress.com/creditcard.prompts" idset="credit"/>
</peml:prompt_output>
```

This signifies that the extraction IDs in the main prompt database begin with the text main and the extraction IDs in the credit card prompt database begin with the text credit. This would allow you to do a look up the ID values and play the specific prompt.

The `<peml:id>` element has one attribute, id, which is required. This tag allows your application to play a specific prompt by using the id value of the prompt. For example, the following PEML would play the prompt with an ID of 001 in the main prompt database.

```
<peml:prompt_output>
    <peml:database fname="http://www.apress.com/main.prompts" idset="main"/>
    <peml:database fname="http://www.apress.com/creditcard.prompts" idset="credit"/>
<peml:id id="main001" />
</peml:prompt_output>
```

The `<peml:div>` element does not have any attributes. It allows you to divide text into different segments, and then search the prompt databases for a prompt and play that prompt. Here is an example:

```
<peml:prompt_output>
    <peml:database fname="http://www.apress.com/main.prompts" idset="main"/>
Did you say <peml:div /> Sales?
</peml:prompt_output>
```

This would look up the phrases "Did you say" and "Sales" in the prompt database. If it does not find a prompt with a transcription of Sales, it will pronounce the word "Sales" using the TTS engine. If it did find a match, it would play the "Sales" prompt after the "Did you say" prompt.

The `<peml:tts>` element tells the prompt engine to use the TTS to render any text in between the tag and not to perform any prompt database searches. Here is an example:

```
<peml:prompt_output>
    <peml:database fname="http://www.apress.com/main.prompts" idset="main"/>
    Did you say <peml:tts> Sales </peml:tts>
</peml:prompt_output>
```

This would perform a database search for the phrase "Did you say," but would not search for "Sales" and would automatically use the TTS engine to render the phrase "Sales."

The `<peml:withtag>` element has one attribute, tag, which is required. It tells the prompt engine to find a prompt with a tag that matches the tag attribute. If no prompt is found using the tag, the Prompt Engine will continue searching for the prompt normally. Here is an example:

```
<peml:prompt_output>
   <peml:database fname="http://www.apress.com/main.prompts" idset="main"/>
   Did you say <peml:withtag tag="department">Sales</peml:withtag>
</peml:prompt_output>
```

The `<peml:withtag>` element can have multiple nested `<peml:withtag>` elements. The Prompt Engine will search for a prompt that contains all of the tags, and continue searching normally if it cannot find a prompt that has all of the tags. The following demonstrates its use.

```
<peml:prompt_output>
   <peml:database fname="http://www.apresss.com/main.prompts" idset="main"/>
...Did you say <peml:withtag tag="department"> <peml:withtag
tag="name">Sales</peml:withtag></peml:withtag>
</peml:prompt_output>
```

The `<peml:rule>` element allows you to reference a JavaScript or VBScript function to do text normalization. Suppose that your prompts have title abbreviations, such as Mr., Dr., Ms., or Mrs. You would probably have a prerecorded prompt that would say each title, so that the prompt said "Mister" rather than "M R period," for example. Using a PEML rule, you could specify a function that would change the title to the proper format before performing a database lookup for the prompt, as in this example:

```
<peml:prompt_output>
<peml:rule name="title">Mr. Joe Smith</peml:rule>
</peml:prompt_output>
```

If no prompt is found, it will render the formatted text using the TTS engine. And that brings us to the topic of the next section: TTS prompts.

Working with TTS Prompts

If you decide to go with TTS for your prompts, you can change the default voice to be male or female. You can also customize the voice by using Speech Synthesis Markup Language (SSML).

Changing the Default Voice

Speech Server includes two voices for TTS in the English language pack: Jill and Tom. Jill is the default voice, but you can configure Tom to be the default during runtime.

InstalledVoices is a collection of installed voices. In the language packs, 0 represents the standard female voice (Jill, in the English language pack), and 1 represents the male voice (Tom in the English language pack). You generally should change the voice of your application in the Initialize event, as in this Voice Response Workflow example:

```
protected override void Initialize(IServiceProvider provider)
{
    base.Initialize(provider);
    host.TelephonySession.Synthesizer.DefaultVoice =
host.TelephonySession.Synthesizer.InstalledVoices[1];
}
```

Using SSML to Modify the TTS Voice

Using SSML, you can customize how the TTS engine renders its voice. You can modify the volume, pitch, rate, and pronunciation of a prompt. Here, we will focus on the SSML for controlling TTS prompts. Implementing SSML in your application will be covered in Chapter 6.

The following SSML elements control how the TTS engine speaks prompts:

- `<ssml:speak>`

- `<ssml:paragraph>`

- `<ssml:sentence>`

- `<ssml:say-as>`

- `<ssml:phoneme>`

- `<ssml:sub>`

- `<ssml:emphasis>`

- `<ssml:break>`

Speak

The `<ssml:speak>` element is the root element: It has three attributes:

- `version`: A required attribute that specifies the version number of the SSML specification that is being used.

- `xml:lang`: An optional attribute, which should include the spoken language that the TTS engine will be using.

- `xmlns`: A required attribute that should contain the URI for the current SSML definition document.

Here is an example:

```
<ssml:speak version="1.0"
xmlns:ssml=http://www.w3.org/2001/10/synthesis
xml:lang="en-US">
</ssml:speak>
```

Sentence Structure

The `<ssml:paragraph>` and `<ssml:sentence>` elements allow you to specifically define the sentence structure for the TSS engine. This allows the TTS engine to properly place sentence and paragraph pauses, as in spoken text. Here is an example:

```
<ssml:speak version="1.0"
xmlns:ssml=http://www.w3.org/2001/10/synthesis
xml:lang="enUS">
    <ssml:paragraph>
        <ssml:sentence>Welcome and thank you for calling.</ssml:sentence>
    </ssml:paragraph>
</ssml:speak>
```

If you do not include these elements, the TTS engine will automatically determine the sentence structure, as in this example:

```
<ssml:speak version="1.0"
xmlns:ssml=http://www.w3.org/2001/10/synthesis
xml:lang="enUS">
    <ssml:paragraph>
        Welcome and thank you for calling.
    </ssml:paragraph>
</ssml:speak>
```

Formatted Prompts

The `<ssml:say-as>` element allows you to produce formatted prompts by assigning the text a type. It has one required attribute: `type`. Speech Server supports the types listed in Table 3-2.

Table 3-2. *SSML:Say-As Types*

Type	Definition
acronym	Renders the element text as an acronym
address	Renders the element text as an address
currency	Renders the element text as a currency amount
date	Renders the element as date using the extension for formatting
name	Sets the element text as a name
net	Renders the element text either as an e-mail or an URI
number	Renders the element text as a number; with the extensions for floats, integers, fractions, and floating points, renders the prompt as a cardinal or ordinal number; with the digits extension, renders the prompt as a series of numbers
spell-out	Renders the element text as individual letters
time	Renders the element text in a time format
phone	Renders the element text as a telephone number

For example, if you have a dollar amount such as $5.50, you could write the following SSML:

```
<ssml:say-as type="currency">5.50</ssml:say-as>.
```

The TTS engine would speak the prompt as "five dollars and fifty cents." This is based on the language defined in `xml:lang` attribute of the root element (`ssml:speak`) of the document.

Pronunciation

The `<ssml:phoneme>` element allows you to set the pronunciation of the text. It has two required attributes:

- `alphabet`: The phonetic alphabet used to pronounce the word.

- `ph`: The pronunciation of the word.

Here is an example:

```
<ssml:phoneme ph="l aa r jh">large</ssml:phoneme>
```

Substitution

The `<ssml:sub>` element allows you to specify spoken text in place of the written text. It has one attribute, `alias`, which is required. For example, you can replace the text "ASP.NET" with "A S P dot net," as follows:

```
<ssml:sub alias="A S P dot net">ASP.NET </ssml:sub>
```

Emphasis

The `<ssml:emphasis>` element tells the TTS engine to put a specific emphasis on certain words in your prompt. The following SSML would put an emphasis on the word "one."

```
You are only allowed <ssml:emphasis>one</ssml:emphasis> item.
```

Pauses

The `<ssml:break>` element allows you to control pauses between words or phrases. You can specify the pause by using either of the element's optional attributes:

- `time`: The length of the pause, in either seconds or milliseconds.

- `size`: The size of the pause. This can be `none` (10 ms), `small` (250 ms), `medium` (1000 ms), or `large` (2500 ms).

For example, for a phone number, such as (123) 555-1212, you may want to add pauses after the area code and the prefix, as follows:

```
123 <ssml:break size="small" />555 <ssml:break time="500ms" /> one two one two.
```

Dynamically Generating Prompts in Web Applications

In web-based speech applications—SALT or VoiceXML—you can use *prompt functions* to dynamically generate prompts. For example, you could prompt the user "You ordered two widgets to be delivered on Wednesday, October 16." The quantity, product, and date are variables in the prompt.

To create prompt functions, you need to add a Prompt Function file to your project in Visual Studio. Right-click the project in the Solution Editor, choose Add New Item, and choose Prompt Function File, as shown in Figure 3-16.

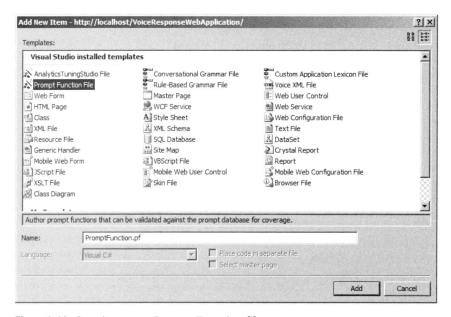

Figure 3-16. *Creating a new Prompt Function file*

Your new Prompt Function file opens in the Prompt Function Editor, as shown in Figure 3-17. This editor has three panes:

- The top pane contains buttons to create and edit the prompt functions.

- The middle pane contains the parameters for a specific prompt function.

- The bottom pane is where you write the JavaScript for your prompt function.

To create a new prompt function, click the New button in top pane. You will be prompted to assign a name to the function.

When you first create a new function, the Prompt Function Editor will automatically create the JavaScript for the wrapper and inner function, along with the History parameter. This parameter holds an array of the last user response and cannot be renamed or deleted.

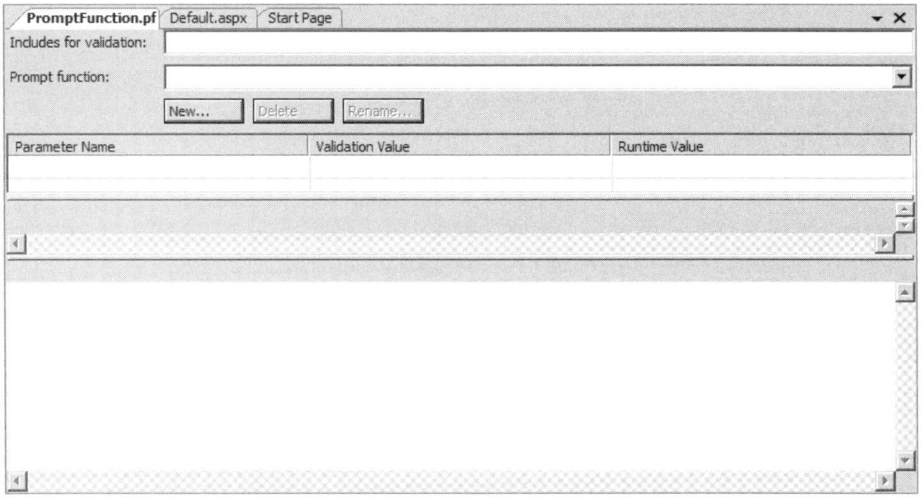

Figure 3-17. *Prompt Function Editor*

When you add a new parameter to your prompt function, the editor adds it as a variable to the wrapper function, and then adds it as a parameter to the inner function. You cannot edit the wrapper function; you can edit only the inner function.

To add a new parameter to the inner function, double-click the Parameter Name column and type the name of the parameter. In the Validation Value column, enter a list of acceptable responses. If the value doesn't matter, this column should contain the default value, such as `""` for a string or `0` for an integer. In the Runtime Value column, enter the name of the object that contains its value, such as a semantic item from the semantic item map.

▓Tip You can also create validation rules in a plain text editor to be used later and reference them via the Includes for Validation field at the top of the Prompt Editor. This allows you to reuse validation rules in more than one prompt function, without needing to re-create them.

After you add your parameters, in the bottom pane of the editor, enter a prompt function to return a string of the prompt you want the user to hear.

For example, suppose you want to prompt the user to confirm an order with something like, "You want to order a widget for $25.99 to be delivered the next day. Is that correct?" For the prompt function, you need to define parameters for the product, price, and delivery date parameters, with the values from semantic items for each. Let's name the parameters `productName`, `deliveryDate`, and `productPrice` with the runtime values `siProductName`, `siDeliveryDate`, and `siProductPrice`, respectively. Each should have `''` as its validation value.

Then write the following function to return a string of the order-confirmation prompt.

```
{
    return "You want to order a " + siProductName + " for "
+ siProductPrice + " to be delivered on " + siDeliveryDate;
}
```

Figure 3-18 shows the sample prompt function defined in the Prompt Function Editor.

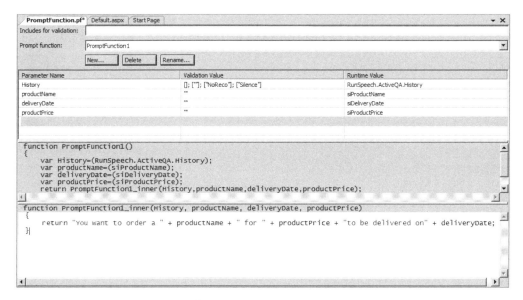

Figure 3-18. *Creating a new prompt function*

Conclusion

This chapter covered how to build prompts for your IVR applications. First, we reviewed some guidelines for creating effective prompts that will make your applications more efficient and give your users a better experience. Then you learned about the three common VUI patterns: system initiative, user initiative, and mixed initiative.

The remainder of the chapter described how to create prompts, focusing mainly on prerecorded prompts, which are recommended over TTS prompts. However, you also saw how to use SSML to modify the TTS voice.

Up to this point, you have learned how to create grammar and prompts. The next three chapters will show you how to use these grammars and prompts in your applications.

CHAPTER 4

Creating SALT Applications

OCS 2007 Speech Server offers two options for developing an IVR application using SALT: you can use the SALT-based ASP.NET controls in Visual Studio, or you can write your own SALT. Both approaches accomplish the same goal, so you should use whichever you prefer.

Speech Server's SALT applications are web-based applications, in that they run on top of an ASP.NET page and IIS. So if you are familiar with ASP.NET applications, you'll find that a lot of the SALT concepts are very similar. SALT is based on client-side code, HTML, and JavaScript.

The advantage of using SALT-based speech controls is that you do not need to know anything about SALT, but having a general understanding of SALT might be helpful. This chapter first covers using the speech controls, and then describes the SALT syntax for speech applications.

Creating a Speech Application Project in Visual Studio

SALT applications are web-based and created as Speech Application projects in Visual Studio. To create a new Speech Application project, select File ➤ New Web Site. Then choose Speech Application in the Templates list, as shown in Figure 4-1.

As with ASP.NET applications, SALT applications have three development views: the designer, the client-side source, and a code-behind. Each of these views provides the same functionality as an ASP.NET application. SALT is mostly client-side code, so you will do most of your development in either the designer or the client-side source.

When you open your new Speech Application project, it starts with an ASP.NET page that has two controls added by default: AnswerCall and SemanticMap. Additionally, a Speech tab is added to your toolbox. The Speech toolbox contains all of the available speech controls, as shown in Figure 4-2.

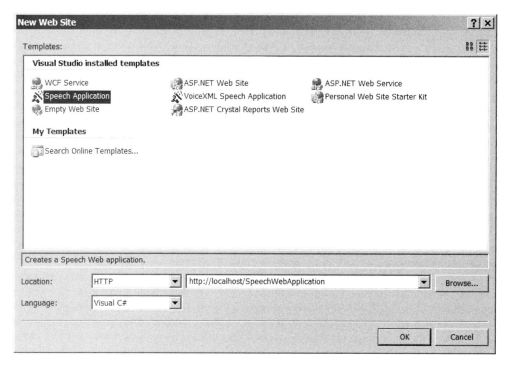

Figure 4-1. *Creating a new Speech Application project*

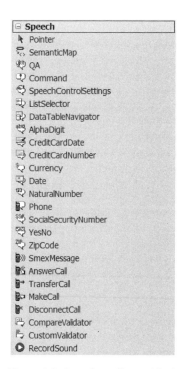

Figure 4-2. *Speech toolbox with the SALT-based speech controls*

To demonstrate how to develop an IVR application using SALT-based speech controls, you'll build a simple sample application that plays a greeting, speaks a main menu, and plays a confirmation prompt. In the designer view, beneath the AnswerCall and SemanticMap controls, add the following controls:

- SpeechControlSettings control

- Three QA controls

- Command control

After you have added the controls to the designer, you can rename them via the Properties window. Your designer view should now look like Figure 4-3.

Figure 4-3. *Speech controls added in the designer*

The AnswerCall control does exactly as its name implies: it answers the call. For most applications, it does not need any configuration. You'll learn more about it in the "Call Control" section later in this chapter. The other controls play prompts and handle user input, as you'll learn while you build the sample application.

Now that you have all the controls on the page, how does your application know which control to play when? SALT has a client-side object called RunSpeech, which manages the order of speech controls, speech dialog controls, and call controls. They are activated automatically based on the position and/or the attributes of the speech elements. However, it's still good practice to set the order manually, using the SpeechIndex property, as you'll do in the "Activating Controls" section later in this chapter.

The RunSpeech object actually does a lot more than determine the order in which controls are played. It also keeps track of the history of the call, such as semantic items and current call properties. You do not need to initialize the RunSpeech object yourself, as it is done automatically as soon as the call is answered. However, this object has several methods and properties that might be useful for your application, which are covered in the "Using the RunSpeech and SpeechControl Objects" section later in this chapter.

Now, let's begin the sample application by configuring the QA control.

Configuring a Simple Speech Application

The QA (for Question and Answer) control is really the heart and soul of a SALT-based application. It is used to ask users questions and get their responses. In your sample application, you have three QA controls, for the greeting, main menu, and confirmation prompt. Now you need to configure these controls. First, you can configure the default behavior, through the SpeechControlSettings control.

Setting Control Defaults

The SpeechControlSettings control allows you to set defaults for the current page's QA, Command, CustomValidator, CompareValidator, and SemanticItem controls. For the sample application, you need to set properties for the QA control. Right-click the SpeechControlSettings control and choose Property Builder. To add a new settings item, click the Add button. Once you have added a new settings item, on the left side of the SpeechControlSettings Properties window, select QAControlSettings, as shown in Figure 4-4. Listed under the QAControlSettings node are several categories of settings.

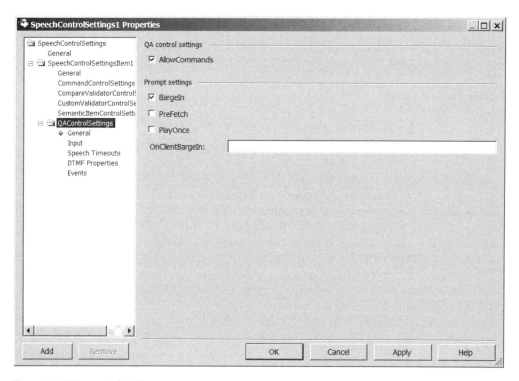

Figure 4-4. *QA control settings*

General Settings

In the General section of the QA control settings, check the AllowCommands check box, since your application will allow commands. Also check the BargeIn check box, to let prompts always barge-in. Do not check the PreFetch or PlayOnce check boxes. Your application will not require these settings for the majority of prompts, so it will handle prefetch and play-once on a prompt-by-prompt basis.

In your application, the majority of your prompts will not be using an onClientBargeIn function. If that were the case, in the OnClientBargeIn text box, you would reference the name of the client-side function that your prompts should always call when the client barges in.

Input Settings

Under the QAControlSettings node, click Input to set defaults for answers and confirmations, as shown in Figure 4-5.

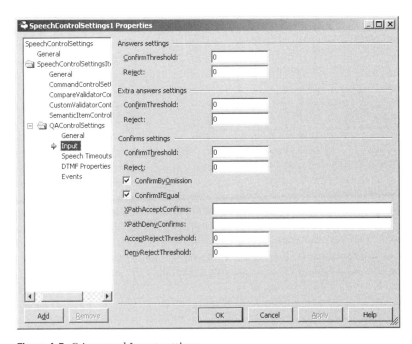

Figure 4-5. *QA control Input settings*

This dialog box has three sections: Answers Settings, Extra Answers Settings, and Confirms Settings. All three sections have two settings in common:

- *ConfirmThreshold*: The confidence value below which the application should confirm the user's response.

- *Reject*: The confidence value below which the application should reject the user input as not recognized.

For both of these values, use a decimal number to represent a percentage; for example, 1 would be 100% and .9 would be 90%.

The Answers Settings section pertains to when the user first responds to a prompt. For your sample application, set ConfirmThreshold to **.75** and Reject to **.6**. This will confirm all prompts for which the confidence value is less than 75% and reject anything under 60%.

The Extra Answers Settings section applies to applications that might support mixed-initiative dialog. This is where you specify settings for answers to questions that your application hasn't asked yet. For your application, these values should probably be a little higher than those in the Answers Settings section, since you aren't asking the question directly. Set ConfirmThreshold to **.8** and Reject to **.69**.

The Confirms Settings section applies only to the confirmation prompts. In addition to the ConfirmThreshold and Reject settings, it has ConfirmByOmission and ConfirmIfEqual properties.

By checking the ConfirmIfEqual option, if the original and the confirmed value of the semantic item are equal, the state will be set to Confirmed. If you do not select ConfirmIfEqual, if the original and confirmed values of the semantic item are equal, the state will be set to Unconfirmed. The ConfirmByOmission setting allows the application to confirm by absence of a correction. Consider the following dialog:

IVR: What size pizza would you like?

User: Large

IVR: What topping would you like?

User: Pepperoni

IVR: OK, a large pepperoni pizza

User: No, a small

The user corrected the size but not the topping. If ConfirmByOmission is enabled, the topping is considered confirmed because the user did not correct it.

The next two Confirms Settings fields, XPathAcceptConfirms and XPathDenyConfirms, refer to the XPath in your SML results, where the Accept and Deny results are located. The AcceptRejectThreshold and DenyRejectThreshold settings determine at what confidence value you want your application to reject the acceptance or denial of the confirmation.

Speech Timeout Settings

In the Speech Timeouts section of the QA control settings, you can specify the following timeouts in milliseconds:

- *FirstInitialTimeout*: Length of time before a silence event is thrown.

- *InitialTimeout*: Length of time between the start of recognition and detection of speech.

- *BabbleTimeout*: Length of time for recognition without speech matching grammars.

- *EndSilence*: Length of time the user can remain silent after giving a response and sending the results to the Speech Recognizer Engine.

- *MaxTimeout*: Maximum length of time between recognition and obtaining results from the Speech Recognizer Engine.

DTMF Properties Settings

In the DTMF Properties section, you can specify properties and events specifically for DTMF input. In the sample application, you will be asking users to enter their PIN via DTMF.

If you select the PreFlush property, the application will flush the prompt queue buffer of any previous input. For example, if you prompt users for their PIN followed by the pound sign (#), and don't set PreFlush, the next prompt will still have the # in the buffer; if your prompt is not expecting #, then an out-of-grammar error will occur. For the sample application, check the PreFlush check box, so that subsequent prompts will flush the buffer of the previously pressed key.

DTMF prompts have unique timeouts that you can set in milliseconds:

- *InitialTimeout*: Specifies the length of time the user has to give input.

- *InterDigitTimeout*: Specifies the length of time the user has in between key presses.

- *EndSilence*: Specifies the maximum time the recognition engine has to match user input to the DTMF grammar.

Activating Controls

Now you need to activate the QA controls. You can do so via the Properties window for each control. Right-click the control and choose Property Builder to access its properties, as shown in Figure 4-6.

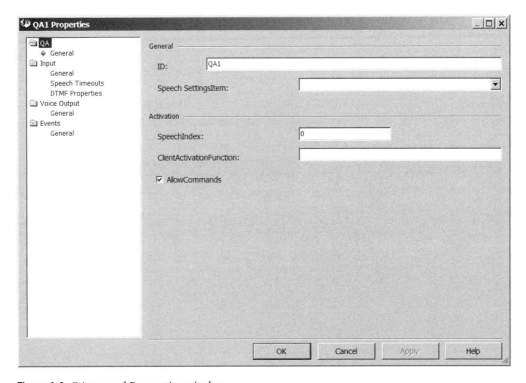

Figure 4-6. *QA control Properties window*

For each of the QA controls, in the Speech SettingsItem drop-down list, select the Speech-ControlsSettings control you added to the page and configured in the previous section. Under the Activation section, set the SpeechIndex value to define the order the prompts should be played. Although the RunSpeech object will determine the order automatically, as explained earlier in the chapter, it is best practice to assign these explicitly. This is a zero- based index, so the control with 0 will be run first, followed by the control with 1. The Greeting QA should be assigned 0, the MainMenu QA should be assigned 1, and the Confirm QA should be assigned 2.

This allows the greeting to be played first, followed by the menu, and then the confirmation. For only the MainMenu QA control, check the AllowCommands check box.

The ClientActivationFunction property allows you to reference an activation function that must be called in order for the control to run. The specified function should return `true` to run the control or `false` to not run the control. This is a client-side function, so the code must be written in JavaScript. For example, you could have the following code:

```
<script language="JavaScript">
var active = false;
function Activation() {
    return active;
}
function Activate() {
    active = true;
}
</script>
```

Configuring Prompts

Next, you need to specify what the QA controls are going to say. This is configured through the Voice Output section of the Properties window, as shown in Figure 4-7. You have two choices for prompts: a static in-line prompt or a more dynamic prompt function.

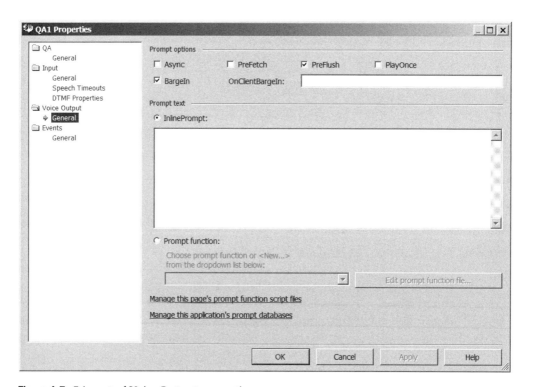

Figure 4-7. *QA control Voice Output properties*

For the Greeting QA, choose the InlinePrompt option, as this will be static and you are not accepting any input from the user. In the InlinePrompt text box, enter the prompt: **Welcome to XYZ Savings and Loan**.

Adding a Prompt Function for the Main Menu

By using a prompt function, you can adapt the prompt to the user, providing the user with more detailed information. If you don't modify the prompt for the MainMenu QA control in the example, the conversation might sound like this:

IVR: Please say Balance, Transactions, or PIN.

User: *(silent)*

IVR: Please say Balance, Transactions, or PIN.

User: *(mumbles)*

IVR: Please say Balance, Transactions, or PIN.

Using prompt functions will allow your prompts to be a little more informative than simply just repeating the prompt, like this:

IVR: Please say Balance, Transactions, or PIN.

User: *(silent)*

IVR: I didn't hear your response. Please say Balance, Transactions, or PIN.

User: *(mumbles)*

IVR: I didn't understand what you said. Please say Balance, Transactions, or PIN.

For the MainMenu QA control, choose the Prompt Function option. Next, if you have not already added a prompt function file, you need to do so by clicking the "Manage this page's prompt function script files" link. This will open a new window, as shown in Figure 4-8.

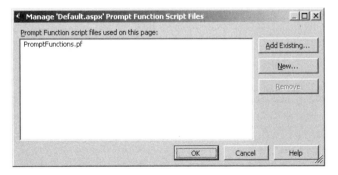

Figure 4-8. *Managing prompt function files*

Click the New button and specify a location where the prompt function file will reside. Next, back in the Properties window, choose New from the drop-down list under the Prompt

Function radio button. You will be prompted for a name for the new prompt function. After you've given the function a name, you will be taken to the Prompt Function Editor, as shown in Figure 4-9.

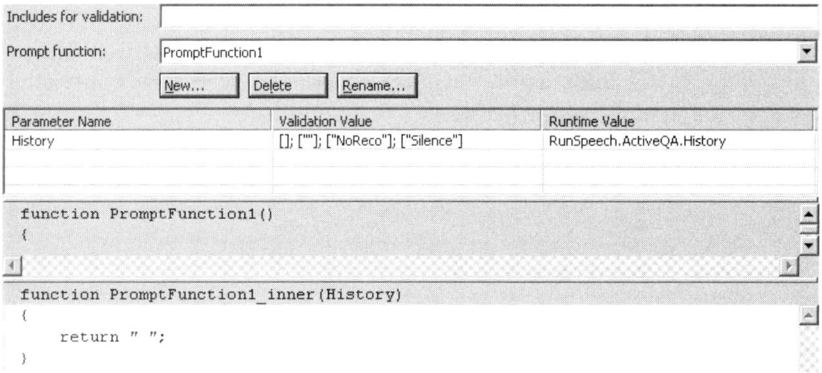

Figure 4-9. *Prompt Function Editor*

Notice that a parameter named History was automatically added with a runtime value of RunSpeech.ActiveQA.History. This refers to the RunSpeech object's History property. As mentioned earlier in the chapter, RunSpeech is a client-side object that determines the order in which controls are played, and also keeps track of the history of the call. In your prompt functions, you can use RunSpeech methods and properties, which are discussed in more detail in the "Using the RunSpeech and SpeechCommon Objects."

You will use this to determine if a NoReco or Silence event has occurred and modify the prompt to reflect that. The code you enter in the editor should look like the following:

```
{
  var sNoReco = "";
  var sSilence = "";
  var sPrompt = "";
  var sMain = "Do you want to hear your current account
Balance, Transaction History or do you want Change
your PIN?";

  var lastException = History.length == 0 ? "" : History[History.length-1];

  if (lastException == "NoReco"){
        sNoReco = "I didn't understand what you said. ";
        sPrompt = sNoReco + sMain;
  } else if (lastException == "Silence") {
        sSilence = "I didn't hear your response. ";
        sPrompt = sSilence + sMain;
  } else {
    sPrompt = sMain;
  }
  return(sPrompt);
}
```

Adding a Prompt Function for the Confirmation Prompt

For the Confirm QA control's prompt, you will also use a prompt function. Open the Prompt Function Editor as you did for the MainMenu QA control's prompt function. Enter the following beneath the row for the `History` parameter:

- In the Parameter Name column, add a parameter named `sMainMenu`.

- In the Validation Value column, enter `"Balance"`; `"Transactions"`; `"Pin"`. These values will be used to validate responses.

- In the Runtime Value column, enter `RunSpeech.GetSemanticItem(siMainMenu)`. This specifies the semantic item from the main menu prompt, which you haven't created yet, whose name will be `siMainMenu`. You use the `RunSpeech` object's `GetSemanticItem` method to return the value of the semantic item, `siMainMenu`. (See the "Using the RunSpeech and SpeechCommon Objects" section later in this chapter.)

Figure 4-10 shows the configuration for the Confirm QA control's prompt function.

Parameter Name	Validation Value	Runtime Value
History	[]; [""]; ["NoReco"]; ["Silence"]	RunSpeech.ActiveQA.History
sMainMenu	"Balance"; "Transactions"; "Pin"	RunSpeech.GetSemanticItem(siMainMenu)

Figure 4-10. *Configuring the confimation prompt function's parameters*

Your code for this prompt function will simply return a string that represents the prompt that the QA control will speak. The code you enter into the editor should look like the following:

```
{
  var sPrompt = "I heard " + sMainMenu + " is that correct?";

  return(sPrompt);
}
```

Your QA controls can now speak, but they aren't configured to get the answers from the user. Handling user input is a two-part process: first you need to set up a place to store the results, and then you need to assign grammar so that the control knows which responses are acceptable.

Configuring the SemanticMap Control to Store Responses

The SemanticMap control was added automatically when you created your new Speech Application project. Now you need to configure the SemanticMap to store the responses the user gives your application. To configure this control, right-click it in the designer and choose Property Builder.

You need to add a semantic item for each answer that you are going to track. In the sample application, the MainMenu page will need a single semantic item to store the user's response to the MainMenu prompt, "Please say Balance, Transactions, or PIN."

Click the Add button in the Properties window to add a semantic item to the SemanticMap control, as shown in Figure 4-11. In the ID text box, enter `siMainMenu`.

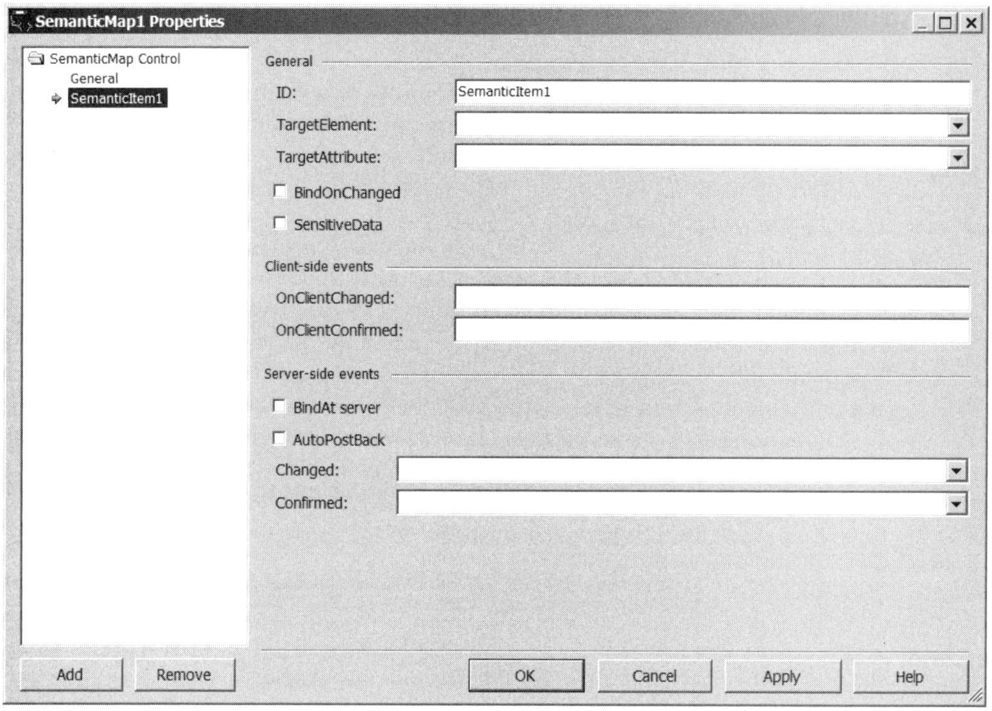

Figure 4-11. *SemanticMap control properties*

Enabling the SensitiveData check box prevents values from being logged. For example, in your sample application, you might want to turn this on for the semantic item that contains a user's PIN.

In the Client-side Events section are options for configuring two events: OnClientChanged and OnClientConfirmed. The values for each of these should be the name of a client-side function, typically written in JavaScript. The specified client-side function will be called when the text of the semantic item has been changed or confirmed, respectively.

In the Server-side Events section, the Changed and Confirmed options are similar to the corresponding client-side events, OnClientChanged and OnClientConfirmed, except they reference server-side managed code. The value should be the name of the managed function that you would like to run when the event fires. For the sample application, you want to add a server-side function for the Changed and the Confirmed events for the `siMainMenu` object. You can do this by selecting New from the drop-down list for each event.

Assigning Grammar and Semantic Items

Next, you need to assign the grammar and the semantic item to the QA controls. You do this via the QA Properties window. Under the Input node, click General, as shown in Figure 4-12.

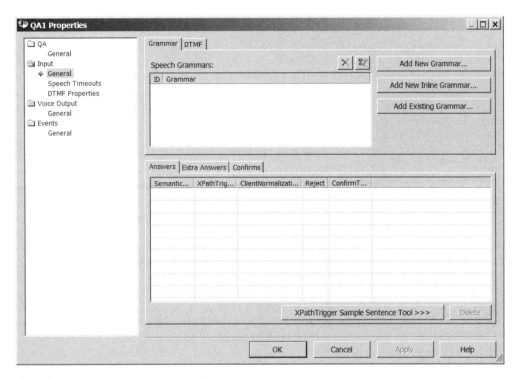

Figure 4-12. *Assigning grammar to a QA control*

To add grammar to a QA control, you have three options: Add New Grammar, Add New Inline Grammar, and Add Existing Grammar. The Add New Grammar option will create a new .grxml document and assign it to this prompt. The Add New Inline Grammar option will prompt you to write the grammar for this prompt, as shown in Figure 4-13.

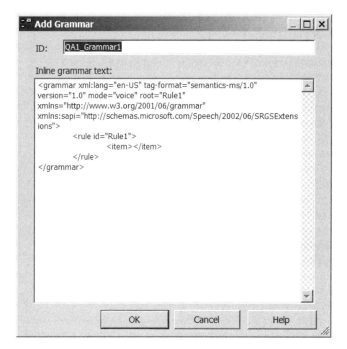

Figure 4-13. *Adding in-line grammar*

Adding Grammar for the Main Menu

For the MainMenu QA control, you will need to create grammar to handle the options Balance, PIN, and Transactions, as described in Chapter 2. Click Add Existing Grammar and choose the grammar file and rule, as shown in Figure 4-14.

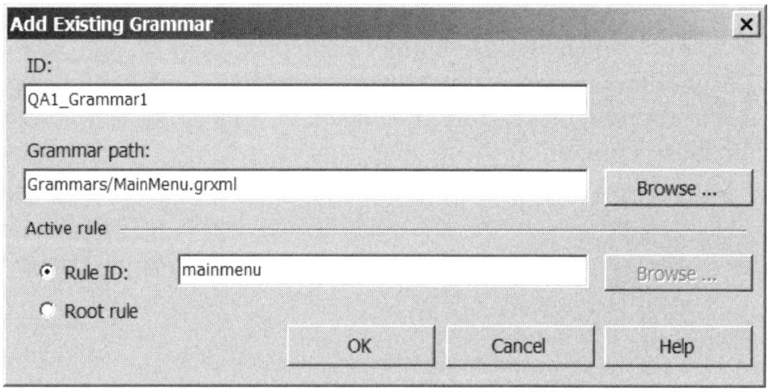

Figure 4-14. *Adding existing grammar*

On the Answers tab at the bottom of the Properties window, add the semantic item by clicking the SemanticItem column. This drop-down list will contain all of the semantic items you created in the SemanticMap control. Choose `siMainMenu`, which you created previously, as shown in Figure 4-15.

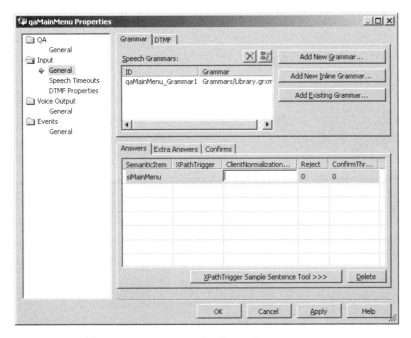

Figure 4-15. *Adding a semantic item for the main menu*

If your prompt needed unique Reject and ConfirmThreshold values, you could set these on the Answers tab as well. However, for the sample application, you have already set these through the SpeechControlSettings control, and this QA control is referencing that control, so you do not need to specify those timeouts here.

Adding Grammar for the Confirmation Prompt

For the Confirm QA control, you can use the `Confirmation_YesNo` rule from the built-in grammar library, `Library.grxml`. Click Add Existing Grammar and specify that grammar file and rule.

On the Confirms tab at the bottom of the Properties window, set the semantic item `siMainMenu` as the item that this control will confirm, as shown in Figure 4-16. You could set the ConfirmByOmission and ConfirmIfEqual properties here as well. However, since you set those in the SpeechControlSettings control, that isn't necessary for this example.

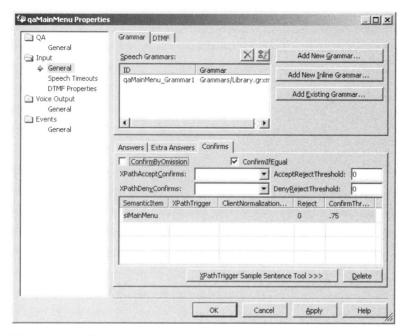

Figure 4-16. *Adding a semantic item for the confirmation prompt*

Configuring the Command Control

You can use the Command control to handle out-of-context dialog. In your sample application, you added a Command control to the page. You now need to configure this control. Right-click it in the designer and select Property Builder to open its Properties window, as shown in Figure 4-17.

In the Command section of the Properties window, two properties are required:

- *Scope*: This should reference the control, form, or panel on which the command can be activated. In the sample application, this should be set to the name of your MainMenu QA control.

- *Type*: This should be a unique name for the type of command. For the sample application, this should be Help.

Each command can reference the same scope but must reference different types.

In the Input section of the Command control Properties window, you need to assign it the grammar. You can assign the grammar by clicking the Add Existing Grammar button and selecting the grammar file and the appropriate rule. You then need to specify the XPath of the SML results. For this example, the XPath would be /SML/Command/Help. You can also set the threshold of when this command will accept a response from the user.

In the Voice Output section for this Command control, add an in-line prompt that tells the users they are being transferred to a real person, as shown in Figure 4-18.

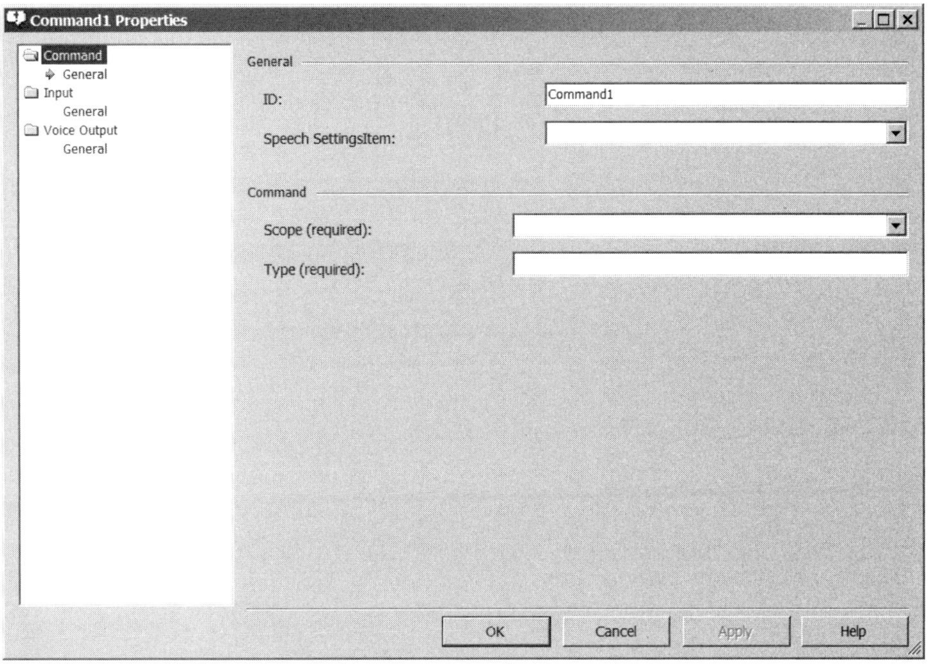

Figure 4-17. *Command control properties*

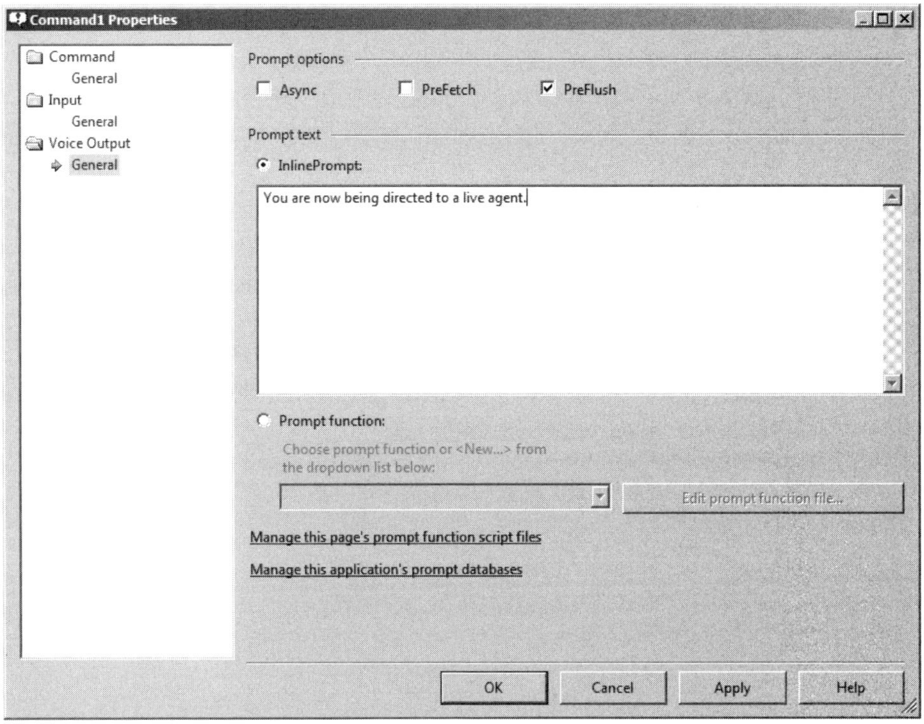

Figure 4-18. *Adding an in-line prompt for a Command control*

This wraps up the basics of creating an application using the SALT-based ASP.NET controls. Next, we'll look at the other speech controls available for SALT applications.

Using Other Speech Controls

Many other SALT-based ASP.NET controls are available for building IVR applications. This section provides brief descriptions of how they work.

Prompt and Recognition Controls

In addition to the QA control, nine other controls can handle both prompting and recognition:

- CreditCardDate
- CreditCardNumber
- Currency
- Date
- NaturalNumber
- Phone
- SocialSecurityNumber
- YesNo
- ZipCode

All of these controls work in the same basic way. They have built-in grammars to support collecting specific information. They also allow you to specify optional grammar rules via their Properties window, as shown in Figure 4-19.

The additional grammar rules refer to user speech before and after the expected answers. For example, a prompt using the CreditCardNumber control might ask the user, "What is your credit card number?" The user might respond, "OK, my credit card number is 123476804." The CreditCardNumber control will recognize only the credit card number, so you may want to create additional grammar for the speech preceding that number: "OK, my credit card number is . . .."

To add optional grammar rules, set the OptionalRulesGrammarUrl field to the location of the grammar file where these rules are located. Then select the rules from that grammar file for each of the applicable fields in the Rules section: OptionalPreAnswerRule, OptionalPostAnswerRule, OptionalPreConfirmRule, and OptionalPostConfirmRule.

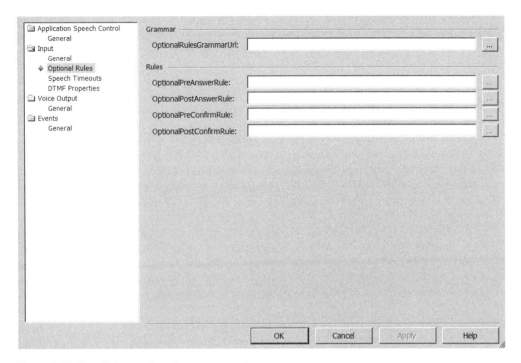

Figure 4-19. *Specifying optional grammar rules*

Data-Bound Controls

Two controls can be bound to the data and automatically use grammar based on the data source: ListSelector and DataTableNavigator.

The ListSelector Control

The ListSelector control allows users to respond to prompts with any answer that is contained in the data source to which it is bound. For example, if you wanted your application's main menu to be data-driven, you could create a table like the one shown in Table 4-1, and then configure a ListSelector control to use that table as a data source.

Table 4-1. *Sample ListSelector Table*

ID	MenuAction
1	Balance
2	Transaction
3	PIN

To use a ListSelector control, first you need to create a data source referencing the table, using a data source control, such as SqlDataSource. Then add a ListSelector control to the page and configure it via its Properties window, as shown in Figure 4-20.

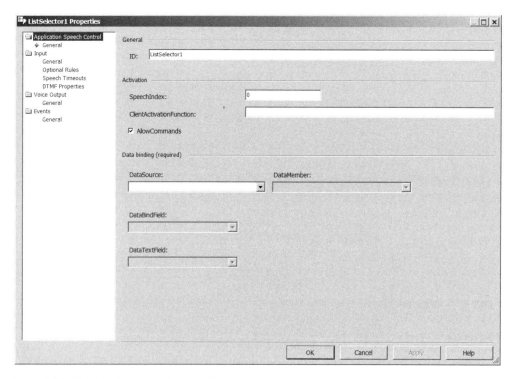

Figure 4-20. *ListSelector control properties*

In the Data Binding section, complete the required information as follows:

- *DataSource*: Choose the data source that references the table you want to use.

- *DataMember*: Select the name of the table that contains the data.

- *DataBindField*: Choose the column of the data source that contains the values of your list items (such as ID for the example in Table 4-1).

- *DataTextField*: Choose the column that contains the values that the user can say to select this item (such as MenuAction for the example in Table 4-1).

Next, select the Input node in the Properties dialog box. In the General section, you need to assign a semantic item that you have created in a SemanticMap control, as explained in the "Configuring the SemanticMap Control to Store Responses" section earlier in this chapter. This will hold the value of the user's response. For the example of the main menu selections in Table 4-1, you would assign `siMainMenu`.

The DataTableNavigator Control

The DataTableNavigator control allows the user to move through rows of a table by using commands. For example, if you had a table with transaction history like the one shown in Table 4-2, the following dialog could occur after the user selected Transactions from your application's main menu:

IVR: Transaction 4 for the amount of $200.50

IVR: Next command?

User: Next

IVR: Transaction 3 for the amount of $21.99

User: Read

IVR: Transaction 3 was a debit purchase for pizza delivery on October 4, 2006, in the amount of $21.99.

Table 4-2. *Sample DataTableNavigator Table*

AccountID	TransID	Date	Amount	Type	Payee
1234	1	10/1/2006	$100.36	Deposit	Null
1234	2	10/2/2006	$50.50	Debit	Grocery Store
1234	3	10/4/2006	$21.99	Debit	Pizza Delivery
1234	4	10/5/2006	$200.50	Deposit	Null

To use a DataTableNavigator control, first you will need to add a new page to the solution (right-click the project in the Solution Explorer, choose Add New Item, and select Web Form). Next, add a SqlDataSource control that references the table that contains the data. Then add a DataTableNavigator control to the page and configure it via its Properties window, as shown in Figure 4-21.

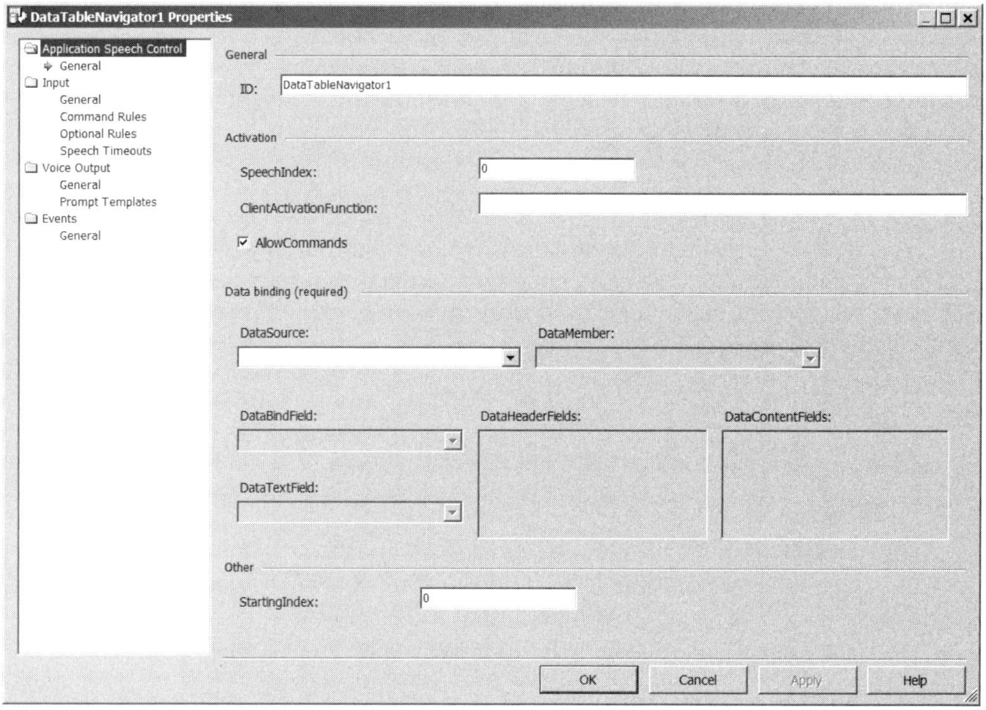

Figure 4-21. *DataTableNavigator control properties*

In the Data Binding section, set the DataSource property to the data source you created and set the DataMember property to the table name. Leave the DataBindField and DataText-Field fields blank. Set the DataHeaderFields to the primary key columns, which are AccountID, TransID, and Date in the example in Table 4-2. Set the DataContentFields to the remaining fields, which are Amount, Type, and Payee in the example in Table 4-2.

Click the Input node in the Properties window. In the General section, choose which access mode you want to use:

- *Ignore:* Ignores the question prompt and plays the no recognition prompt. The user can say anything that the data source contains.

- *Select*: Navigates to the first row of the data source and asks the user "Next command?" This allows the user to navigate through the table without leaving the control. This is the mode used in this section's example.

- *Fetch*: Stores the recognized user speech in the specified semantic item and moves to the next control.

In the Command Rules section under Input, you can specify additional grammars that the DataTableNavigator will support, as shown in Figure 4-22. For example, for the Next command, you can add grammar that will trigger the Next command when a user says "More."

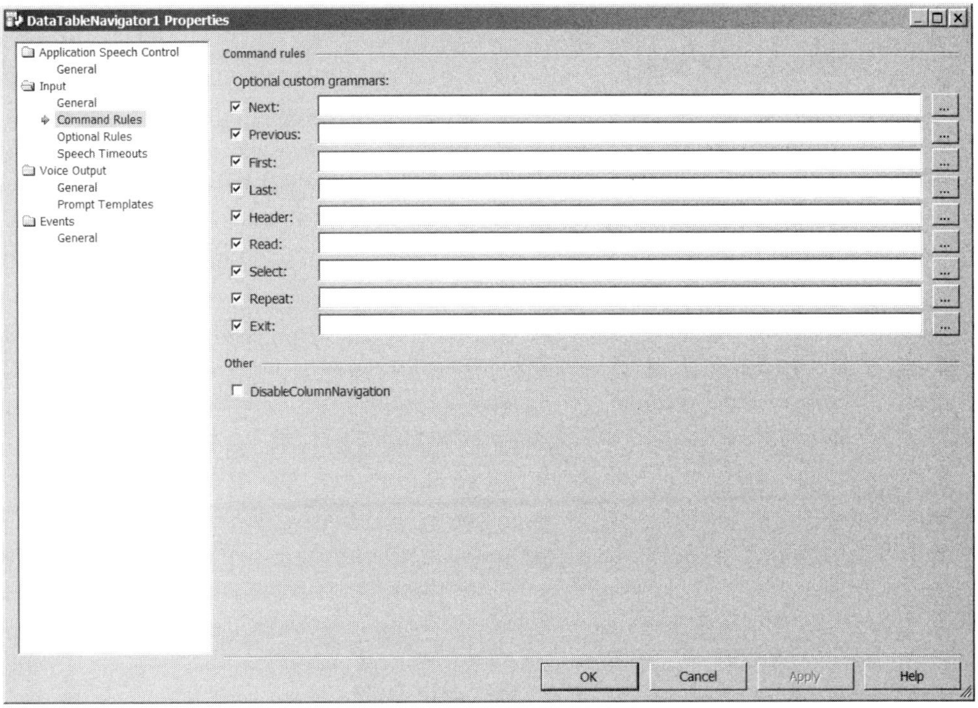

Figure 4-22. *DataTableNavigator control Command Rules properties*

Validators

The CompareValidator and CustomValidator controls can validate a semantic item's value. When the validation rules are broken, the validator control will play a prompt and then play the original QA control with which the rules are associated. The CompareValidator control supports validation with a fixed set of operators, and the CustomValidator control supports validation by application-specific client-side scripts.

Your validator control should play immediately after its associated QA control. You can ensure this by placing it directly after the QA control on the designer or by setting its SpeechIndex property to the next index value after the QA control's index value.

The CompareValidator Control

To use a CompareValidator control, add it after its associated QA control and configure it via its Properties window, as shown in Figure 4-23.

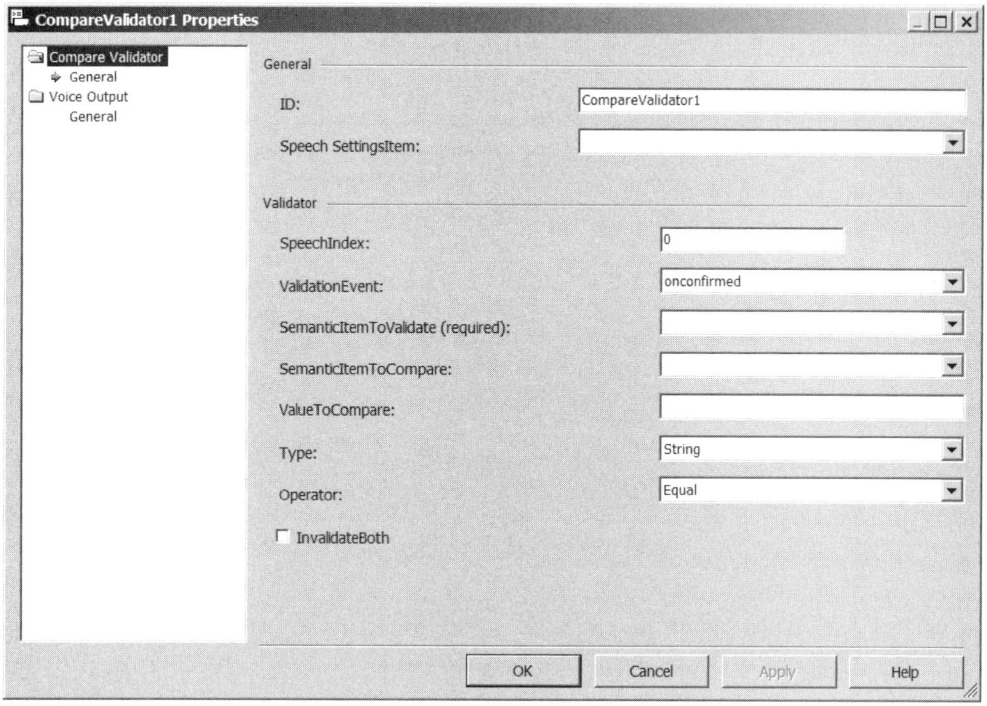

Figure 4-23. *CompareValidator control properties*

Set the ValidationEvent property to either the `onconfirmed` or `onchange` event. When the validation event fires, the CompareValidator is activated and will compare the SemanticItemToValidate value to either the SemanticItemToCompare value or a constant value in the ValueToCompare property. The Operator property specifies the type of comparison, which can be either equal to or less than.

If the result of the comparison is false, CompareValidator invalidates the item specified by SemanticItemToValidate. If the result is false and you've selected the InvalidateBoth option, the SemanticItemToValidate and SemanticItemToCompare properties are both invalidated. When the result of the comparison is false, the CompareValidator control plays an associated prompt to inform the user that the data is not valid.

The CustomValidator Control

The CustomValidator control is similar to the CompareValidator control, except that it uses a custom function to validate the results. Figure 4-24 shows its Properties window.

The ClientValidationFunction field should reference a client-side script that returns either true or false. If it returns false, the CustomValidator control will play the prompt specified in the Voice Output section. Typically, this prompt tells users that data they gave is invalid.

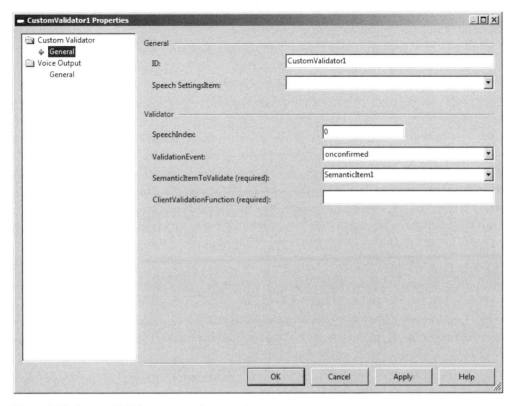

Figure 4-24. *CustomValidator control properties*

Call Controls

Four controls can handle calls: AnswerCall, TransferCall, MakeCall, and DisconnectCall.

The AnswerCall Control

The AnswerCall control is generally the first control on a page for an inbound application (the user calls the application). It handles picking up the telephone call from the user. For most applications, you will not need to configure this control. However, you can set the following properties to expand the functionally of the control:

- OnClientConnected
- OnClientDelivered
- OnClientError
- OnClientFailed
- OnClientTimeout

These properties allow you to specify a client-side function to handle the different events. For example, you may want to log client information when a call is answered. You could use the following JavaScript function and set the OnClientConnected property to the name of the function.

```
function OnClientConnected(obj, CallID, CallingDevice,
CalledDevice, cstaMessageDomObject) {
    LogMessage("", "Client Connected: " +  CallID +
" - " + CallingDevice + " - " + CalledDevice);
    return true;
 }
```

The TransferCall Control

The TransferCall control is used if you want your application to transfer the user to another line. For example, your application might allow the user to be transferred to a live operator. You can specify the extension or number to transfer the user to via the TransferredTo property of the TransferCall. This control allows for blind transfers only—meaning when the RunSpeech object encounters the TransferCall control, it stops all other dialog until the transfer has completed. Telephony Application Services (TAS) then terminates the call and closes the application.

For example, suppose that you want to transfer the user to a real person when the user says, "Help." For this, you need a Command control that accepts the Help command, as described earlier in this chapter. Then you need to define two client-side functions: one that is called after the user triggers the command and one for the activation function of the TransferCall control.

```
<script language="JavaScript">
var activeTransfer = false;
function TransferActivation() {
    return activeTransfer;
}
function HelpCommandTriggered() {
    activeTransfer = true;
}
</script>
```

In the Command control, set the OnClientCommand property to the HelpCommandTriggered function and the ClientActivationFunction property of the TransferCall control to the TransferActivation function. This way, the TransferCall control is activated only if the command is triggered.

The MakeCall Control

The MakeCall control is used for outbound applications, such as an application that calls users to let them know that their prescription is ready to be picked up. For an outbound calling application, replace the AnswerCall control that was added automatically with a MakeCall control. No other controls will be activated until the call has been answered by the dialed party. Specify the number to call via the CalledDirectoryNumber property.

The DisconnectCall Control

The DisconnectCall control is used for the application to terminate the call, when the application is finished. This is generally the last control of the application. Here is another example where you might need to use the control's activation function to determine when this control should be activated and disconnect the call.

Using the RunSpeech and SpeechCommon Objects

SALT provides two built-in client-side objects: RunSpeech and SpeechCommon. These typically run in the background; you do not need to interact with them at all. However, they both have publicly accessible methods and properties that you can use in your JavaScript code.

The RunSpeech Object

As you've learned, RunSpeech manages the order of your speech application controls, and also maintains call history. The RunSpeech object is initialized automatically as soon as the call is answered.

Earlier in this chapter, you learned how you can use RunSpeech in prompt functions to generate dynamic prompts. You can use the methods listed in Table 4-3 (in JavaScript or another client-side scripting language) to interact with the RunSpeech object. For example, you can use the Get method to return any property of the CallInfo object, such as the ID of the device the caller is using to call your application:

```
RunSpeech.CurrentCall().Get("DeviceID");
```

Table 4-3. *RunSpeech Methods*

Method	Description
Pause()	Stops the current Prompt, Listen, or DTMF object of the application.
Resume()	Resumes play back after the Pause method has been called.
Reset()	Resets all the application's semantic items, validators, and the HasPlayed property of all QA objects.
CurrentCall()	Returns a CallInfo object that contains information specific to current call. The CallInfo object properties include DeviceID, CallID, CallState CalledDevice CallingDevice, CorrelatorData (the correlator information that may be provided with the call by Computer Telephony Integration), and MonitorCrossRefID (the ID returned by the MonitorStart on the Start page).
GetEventSource()	Returns the SALT object that caused the most recent event.
GetSemanticItem()	Returns the semantic item based on the ID you provide.

The RunSpeech object also has several properties that you can access, as listed in Table 4-4.

Table 4-4. *RunSpeech Properties*

Property	Description
ActiveQA	Returns the most recent active QA object
History	Returns exceptions of a QA object
OnUserDisconnected	Used to set the method that should be called when the user hangs up

The SpeechCommon Object

The SpeechCommon object is another client-side object. It can be used to persist data across pages and postbacks. Up to this point, the examples have stayed on one page, but what if you wanted to divide your code across multiple pages? You could use the SpeechCommon object in your client-side code to do just that. The SpeechCommon object has Navigate and Submit methods, which are similar to the Navigation and Submission methods in ASP.NET.

You can use the Navigate method to navigate between speech pages. This allows you to structure your menus on different pages and navigate between them. For example, on the MainMenu.aspx page, the user might choose Balance, which would then navigate to the Balance.aspx page.

```
SpeechCommon.Navigate("Balance.aspx");
```

The Submit method is similar to an HTML form submit; it causes the page to post back to the server. For example, you could have a single page, MainMenu.aspx, to handle all of the menu options that will post back to the server to determine what action to perform next. The client-side objects will be persisted in the ClientViewState object when the Submit method is called.

```
SpeechCommon.Submit();
```

Writing Your Own SALT

Rather than using the SALT controls to build your speech application, you can write your own SALT, by creating a new text file and saving it with a .salt extension. This can be a good choice if you are familiar with SALT or you already have an existing SALT application.

The SALT syntax is made up of a small number of XML elements and objects that extend HTML and XHTML. The <prompt> element is used to play prompts. Three main elements support collecting user responses: the <listen> element allows for speech recognition, the <dtmf> element allows for DTMF recognition, and the <record> element allows you to record the user and save the recording.

The Prompt Element

The <prompt> element controls what the user is going to hear. You will need to decide which prompts your application will need. For example, you might want the main page of your application to have the prompts "Welcome to XYZ Savings and Loan" and "Please say Balance, Transactions, or PIN."

Each `<prompt>` element begins with the `id` attribute, which is the only required attribute.

```
<salt:prompt id="Greeting" />
```

Prompt String Specification

Now you need to decide how you are going to provide the prompt string to the `<prompt>` element. There are four ways you can provide this information:

- In-line text

- Referenced

- PEML

- Parameter text

If you want to use a static TTS prompt, you can add in-line text to specify what the prompt is going to say.

```
<salt:prompt id="Greeting">
    Thank you for calling XYZ Savings and Loan.
</salt:prompt>
```

If you want to reference an external resource for the prompt, such as an SSML file or a wave file, you can do so by using the `<content>` subelement and specifying the type and location of the external resource. Here is an example of referencing an SSML file:

```
<salt:prompt id="Greeting">
    <salt:content type="application/ssml+xml" href="greeting.ssml" />
</salt:prompt>
```

And here is an example of referencing a wave file:

```
<salt:prompt id="Greeting">
    <salt:content type="audio/wav" href="http://localhost/greeting.wav" />
</salt:prompt>
```

You also have the option of using PEML (discussed in Chapter 3) to specify a prompt database to use in the prompt.

```
<html xmlns:salt="http://www.saltforum.org/2002/SALT"
    xmlns:pe="http://schemas.microsoft.com/Speech/2003/03/PromptEngine">
    <salt:prompt id="Greeting">
        <pe:prompt_output>
            <pe:database fname="http://xyzsavings.com/Prompts/SALT.prompts" />
            Thank you for calling XYZ Savings and Loan.
        </pe:prompt_output>
    </salt:prompt>
</html>
```

Finally, you could just have an empty `<prompt>` element and pass the prompt text via the parameter of the `Start` method using JavaScript.

```
<salt:prompt id="Greeting"></salt:prompt>

   <script language="JScript">
           function StartPrompt() {
              Greeting.Start("Welcome to XYZ Savings and Loan.");
           }
   </script>
```

Tip It is a good idea to include the in-line text even for prerecorded prompts. If the recording failed, the application would use the TTS engine to produce the prompt, instead of throwing an error.

Bargeln and Prefetch Attributes

If you want to allow the users to give responses before they have heard the entire prompt, set the bargein attribute to true.

```
<salt:prompt id="MainMenu" bargein="true" >
Please say Balance, Transaction or PIN</salt:prompt>
```

If you do not specify the bargein attribute, it will use the default value of false.

If you are referencing files in your prompts, a file such as a wave file could be fairly large and take additional time to download. You can use the prefetch attribute to download an external resource before it is used. You just need to set the attribute to true and specify the location of resource that needs to be downloaded.

```
<salt:prompt id="Greeting" prefetch="true" >
    <salt:content href="greeting.wav" >
        Welcome to XYZ Savings and Loan
    </salt:content>
</salt:prompt>
```

Prompt Events

The next step is to decide which event(s) you want to handle for each `<prompt>` element. To handle events, you will need to write a JavaScript function for each event and specify the function name in the event handler. You can handle three events: onbargein, oncomplete, and onerror.

Onbargein Event

You should handle the onbargein event if you want to do any processing on what the user has said before the prompt has finished playing. You do not need to specify bargein="true" to handle the onbargein event. Setting the bargein attribute to true just stops the playing of the prompt when a barge-in occurs. If the bargein attribute is set to false and you specify a handler for the event, the event will still fire but the prompt will continue to play. The benefit of doing this is that you can match what the user said to the grammar before stopping the prompt; otherwise, you might pick up background noise from the user, which would trigger a no recognition error. This way, you can make sure that the user said something valid before stopping the prompt. Here is an example of handling the onbargein event:

```
<salt:prompt id="MainMenu" bargein="false"
onbargein="HandleOnBargeIn()" >Please say Balance,
Transaction, or PIN</salt:prompt>

<script language="JScript">
    function HandleOnBargeIn() {
    //Handle Barge In
    }
 </script>
```

You can specify the type of barge-in allowed for the prompt by using the <param> subelement with a name of bargeintype and one of the three valid bargeintype values:

- speech: A speech type (the default) will raise the onbargein event whenever it hears anything from the user.

- grammar: A grammar type will raise the onbargein event if the user response partially matches the grammar; this is based on the reject value of the <listen> element.

- final: A final type raises the onbargein event only if recognition was successful. If you choose final, the onbargein event fires before the onreco event of the <listen> element.

Here is an example of using a bargeintype of final:

```
<salt:prompt id="MainMenu" bargein="true" onbargein="HandleOnBargeIn()" >
    <salt:param name="bargeintype">final</salt:param>
    Please say Balance, Transaction, or PIN
</salt:prompt>

<script language="JScript">
    function HandleOnBargeIn() {
    //Handle Barge In
        }
 </script>
```

Oncomplete Event

The oncomplete event fires after the prompt has played successfully. You can use this event to start recognition or to play another prompt.

```
<salt:prompt id="Greeting" oncomplete="HandleOnComplete()" >
Welcome to XYZ Savings and Loan</salt:prompt>
<salt:prompt id="MainMenu" bargein="true" >
    Please say Balance, Transaction, or PIN
</salt:prompt>
```

```
<script language="JScript">
     function HandleOnComplete() {
     //Play MainMenu Prompt
     MainMenu.Start();
          }
 </script>
```

Onerror Event

The onerror event fires after an error has occurred with the prompt. You can handle this event and find out which error has occurred by using the status property of the <prompt> element. The status property returns a numeric value that signifies which error has occurred. The status value definitions are listed in Table 4-5.

Table 4-5. *Error Status Value Definitions*

Status Value	Description
0	No errors occurred. Speech concluded normally.
–1	Failed to queue the prompt onto the speech subqueue or the PromptQueue object.
–2	Failed to find a speech output resource (for distributed architectures).
–3	An invalid property/attribute setting caused a problem within the prompt request.
–4	Failed to resolve content. This is likely to be an unreachable Uniform Resource Identifier (URI) or malformed markup content.

You can check the error status by using the status property of the prompt at anytime— it doesn't have to be on the onerror event. If the onerror event fires, you will not get a status value of 0. You will get a 0 status value only if you check the status at any other time.

The following code demonstrates how to handle the onerror event and get the error status code.

```
<salt:prompt id="Greeting" onerror="HandleOnError()" >
Welcome to XYZ Savings and Loan</salt:prompt>
<salt:prompt id="MainMenu" bargein="true" >
     Please say Balance, Transaction, or PIN
</salt:prompt>

<script language="JScript">
     function HandleOnError() {
          if (Greeting.status == 0){
               Greeting.Start("No Error has occurred");
          }
```

```
        else{
            Greeting.Start("An Error has occurred
with a status value of  "  + Greeting.status);
            }
        }
</script>
```

Confidential Information

OCS 2007 Speech Server is automatically set to log almost every prompt and reply by the user, based on how you configured logging in the Administrator Console. If your prompt is going to play confidential information, such as an account number or PIN, you will want to turn off logging. You can do this by using the <param> subelement and the confidential parameter name. You simply need to set this value to true.

```
<salt:prompt id="ConfirmPIN">
     <salt:param name="confidential">true</salt:param>
</salt:prompt>
```

Prompt Methods and the PromptQueue Object

The <prompt> element has two methods: Start and Queue. The Start method should be called when you want the prompt to start playing.

```
<salt:prompt id="Greeting">Welcome to XYZ Savings and Loan</salt:prompt>

    <script language="JScript">
            function StartPrompt() {
                Greeting.Start();
            }
    </script>
```

The Queue method allows you to play prompts sequentially. For example, you may want to play your greeting prompt and then your main menu prompt. You could do this with the following code:

```
<salt:prompt id="Greeting">Welcome to XYZ Savings and Loan</salt:prompt>
<salt:prompt id="Greeting2">Please Listen the following menu carefully</salt:prompt>
<salt:prompt id="MainMenu">Please say Balance, Transactions, or PIN</salt:prompt>

    <script language="JScript">
            function StartPrompts() {
                Greeting.Queue();
                Greeting2.Queue();
                MainMenu.Queue ();
                window.PromptQueue.Start();
            }
    </script>
```

Once you have added prompts to the queue, you need to use the PromptQueue object to play those prompts. The PromptQueue object is a client-side object and must be used via client-side code, as it has no SALT syntax. It has six methods, which are listed in Table 4-6.

Table 4-6. *PromptQueue Methods*

Method	Description
Start	Triggers the PromptQueue to start playing prompts in the queue (must be called explicitly)
Pause	Pauses the playback of the current prompt without flushing the audio or removing any prompts from the queue
Resume	Resumes playback of the currently paused prompt and then continues playing prompts in the queue
Flush	Stops playing the current prompt and removes all other prompts from the queue
Stop	Stops the playback and flushes the queue
Change	Allows you to change the volume and speed of the prompts

The following code demonstrates the use of these methods together.

```
function checkListen() {
    if (keyword.value == "") {
        menu.Change(1.0, 2.0);
        keyword.Start();
    } else {
        PromptQueue.Stop();
    }
}
<salt:prompt id="menu" bargein="false" onbargein="menu.Change
(1.0, 0.5);" >Please say Balance, Transactions or
PIN</salt:prompt>

<salt:listen id="keyword" reject=".8"
onreco="checkListen()" onnoreco="checkListen()" >
        <salt:grammar src="mainmenu.grxml" />
</salt:listen>
```

This example demonstrates handling the onbargein event while setting the bargein to false, which allows the user to give a response and for you to check the response before stopping the prompt. Here, the onbargein handler, onbargein-"menu.Change(1.0, 0.5);", calls the Change method to keep the speed of the prompt the same and lower the volume by half, if the user says anything while the prompt is playing. The next section of SALT markup allows the user to give a response. It calls the defined function checkListen on the onreco and onnoreco events. This function checks the given input. If the user didn't give a valid response, it calls the Change method, to play the prompt at a normal speed and double the current volume. If the user gives a valid response, it stops playing the prompt. The `<listen>` element is covered in more detail in the next section.

The Listen Element

The `<listen>` element is how your application will implement your grammar and collect the response from the user via speech.

Grammar Specification

To implement grammar inside a `<listen>` element, you need to create a nested `<grammar>` element.

```
<salt:listen id="listenMainMenu">
    <salt:grammar name="mainmenu" />
</salt:listen>
```

You have two options to implement the grammar: reference an external grammar or use in-line grammar.

You can access an external SRGS-formatted grammar by referencing it using the src attribute.

```
<salt:listen id="listenMainMenu">
    <salt:grammar name="mainmenu" src="mainmenu.grxml" />
</salt:listen>
```

This sets the grammar to the root rule of the mainmenu.grxml document. Alternatively if you wanted to specify which public rule to apply, you could do so with the following code:

```
<salt:listen id="listenMainMenu">
        <salt:grammar src="mainmenu.grxml#firstmenu" />
</salt:listen>
```

You also have the option of developing your GRXML grammar in-line, within the `<grammar>` element itself.

```
<grammar version="1.0" tag-format="semantics-ms/1.0" lang="en-US"
xmlns="http://www.w3.org/2001/06/grammar" root="firstmenu">
    <rule id="firstmenu">
        <one-of>
            <item>Balance Inquiry</item>
            <item>Transaction History</item>
            <item>Change PIN</item>
        </one-of>
    </rule>
</grammar>
```

Listen Events

The `<listen>` element has five events that you can handle: onreco, onsilence, onspeechdetected, onnoreco, and onerror. To handle any of these events, you need to write JavaScript functions and then reference those functions in the `<listen>` element.

Onspeechdetected and Onsilence Events

The onspeechdetected event is fired when the application detects any speech from the user; it hasn't recognized any speech at this point, only that the user has said something. The next event is onsilence, which fires when the initialtimeout property of the <listen> element has expired. If the initialtimeout property isn't specified, it defaults to 3000 milliseconds. Valid values for this property are 1 to 60,000. To disable this property, set the value to 0.

```
<salt:listen id="listenMainMenu" initialtimeout="4000"
 onsilence="Handleonsilence()"
 onspeechdetected="Handleonspeechdetected()" >
    <salt:grammar name="mainmenu" src="mainmenu.grxml" />
</salt:listen>

        <script language="JScript">
            function Handleonsilence() {
                //Handle On Silence
            }
            function Handleonspeechdetected () {
                //Handle On Speech Detected
            }
    </script>
```

Onerror Event

The onerror event fires when an error has occurred. It will return an error code that describes the error. There are two sets of error codes for the <listen> element: recognition errors and recording errors. The recording errors are discussed in the "The Record Element" section later in this chapter. You can check the error code via the status property of the <listen> element. Table 4-7 lists the error codes for recognition.

Table 4-7. *Recognition Errors*

Error Code	Description
−1	Generic Speech Server error
−2	Speech application platform not found
−3	Inappropriate property/attribute setting causes a problem with the recognition request
−4	Failed to find a resource
−5	Failed to load a grammar resource
−6	Failed to activate or deactivate rules or grammars
−7	There are no active grammars
−8	There are no active grammars
−9	Recognition was attempted while another recognition was in progress

For example, in your application, you might have a <listen> element that speaks the error code that occurred.

```
<salt:prompt id="MainMenu"></salt:prompt>
<salt:listen id="listenMainMenu" onerror="HandleOnError()">
     <salt:grammar name="mainmenu" src="mainmenu.grxml" />
</salt:listen>

<script language="JScript">
 function HandleOnError() {
var Status = event.srcElement.status;
              MainMenu.Start("Error detected, status: " + Status);
}
</script>
```

Onreco and Onnoreco Events

The onreco and onnoreco events fire after the onspeechdetected event. If the user said something that matches the <listen> element's grammar, the onreco event will fire. If the user said something that doesn't match the <listen> element's grammar, the onnoreco event will fire. If the onnoreco event fires, you should reprompt the user in a more direct manner. If the onreco event fires, you should collect and process what the user said.

You can access the response of the user with the text property. The text property will contain the word or phrase the user said that was recognized from your grammar. You can also access the SML results via the recoresult property.

```
<salt:listen id="listenMainMenu"
onreco="HandleMainMenuonreco()" onerror="Handleonerror" >
     <salt:grammar src="mainmenu.grxml" />
</salt:listen>

<script language="JScript">
function HandleMainMenuonreco() {
    var sml = event.srcElement.recoresult;
    var confidence = sml.selectSingleNode("/@confidence").nodeValue;
}
function Handleonerror() {
     var errorStatus = event.srcElement.status;
}
</script>
```

You can set the confidence value that triggers an onnoreco event via the reject attribute. For example, if you want your application to trigger an onnoreco when the confidence value is less than 80% positive for the main menu, you could set the reject value to .8.

```
<salt:listen id="listenMainMenu" onreco="HandleMainMenuonreco()"
 onerror="Handleonerror" reject=".8" >
     <salt:grammar src="mainmenu.grxml" />
</salt:listen>
```

Timeout Attributes

The `<listen>` element has four timeout attributes: `initialtimeout`, `babbletimeout`, `maxtimeout`, and `endsilence`.

Initialtimeout Attribute

The `initialtimeout` attribute represents the maximum amount of time that the user has to say something before the `onsilence` event fires.

```
<salt:listen id="MainMenu" initialtimeout="10000"
 onsilence="Handleonsilence()">
     <grammar src="mainmenu.grxml" />
</salt:listen>
```

Babbletimeout Attribute

The `babbletimeout` attribute represents the maximum amount of time that the user can speak without saying anything that matches the grammar. When this timeout is exceeded, it will fire the `onnoreco` event with an error code of –15. Here is an example:

```
<salt:listen id="MainMenu" babbletimeout="10000"
 onreco="Handleonreco()" onnoreco="Handleonnoreco()" >
     <grammar src="mainmenu.grxml" />
</salt:listen>
```

This would handle the following dialog:

IVR: Please say Balance, Transactions, or PIN.

User: Umm, I am not sure. I think I need to see how much money is in my account. *(10 seconds elapse)*

IVR: Please say Balance, Transactions, or PIN. *(onnoreco fires)*

Endsilence Attribute

The `endsilence` attribute allows you to specify how long the user can pause. This can help determine if the user is actually finished speaking. After this time, it will then pass the speech to the Speech Recognizer Engine. It has a default value of 1000 milliseconds. Valid values are between 50 and 60,000 milliseconds. Here is an example:

```
<salt:listen id="MainMenu" babbletimeout="5000"
 onreco="Handleonreco()" onnoreco="Handleonnoreco()" >
     <grammar src="mainmenu.grxml" />
</salt:listen>
```

Consider the following dialog:

IVR: Please say Balance, Transactions, or PIN.

User: Umm, I am not sure . . . *(5 seconds elapse)*

IVR: Please say Balance, Transactions, or PIN. *(onnoreco fires)*

If you were to extend the endsilence timeout to 10 seconds, the user would be able to give a longer pause, and this dialog could occur:

IVR: Please say Balance, Transactions, or PIN.

User: Umm, I am not sure . . . *(5 seconds elapse)* I think I need to hear my balance.

IVR: Your account balance is 153.98. *(onreco fires)*

Maxtimeout Attribute

The maxtimeout attribute allows you to specify the maximum time to wait for the recognition results. If these results are taking too long to return, this can indicate a networking or server problem. If the maximum amount of time elapses, the onerror event is fired. The default value is 120,000 milliseconds. Valid values are between 5051 and 2,147,483,647.

■**Note** While the minimum value of 5051 seems like a strange number, it has a practical reason behind it. The maxtimeout cannot be less than the total of other timeouts. When you add the minimum values of the other timeouts together, the result is 5051.

Here is an example:

```
<listen id="MainMenuu" maxtimeout="10000" onreco="Handleonreco()"
 onnoreco="Handleonnoreco()"
    onsilence="Handleonsilence()" onerror="Handleonerror()">
    <grammar src="mainmenu.grxml" />
</listen>
```

This would handle the following dialog:

IVR: Please say Balance, Transactions, or PIN.

User: Balance *(10 seconds elapse)*

IVR: I'm sorry but a network error has occurred. Please try your call again. *(onerror fires)*

Listen Methods

The <listen> element has five methods: Start, Stop, Cancel, Activate, and Deactivate.

Start Method

The Start method tells the <listen> element to start listening for speech that matches the specified grammar. For example, here is a <listen> element for a main menu:

```
<body onload="StartRecognition()">
<salt:prompt id="MainMenuPrompt">
</salt:prompt>
<listen id="MainMenuListen" onreco="Handleonreco()" onnoreco="Handleonnoreco()"
```

```
      onsilence="Handleonsilence()" onerror="Handleonerror()">
      <grammar name="MainMenuGrammar" src="mainmenu.grxml" />
</listen>

<script language="JavaScript">
function StartMainMenu() {
    MainMenuPrompt.Start("Please say Balance, Transactions, or PIN");
    MainMenuListen.Start();
}
</script>
</body>
```

Stop Method

You can use the Stop method to stop the <listen> element's recognition and get the recognition results up to that point, at which time either the onreco or onnoreco event will fire. For example, you could use the Stop method on the onerror event, which will then decide to call the onreco or onnoreco event based on the results up to the point that the error occurred.

```
<salt:prompt id="MainMenuPrompt">
</salt:prompt>
<listen id="MainMenuListen" onerror="MainMenuListen.Stop()"
 onreco="HandleOnReco()" onnoreco="HandleOnNoReco()">
    <grammar src="mainmenu.grxml" />
</listen>
```

Cancel Method

You can use the Cancel method to stop the <listen> element's recognition and release the recognizer, which will destroy any recognition results up to that point. For example, the following code will call the Cancel method when an error occurs and will not save any recognition results.

```
<salt:prompt id="MainMenuPrompt">
</salt:prompt>
<listen id="MainMenuListen" onerror="MainMenuListen.Cancel()">
    <grammar src="mainmenu.grxml" />
</listen>
```

Deactivate Method

You can use the Deactivate method to disable the recognition for a <listen> element; however, the Deactivate method must be called before the Start method is called. For example, you could deactivate all of the commands for the MainMenuListen <listen> element with the following code:

```
<salt:prompt id="MainMenuPrompt" oncomplete="StartReco()">
</salt:prompt>
<listen id="MainMenuListen">
    <grammar name="mainmenu" src="mainmenu.grxml" />
    <grammar name="commands" src="commands.grxml" />
</listen>

<script language="JScript">
         function StartReco() {
             MainMenuListen.Deactivate("commands");
             MainMenuListen.Start();
         }
 </script>
```

Activate Method

You can use the Activate method to activate recognition on a <listen> element that was previously deactivated. However, like the Deactivate method, the Activate method must be called before the <listen> element's Start method. For example, you could reactivate just the Help rule for the command grammar with the following code:

```
<salt:prompt id="MainMenuPrompt" oncomplete="StartReco()">
</salt:prompt>
<listen id="MainMenuListen">
    <grammar name="mainmenu" src="mainmenu.grxml" />
    <grammar name="commands" src="commands.grxml" />
</listen>
<script language="JScript">
         function StartReco() {
             MainMenuListen.Deactivate ("commands");
             MainMenuListen.Activate ("commands", "help");
             MainMenuListen.Start();
         }
 </script>
```

The Record Element

In your application, you can record and save what the user said. This might be useful in a voice-mail application or an application where you need to save a user's response for legal purposes. To do this in SALT, use the <record> element inside a <listen> element. If your <listen> element also contains grammar, the grammar is ignored and the <record> element is used instead. The <record> element has one optional attribute: type. If the type attribute isn't defined, the default value of audio/wav will be used. The type describes the format of the audio that it will be recording. Table 4-8 lists the acceptable type values.

Table 4-8. *Record Type Values*

Type	Description
audio/basic	Headerless 8kHz, 8-bit mono (PCM) single-channel compressed audio based on the telephony standard of the locale where it is used. This can either be -law or u-law.
audio/wav	8kHz, 8-bit mono (PCM) single-channel compressed audio based on the telephony standard of the locale where it is used. This can either be a-law or u-law. This is the default for telephony applications.
audio/x-wav	16kHz PCM, 22kHz PCM, 8kHz PCM.

When using the <record> element, you should use the <listen> element's events to complete actions for the <record> element. For example, you might want to save a recording that a user has completed.

```
<salt:prompt id="RecordPrompt" oncomplete="RecordListen.Start()">
    For security purposes, please say your full name to
confirm that you want to change your PIN.
</salt:prompt>

<salt:listen id="RecordListen" initialtimeout="3000"
endsilence="1500" babbletimeout="60000"
onreco="RecordSaved()" onnoreco="RecordSaved()">
      <salt:record type="audio/x-wav" />
 </salt:listen>
```

Recording Properties

You may also want to get properties of the recording. You can access those via the properties of the <listen> element to which the <record> element belongs, as listed in Table 4-9.

Table 4-9. *Recording Properties*

Property	Description
recordlocation	Returns the location of the recorded audio
recordtype	Returns the MIME type of the recorded audio
recordduration	Returns the duration in milliseconds of the recorded audio
recordsize	Returns the size in bytes of the recorded audio

The following example demonstrates how to access these properties.

```
<salt:prompt id="RecordPrompt" oncomplete="RecordListen.Start()">
    For security purposes, please say your full name to
confirm that you want to change your PIN.
</salt:prompt>

<salt:listen id="RecordListen" initialtimeout="3000"
endsilence="1500" babbletimeout="60000"
onreco="RecordSaved()" onnoreco="RecordSaved()">
    <salt:record type="audio/x-wav" />
 </salt:listen>

<script language="JavaScript">
            function RecordSaved () {
                //Retrieve Recording Properties
                var recordingDuration = RecordListen.recordduration;
                var recordingLocation = RecordListen.recordlocation;
                var recordingSize = RecordListen.recordsize;
                var recordingType = RecordListen.recordtype;
            }
 </script>
```

Recording Errors

If your application encounters an error during recording, you can get the error from the parent <listen> element's status property. You can capture the error codes using the sample code presented earlier in the section about the <listen> element. Table 4-10 lists the recording error codes.

Table 4-10. *Recording Errors*

Error Code	Description
–20	Failed to record on the local platform
–21	Unsupported codec
–22	Unsupported format
–23	Error occurred during streaming to a remote server
–24	An invalid property/attribute setting caused a problem with the recording request
–30	Recording was attempted after a disconnect

Beep Attribute

Generally before starting recognition for recording, you should signal the user when to begin speaking. You can accomplish this by setting the beep attribute to true on the <listen> element to which the <record> element belongs.

```
<salt:prompt id="Record" >
          Change your PIN after the beep.
</salt:prompt>
<salt:listen beep="true" id="recordName" >
      <salt:record type="audio/x-wav" />
</salt:listen>
```

While you cannot change the way the beep sounds, you could set the beep attribute to false, and have the preceding <prompt> element to play a recorded sound.

```
<salt:prompt id="Record" >
          For security purposes, please say your full
name after the tone.
 </salt:prompt>
<salt:prompt id="CustomBeep">
    <salt:content type="audio/wav"
 href="beep.wav" />
</salt:prompt>
 <salt:listen beep="false" id="recordName" >
      <salt:record type="audio/x-wav" />
</salt:listen>
```

The DTMF Element

The <dtmf> element is similar to the <listen> element. Instead of speech, the <dtmf> element is looking for Touch-Tone keys being pressed on the telephone. As discussed in previous chapters, you generally want to use DTMF only when you are prompting users for sensitive information, such as a PIN, that others might overhear if they speak it aloud.

The <dtmf> element has only one required attribute, id, which must be unique to the page.

```
<salt:dtmf id="PIN" />
```

DMTF Events

The <dtmf> element has five events: onkeypress, onsilence, onnoreco, onreco, and onerror.

Onkeypress and Onsilence Events

The onkeypress event is similar to the onspeechdetected event for the <listen> element. The onkeypress event is fired after the user presses any telephone key. It does not represent that the key was recognized from the grammar, only that the user pressed a key.

```
<salt:dtmf id="PIN" onkeypress="HandleKeyPress()" >
      <salt:grammar src="fourdigitpin.grxml" />
</salt:dtmf>

<script language="javascript">
      function HandleKeyPress() {
          //Handle Key Presses
      }
</script>
```

The `onsilence` event is fired if the user has not pressed any key before the initial timeout period. You can specify the `initialtimeout` attribute. If you do not specify the value, a default of 5 seconds is used. For example, you could prompt users to enter their PIN, and if they do not enter anything within 6 seconds, replay the prompt.

```
<salt:prompt id="PINPrompt">Please enter your PIN now.</salt:prompt>
<salt:dtmf id="PIN" initialtimeout="6000" onsilence="PINPrompt.Start()" >
    <salt:grammar src="fourdigitpin.grxml" />
</salt:dtmf>
```

Onreco and Onnoreco Events

The `onreco` event fires when the user's input matches the grammar. The `onnoreco` event fires when either the user's input doesn't match the grammar or the `interdigittimeout` attribute has expired. The `interdigittimeout` attribute is the time between key presses. If you don't specify this attribute, it will default to 10 seconds. You can disable this timeout by setting its value to 0.

```
<salt:prompt id="PINPrompt">Please enter your PIN now.</salt:prompt>
<salt:dtmf id="PIN" interdigittimeout="6000"
 onnoreco="PINPrompt.Start()" onreco="HandleOnReco()">
    <salt:grammar src="fourdigitpin.grxml" />
</salt:dtmf>

<script language="javascript">
function HandleOnReco() {
    //Get Results and Do Next Action
 }
</script>
```

Onerror Event

The `onerror` event for the `<dtmf>` element is similar to the `onerror` event of the `<listen>` element, in that you can use the `status` property to check the error code. Table 4-11 lists the `status` value codes for DTMF errors.

Table 4-11. *DTMF Error Codes*

Value	Description
−1	A generic Microsoft speech application platform error occurred during DTMF collection
−3	An invalid property/attribute setting caused a problem with the DTMF collection request
−4	Failed to find the URI of a DTMF grammar resource
−5	Failed to load or compile a grammar resource
−8	DTMF collection was attempted without an active grammar element
−9	DTMF collection was attempted while another DTMF collection was in progress

Table 4-11. *DTMF Error Codes (Continued)*

Value	Description
–11	No DTMF input was detected within the period specified by the `initialtimeout` attribute
–13	An invalid (out-of-grammar) key press was detected
–16	No DTMF input was detected within the period specified by the `interdigittimeout` attribute
–18	SML generation failure; the DTMF grammar script might contain invalid code or might be taking too long to execute
–30	DTMF collection was attempted after a disconnect

Accessing Results

To access the results of a `<dtmf>` element, you can use either the `text` property or the `dtmfresult` property. The `text` property will give you exactly what the user has pressed. For example, a four-digit PIN might return 1 2 3 4.

```
<salt:prompt id="PINPrompt">Please enter your PIN now.</salt:prompt>
<salt:dtmf id="PIN" onnoreco="PINPrompt.Start()" onreco="HandleOnReco()">
    <salt:grammar src="fourdigitpin.grxml" />
</salt:dtmf>

<script language="javascript">
function HandleOnReco() {
    var text = PIN.text;
}
</script>
```

The `dtmfresult` property returns the SML results, which your grammar might have formatted to remove the empty spaces, as in 1234.

```
<salt:prompt id="PINPrompt">Please enter your PIN now.</salt:prompt>
<salt:dtmf id="PIN" onnoreco="PINPrompt.Start()" onreco="HandleOnReco()">
    <salt:grammar src="fourdigitpin.grxml" />
</salt:dtmf>

<script language="javascript">
function HandleOnReco() {
    var results = PIN.dtmfresult;
}
</script>
```

DMTF Methods

The <dtmf> element has three methods: Start, Stop, and Flush.

The Start method starts the recognition of DTMF input. If the <dtmf> element is used before the Start method, it will clear the results before beginning recognition again. Calling the Start method on any <dtmf> element if another <dtmf> element is still started will cause an error to occur.

The Stop method stops the recognition of DTMF input and returns partial recognition results. For example, you may want to stop recognition as soon as an error occurs. You could do so with the following code.

```
<salt:prompt id="PINPrompt">Please enter your PIN now.</salt:prompt>
<salt:dtmf id="PIN" onerror="PIN.Stop()" >
    <salt:grammar src="fourdigitpin.grxml" />
</salt:dtmf>
```

The Flush method flushes the DTMF buffer of the user's input. In the previous example. the DTMF recognition was stopped, but the DTMF buffer wasn't cleared. You could use the following code to stop recognition and then flush the results.

```
<salt:prompt id="PINPrompt">Please enter your PIN now.</salt:prompt>
<salt:dtmf id="PIN" onerror="HandleOnError()">
    <salt:grammar src="fourdigitpin.grxml" />
</salt:dtmf>

<script language="javascript">
function HandleOnError() {
        PIN.Stop();
        PIN.Flush();
 }
</script>
```

Conclusion

This chapter has covered the two methods for developing SALT applications. If you don't know SALT and do not want to learn SALT, you can use the ASP.NET SALT-based controls. If you already know or want to learn SALT, you have the option of writing SALT on your own.

The next chapter covers the VoiceXML application development model. VoiceXML is an older development language for IVR applications than SALT. They both can accomplish the same objective, and which you use is really a developer preference.

CHAPTER 5

■■■

Creating VoiceXML Applications

New to OCS 2007 Speech Server is support for VoiceXML applications. VoiceXML is a markup language that extends HTML and XHTML. Unlike SALT, VoiceXML doesn't *need* to use JavaScript. Whereas SALT relies heavily on JavaScript to make any decisions programmatically, VoiceXML allows you to do simple conditional statements directly without calling any JavaScript.

So what does a VoiceXML application look like? Well, it looks very similar to a SALT application, as they both extend HTML for a similar purpose. VoiceXML is fairly easy to read, even if you haven't used it before. Consider the following VoiceXML code:

```
<vxml version="2.0" xml:lang="en-US" xmlns=http://www.w3.org/2001/vxml
 xmlns:xsi=http://www.w3.org/2001/XMLSchema-instance
 xsi:schemaLocation="http://www.w3.org/2001/vxml
http://www.w3.org/TR/voicexml20/vxml.xsd">

<var name="strCompany" expr="'XYZ Savings and Loan'" />

<form id="Welcome">
    <block>
        <prompt>
            Welcome to <value expr="document.strCompany" />
        </prompt>
    </block>
</form>

</vxml>
```

Af first glance, you probably made the reasonable assumption that this VoiceXML application says, "Welcome to XYZ Savings and Loan." You also can see that `'XYZ Savings and Loan'` is a document variable, defined by the `var` element and its `expr` attribute.

In this chapter, you'll learn the details of creating VoiceXML applications, beginning with an overview of their scopes and interactions.

Understanding VoiceXML Scopes and Interaction

No matter the programming language, it is important to understand the scopes that are available. Also fundamental is how user and application interactions are controlled.

VoiceXML Scopes

The scope determines how actions are performed and variables are handled. VoiceXML has the following four scopes:

Session: A session starts as soon as the user's call is connected, before the first application is loaded, until the user is disconnected. Anything declared in this scope is available throughout the entire session.

Application: An application is simply one or more VoiceXML documents that contain the same root document. During a session, a user may interact with multiple applications. When the user is transitioned to another application, the previous application is unloaded before the new application is loaded. Anything declared in this scope is available only for the user's current application.

Document: A document contains one or more dialogs. At any point, the user can be in only one dialog. The session is terminated when the dialog no longer specifies the dialog to continue to next. Anything declared in the document scope is available to any dialog in the same document.

Dialog: Anything declared in the dialog scope will be available only to the declaring dialog.

VoiceXML Interaction Control

The form interpretation algorithm (FIA) controls the interaction between the caller and the forms or menus of your VoiceXML application. It decides which element should be visited and played at any given time. The FIA has two phases in which to determine what element needs to be played:

Initialization phase: This phase happens when a form is loaded or reloaded. It initializes all of the form-level variables, to undefined or to their defined default value. The FIA is part of the document scope, so the initialization phase will typically happen once per document load.

Main loop: After the initialization phase completes, the main loop phase starts. It loops through the form, choosing which element to visit, which grammar to activate, and what to do with the information collected from the user. The main loop is broken down into three phases:

- The *select phase* selects the next unfilled form item. It then looks at the condition attribute of the unfilled form item, and if it is evaluated to be true, it selects that form element and starts the collect process.

- The *collect phase* visits the selected form item from the select phase. Depending on the form item, it will play prompts, enable grammars, and collect input from the user.

- The *process phase* processes the input by executing the filled elements for the selected form item. The select phase then repeats, selecting the next unfilled form item.

You'll see the FIA in action as we go through building the parts of a VoiceXML application. But before you begin coding, you need to create a VoiceXML project in Visual Studio.

Creating a VoiceXML Project in Visual Studio

Like SALT, VoiceXML follows the web-based paradigm. So, in Visual Studio, VoiceXML projects are found under the Web Site project types. To create a new VoiceXML project in Visual Studio, choose File ➤ New ➤ Web Site. Then select VoiceXML Speech Application in the Templates list, as shown in Figure 5-1.

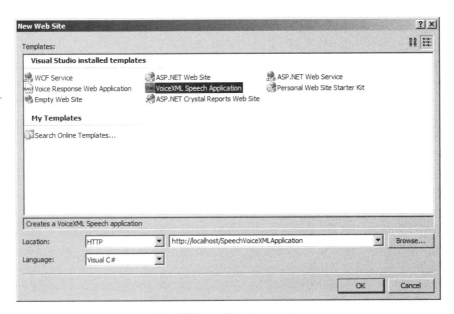

Figure 5-1. *Creating a new VoiceXML application project*

You have a couple of options when writing VoiceXML in Visual Studio. You can write VoiceXML on an .aspx page or on a .vxml page. Using an .aspx page allows you to control server-side events and dynamically create VoiceXML code via the code-behind page using either C# or Visual Basic .NET. If you do not need to control any server-side events, you can create a static .vxml page.

For either approach, you should enable the VoiceXML IntelliSense. To do this, from your .aspx or .vxml page, select VoiceXML 2.0 from the Target Schema for Validation drop-down list in the Visual Studio toolbar, as shown in Figure 5-2.

After creating your new project, you are ready to start coding your application. First up is specifying prompts and grammar, which you learned how to build in Chapters 2 and 3.

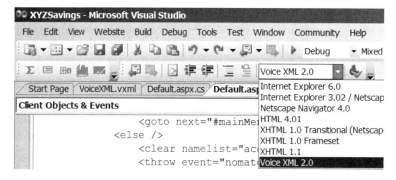

Figure 5-2. *Enabling VoiceXML IntelliSense*

Specifying Prompts and Grammar

To examine VoiceXML syntax, we'll use the following sample VoiceXML application excerpt:

```
<form id="login">
    <prompt>Welcome to XYZ Savings and Loan</prompt>
    <field name="accountNumber">
            <grammar src="PinDTMF.grxml#fourdigits"/>
            <prompt count="1">Please enter
your account number</prompt>
            <prompt count="2">Using your Touch-Tone
keypad, please enter your four-digit
account number</prompt>
            <filled>
                <prompt>Got it!</prompt>
            </filled>
        </field>
</form>
```

Adding Prompts

In VoiceXML, prompts are specified using the `<prompt>` element. Here is the first prompt in the sample application:

```
<prompt>Welcome to XYZ Savings and Loan</prompt>
```

This will use the TTS engine to render the prompt. This simple prompt will speak only the in-line text, "Welcome to XYZ Savings and Loan."

By using `<prompt>` element attributes, you can control various aspects of your prompts, as described in the following sections.

Playing Prompts Based on Count

In the example, two prompts ask for an account number:

```
<prompt count="1">Please enter your account number</prompt>
<prompt count="2">Using your Touch-Tone keypad, please
enter your four-digit account number</prompt>
```

These use the count attribute to control when they are played. The FIA keeps a count of how many times the prompt is played. You can specify a different prompt to be played for each count.

In the sample application, the user will always hear "Please enter your account number." If the user provides the requested input, the user will never hear the prompt specified with a count of 2. However, if the user doesn't provide input, the application will then play the second prompt. As another example, using the count attribute, an application might prompt a user, "Please say Balance, Transactions, or PIN." If the user didn't respond, the application may then say, "Using your Touch-Tone keypad, please enter your four-digit account number."

Allowing Barge-Ins

By setting the bargein attribute to true, you allow users to interrupt the prompt to give input immediately. The bargeintype attribute specifies how the barge-in can happen. The barge-in type can be either speech or hotword. Here is an example of using the former:

```
<prompt bargein="true" bargeintype="speech">Please enter your PIN</prompt>
```

This will stop playing the prompt as soon as any speech or DTMF input is entered by the user. So, the user could enter his PIN anytime after the first word of the prompt.

The following prompt specifies a bargeintype of hotword:

```
<prompt bargein="true" bargeintype="hotword">
Main Menu. Please say one of the following options:
<enumerate/>
</prompt>
```

This will stop the prompt only when the input matches the grammar. For example, the following conversation might occur:

IVR: Please say one of the . . .

Caller: Umm

IVR: . . . following options: Balance Inquiry, Recent

Caller: Balance Inquiry

After the first response, the prompt continued because the caller response did not match the grammar. After the user barged in again with a recognized response, the prompt stopped playing.

Timing Out

The timeout attribute allows you to specify either in seconds or milliseconds how long the user can remain silent until a nomatch error is thrown (nomatch and other errors are discussed in the "Error Handling and Logging" section later in this chapter). For example, you may want to give the user 20 seconds to answer, as follows:

```
<prompt timeout=20s>Main Menu. Please say one from the following options:</prompt>
```

Specifying Conditions

Using the cond attribute, you can specify a condition to determine whether a prompt will play. For example, you might have a variable named replay, which will determine whether a certain prompt is played. The cond attribute will have a valid JavaScript expression statement, as in the following example, which must evaluate to true in order for the prompt to play.

```
<var name="replay" expr="1"/>
<prompt cond="replay = 1">Your account balance is $123.55</prompt>
```

Playing Prerecorded Prompts

To play prerecorded prompts, you use the <audio> element and set the src attribute to the location of the recording file. You should also specify the spoken text, so that the TTS engine will play the prompt if the recording fails. Here is an example:

```
<prompt>
<audio src="Greeting.wav">
Welcome to XYZ Savings and Loan
</audio>
<prompt>
```

You can also use the expr attribute of the <audio> element to retrieve the value of the audio to be played, via JavaScript or a <var> element. Here is an example of using a <var> element:

```
<var name="Greeting" expr="'Greeting.wav'"/>
<prompt>
<audio expr="Greeting">
Welcome to XYZ Savings and Loan
</audio>
<prompt>
```

And here is an example of using a <script> element:

```
<script language="javascript">
    GetAudio(string audio){
        //Get and return based on input string
    }
</script>
```

```
<prompt>
    <audio expr="GetAudio(Greeting)">
            Welcome to XYZ Savings and Loan
    </audio>
<prompt>
```

Ideally, you should use a prompt database, as discussed in Chapter 3. To use a prompt database in a VoiceXML application, you need to use PEML, also introduced in Chapter 3. For example, if you had a prompt database with a recording of "Welcome to XYZ Savings and Loan," you could access it in your VoiceXML application with the following code.

```
<prompt>
    <peml:prompt_output
xmlns:peml="http://schemas.microsoft.com/Speech/2003/03/PromptEngine">
        <peml:database
fname="http://localhost/VoiceXMLApplication/Prompts.prompts" />
            Welcome to XYZ Savings and Loan
        </peml:prompt_output>
</prompt>
```

Specifying Grammar

The `<grammar>` element in VoiceXML supports only XML-formatted grammars (GRXML). You can use the Grammar Editor to create grammars for VoiceXML applications, as discussed in Chapter 3.

Adding In-Line Grammar

You can write the grammar rules directly in the `<grammar>` element itself, which is referred to as *in-line grammar*. For example, the main menu of an application might look like the following:

```
<grammar mode="voice" xml:lang="en-US" version="1.0" root="mainmenu">
    <rule id="mainmenu" scope="public">
        <one-of>
            <item>Balance Inquiry</item>
            <item>Recent Transactions</item>
            <item>Change PIN</item>
        </one-of>
    </rule>
</grammar>
```

■**Note** This example is for demonstration purposes. In this case it probably would be better to use the `<menu>` element, as discussed in the "Using Menus" section later in this chapter.

Using External Grammar

In the `<grammar>` element, you can reference external grammars, such as grammars designed using the Grammar Editor. Consider the following code:

```
<grammar type="application/srgs+xml" src="PinDtmf.grxml#fourdigits" />
```

This will reference and activate the `PinDtmf.grxml` file and the rule named `fourdigits`.

Grammar Scope

The scope of the grammar is determined by its parent element. If the parent element is an input item, the grammar is active only while the input item is active. You cannot specify a scope for grammars on an input item.

If the parent is a `<form>` or `<menu>` element, the grammar is automatically scoped to dialog. A dialog scope will keep the grammar active as long as the user is in the form or menu. If you specify a scope of document of a form-level grammar, the grammar is active as long as the user is in the same document. You cannot specify a scope on the menu `<choice>` elements.

Using Forms

Most VoiceXML dialogs are created either using the `<form>` element or `<menu>` element. A menu dialog presents the user with a list of options and ask the user to select one. A form dialog contains multiple fields. The user is asked a question for each field, so that each field is filled. A menu is basically a form, with a single field that determines where to navigate to next. We'll look at forms first, and then cover how to use menus in the next section.

The form dialog is similar to a paper form. It has multiple fields for which the user must supply input. A form is constructed with the `<form>` element, and it must contain a unique `id` attribute:

```
<form id="login" scope="dialog">
```

The `scope` attribute of the `<form>` element determines when the grammar is active. Two `scope` attributes are valid for forms:

- `document`: The grammar will remain active throughout the entire document. If the document is also the root document, the grammar will remain active throughout the entire application.

- `dialog`: The grammar is active only within the defined element. In the previous code example, the grammar will remain active as long as the `<form>` element is active.

A form contains multiple items, which are divided into two groups: input items and control items.

Adding Input Items

As the name implies, input items allow the user to give input. Four input items can be used within a `<form>` element: `< field>`, `<record>`, `<transfer>`, and `<subdialog>`. The input elements may also contain one or more of the children elements `<filled>`, `<prompt>`, `<grammar>`, and

`<catch>`. The `<prompt>` and `<grammar>` elements were covered earlier in this chapter. The `<filled>` element is discussed in this section, and the `<catch>` element will be discussed in the "Error Handling and Logging" section later in this chapter.

Adding Fields

A `<field>` element prompts the user for input and stores the input. Each field in a form is selected by the FIA in the order in which it appears and then by the cond attribute. If the cond attribute evaluates to false, the FIA selects the next form item. Consider the following code:

```
<field name="accountNumber">
    <grammar src="PinDTMF.grxml#fourdigits"/>
    <prompt count="1">Please enter your account number</prompt>
    <prompt count="2">Using your Touch-Tone keypad, please
enter your four-digit account number</prompt>
    <filled>
        <prompt>Got it!</prompt>
    </filled>
</field>

<field name="pinNumber">
    <grammar src="PinDTMF.grxml#fourdigits"/>
    <prompt bargein="true" bargeintype="speech">
Please enter your PIN</prompt>
    <filled>
        <prompt>Got it!</prompt>
    </filled>
</field>
```

Each `<field>` element is also a variable. Before user input, the field's value is undefined. Once the field has been filled, the value is equivalent to the SML results from the grammar.

The modal attribute of the `<field>` element allows you to ignore active grammars that are outside the `<field>` element itself. For example, the form's scope attribute might be set to document, in which case the `<field>` element would automatically use the grammar specified for the entire document. If you wanted to have grammar specific to one `<field>` element and ignore the document grammar, you would set the modal attribute to true.

```
<field name="accountPin" modal="true">
    <grammar></grammar>
</field>
```

Recording Input

The `<record>` element allows you to record the user and then save the recording. Consider the following code:

```
<record  name="confirmPin" beep="true" maxtime="10s" finalsilence="4000ms"
dtmfterm="true" type="audio/x-wav">
<prompt timeout="5s">
        For security reasons please state your full name after the tone.
</prompt>
</record>
```

The `<record>` element has two `timeout` attributes: `maxtime` and `finalsilence`. The `maxtime` attribute specifies either in seconds or milliseconds the maximum time for the recording. The `finalsilence` attribute allows you to specify how long the user can pause before the application considers that the user has finished speaking. In the sample code, if any of the timeouts expire, the `<record>` element will simply stop recording.

The `beep` attribute allows you to specify whether a beep should sound after the containing prompt is played.

You can specify the media format in which the recording will be stored via the `type` attribute. In the example, the recording will be stored in the `.wav` format.

Transferring the User

The `<transfer>` element allows you transfer the caller to either another line or another application.

A *blind transfer* only attempts to connect the caller to a destination; it does not know the status or outcome of the transfer. A blind transfer will play any prompts that are before and within the `<transfer>` element before transferring. For example, if you wanted to blind transfer the caller to the telephone number 555-1212, the code would look like this:

```
<transfer name="supportTransfer" dest="5551212" bridge="false" />
```

A *bridge transfer* connects the caller to the destination but maintains the outcome of the transfer attempt. For example, you may want to give the user options if the transfer destination line is busy or it doesn't pick up. You could do so with the following code:

```
<transfer name="supportTransfer" bridge="true" dest="tel:5551212">
    <prompt> Transferring you to support</prompt>
      <filled>
        <if cond="supportTransfer == 'busy'">
            <prompt>The line is busy. Please try your call again. </prompt>
            <exit/>
        <elseif cond="supportTransfer == 'noanswer'"/>
            <prompt> There is no answer. Please try your call again. </prompt>
        </if>
      </filled>
</transfer>
```

■**Note** OCS 2007 Speech Server directly supports blind transfers, but bridge transfers are dependent on your telephony hardware. Check with the manufacturer of your hardware to see if bridge transfers are supported.

Calling Other Dialogs

The `<subdialog>` element allows you to call common dialogs for the purpose of reuse. So first, you need to define a form that you will call from another form. You can compare this to making a method call in C#, as in *MyMethod(parameters)*. Consider the following form, which can be called from another form:

```
<form id="askLogin">
    <var name="ask" />
    <field name="accountNumber" cond="ask == 'yes'" >
          <grammar src="PinDTMF.grxml#fourdigits"/>
          <prompt count=1>Please enter your account number</prompt>
          <prompt count=2>Using your Touch-Tone keypad, please
           enter your four-digit account number</prompt>
          <filled>
              <prompt>Got it!</prompt>
          </filled>
    </field>
     <field name="pinNumber" cond="ask == 'yes'" >
          <grammar src="PinDTMF.grxml#fourdigits"/>
          <prompt bargein="true" bargeintype="speech">Please enter your PIN</prompt>
          <filled>
              <prompt>Got it!</prompt>
          </filled>
      </field>
    <filled mode="all">
          <return namelist="accountNumber pinNumber"/>
    </filled>
</form>
```

The three important parts of this form definition for this example are highlighted:

- The `<form>` element, `<form id="askLogin">`. This will act as your method.

- The undefined variable, `<var name="ask" />`. This will act as your parameter.

- The values to return to the calling form—in the example, the account number and PIN number. These are returned via the `<return>` element: `<return namelist="accountNumber pinNumber"/>`.

In the invoking form, you need to specify which form to call via the `src` attribute of the `<subdialog>` element—in this case, `"askLogin"`. To specify parameters to pass, you define a `<param>` element as a child element of the `<subdialog>` element. The name attribute of the `<param>` element should reflect the undefined variable in the invoked form, and the `value` attribute should contain the value you want to pass. So, to invoke the `askLogin` form from another form, the code might look like the following:

```
<form id="login">
    <prompt>Welcome to XYZ Savings and Loan</prompt>
    <subdialog name="login" src="#asklogin">
        <param name="ask" expr="yes" />
    </subdialog>
      <filled mode="all">
          <if cond="accountNumber == pinNumber">
              <goto next="#mainMenu" />
          <else />
              <clear namelist="accountNumber pinNumber" />
              <throw event="nomatch" />
          </if>
      </filled>
</form>
```

After the subdialog has been called, you can use the variables, accountNumber and pinNumber, which were returned from the called form, askLogin.

Performing Actions After Items Are Filled

The <filled> element allows you to perform an action after the input items are filled in by the user. You can put a <filled> element either in an input item or in the form itself.

If you put a <filled> element inside a <form> element, you can specify when you want it to execute via the mode attribute. The mode attribute has two values: all or any. Specifying all executes the <filled> element only when all of the form's input items have been filled. Specifying any will execute the <filled> element when any of the form's input items are filled. Also, you can define which fields the form's <filled> element applies to by specifying the name of the input item in the namelist attribute. In the XYZ Savings and Loan example, the login page might contain a form-level <filled> element, which would process the results of the user-entered account number and PIN.

```
<form id="login" scope="dialog">
    <field name="accountNumber" type="digits">
        <prompt>Please enter your account number</prompt>
    </field>

    <field name="accountPin" type="digits">
        <prompt>Please enter your PIN code</prompt>
    </field>

    <filled mode="all" namelist="accountNumber accountPin">
          'Check Results
    </filled>
 </form>
```

If you put a <filled> element inside an input item, it will execute after that item has been filled. The following example illustrates the input item-level <filled> element, which checks the account number and PIN lengths, and then a form-level <filled> element to submit the information to the server for validation.

```
<form id="login" scope="dialog">
    <field name="accountnumber" type="digits">
        <prompt>Please enter your account number</prompt>
            <filled>
                'Check Results
            </filled>
    </field>
    <field name="accountpin" type="digits">
        <prompt>Please enter your PIN code</prompt>
            <filled>
                'Check Results
            </filled>
    </field>
    <filled mode="all" namelist="accountnumber accountpin">
        'Check Results
    </filled>
</form>
```

Adding Control Items

The other group of form items are control items. Control items do not accept input from the user, but are used to control which input items are played and when. The three control items are `<block>`, `<initial>`, and `<exit>`.

Adding Blocks for Conditions

The `<block>` element contains code that will be executed if the expression statement is undefined and if the conditional expression evaluates to true. After the block is executed, the form item's variable is set to `true`; therefore, the block will not be visited again. Here is an example:

```
<form id="blockExample">
  <block name="blockOne" expr="'value'">
    <prompt>
    This prompt will NOT play because the expr attribute is not undefined.
    </prompt>
  </block>

  <block name="blockTwo" cond="false">
    <prompt>
        This prompt will NOT play because the cond attribute is set to false.
    </prompt>
  </block>

  <block name="blockThree" cond="true" expr="">
    <prompt>
        This prompt will play because the cond attribute is set to true.
    </prompt>
  </block>
</form>
```

Setting an Initial Prompt

The `<initial>` element is generally used in a mixed-initiative dialogs (described in Chapter 3). It contains the first prompt, typically a HMIHY question. It is similar to an input item, in that it has `<prompt>`, `<catch>`, and `<counter>` elements, but it cannot have `<grammar>` or `<filled>` elements. For example, you might use a mixed-initiative form on an account balance transfer page, as in the following code. This would allow the user to transfer a balance from one account to another.

```
<form id="balanceTransfer">
    <grammar src="fromto.grxml"  type="application/srgs+xml"/>
    <initial name="bypassInit ">
      <prompt>
        What would you like to transfer?
      </prompt>
      <nomatch count="1">
        <prompt>Please say something like $100.00 from Savings to Checking</prompt>
      </nomatch>
      <nomatch count="2">
        <assign name="bypassInit" expr="true"/>
        <reprompt/>
      </nomatch>
    </initial>
    <field name="amount">
      <grammar src="amount.grxml" type="application/srgs+xml"/>
      <prompt>How much do you want to transfer?</prompt>
    </field>
    <field name="from">
      <grammar src="accountType.grxml" type="application/srgs+xml"/>
      <prompt>From which account?</prompt>
    </field>
    <field name="to">
      <grammar src="accountType.grxml"  type="application/srgs+xml"/>
      <prompt>To which account?</prompt>
    </field>
</form>
</vxml>
```

Exiting

The `<exit>` element returns control to the interpreter. This is different from the `<return>` element, as the `<exit>` element terminates all loaded documents; `<return>` simply goes back to the calling document. Once the `<exit>` element has been called, you will have no control over what happens next. Here is an example:

```
<block>
      <exit/>
      <prompt> You will not hear this prompt </prompt>
</block>
```

Using Menus

A menu is basically a form with a single field that determines where to navigate to next. The <menu> element contains one or more <choice> elements, each representing a choice in the menu. Using the <enumerate> element automatically returns each <choice> element's in-line text and sets up the grammar. For example, your application might use the <menu>, <choice>, and <enumerate> elements for the main menu, like this:

```
<menu id="mainMenu" scope="dialog" dtmf="true" accept="approximate">
        <prompt bargein="true" bargeintype="hotword">
            Main Menu. Please say one from the following options:
        <enumerate/>
        </prompt>

        <choice next="#balance" accept="approximate">Balance Inquiry</choice>
        <choice next="#transaction" accept="approximate">
                Recent Transactions
        </choice>
        <choice next="#pin" accept="approximate">Change PIN</choice>
</menu>
```

This would produce the prompt, "Please say one from the following options: Balance Inquiry, Recent Transactions, Change PIN."

Inheriting from a Root Document

VoiceXML has a sense of inheritance, in that you can inherit from a parent document called a *root document*. For example, your application might have the following root document, root.vxml:

```
<?xml version="1.0" encoding="UTF-8"?>
<vxml xmlns="http://www.w3.org/2001/vxml"
  xmlns:xsi="http://www.w3.org/2001/XMLSchema-instance"
  xsi:schemaLocation="http://www.w3.org/2001/vxml
    http://www.w3.org/TR/voicexml20/vxml.xsd"
    version="2.0">
 <var name="loggedin" />
 <link next="transfer.vxml">
   <grammar type="application/srgs+xml" root="root" version="1.0">
     <rule id="root" scope="public">operator</rule>
   </grammar>
 </link>
</vxml>
```

This root document declares one variable, <var name="loggedin">, and one link element, <link next="transfer.vxml">, with a grammar rule of operator. In a child VoiceXML document, you can set the application attribute of the <vxml> element to the relative path of your root document.

```
<vxml xmlns="http://www.w3.org/2001/vxml"
  xmlns:xsi="http://www.w3.org/2001/XMLSchema-instance"
  xsi:schemaLocation="http://www.w3.org/2001/vxml
  http://www.w3.org/TR/voicexml20/vxml.xsd"
  version="2.0" application="root.vxml" >
```

If you set the root document to the previous VoiceXML code, it will allow the user at any time during the application to say "Operator," which will trigger the <link> element to transfer the user to an operator.

The next section explains the use of variables in more detail.

Scripting

VoiceXML supports JavaScript, which allows you to create simple scripts to handle variables, conditions, and errors. However, typically you will not need to create complex JavaScript functions for your applications, as you would with SALT.

Using Variables

The variable element, <var>, is basically a JavaScript variable. Whether you declare a variable in a <script> element or in a <var> element, you can still reference the variable the same way with the same results. VoiceXML provides several built-in variables that you can reference, as listed in Table 5-1.

Table 5-1. *Built-in Session and Application Variables*

Session and Application Variables	Returns
session.connection.local.uri	URI of the called application
session.connection.remote.uri	URI of the remote caller
session.connection.protocol.name	Protocol currently being used
session.connection.protocol.version	Version of the protocol currently being used
session.connection.redirect	An array of connection redirection paths
session.connection.aai	Application-to-application information
session.connection.originator	Party who initiated the call
application.lastresult$[i].confidence	Confidence score of the last utterance
application.lastresult$[i].utterance	Raw text of the recognized text
application.lastresult$[i].inputmode	Input mode: DRMF or Voice
application.lastresult$[i].interpretation	Semantic results of the recognized speech

The scope of the variable depends on the parent element of the variable. Any variable declared in a root document can be accessed by a leaf (child) document by using the application prefix, as in this example:

```
/* RootDoc.vxml */
<vxml>
        <var name="account" />
        <assign name="account" expr="1234" />
</vxml>

/* LeafDoc.vxml */
<vxml application="RootDoc.vxml">
        <value expr="application.account" />
</vxml>
```

A variable whose parent element is `<vxml>` and is not a root document can be accessed anywhere in the document by using the `document` prefix.

```
<vxml>
<var name="account" />
    <form id="form1">
          <assign name="document.account" expr="1234" />
    </form>
    <form id="form2">
          <assign name="document.account" expr="5678" />
    </form>
</vxml>
```

Several elements are used with variables: `<assign>`, `<clear>`, and `<value>`.

The `<assign>` element is used to assign a value to a variable, which has been previously declared in either a `<var>` element or a `<script>` element. The `name` attribute should be unique to the scope in which the variable is being declared. If your variable needs an initial value, you can assign it via the `expr` attribute, as in this example:

```
<assign name="accountNumber" expr="1234" />
```

The `<clear>` element can be used to reset variables and form items. You can specify the variables or form items to be cleared by specifying the names in the `namelist` attribute. If you do not specify a `namelist`, `<clear>` will clear all of the form items that belong to the parent `<form>` element. For example, you could use the `<clear>` element to clear the form items if the account number and PIN do not match.

```
<clear namelist="accountNumber pinNumber" />
```

This sets the `<field>` element back to undefined and available for selection by the FIA. The FIA will select the fields and play the associated prompts.

You can use the `<value>` element to retrieve the value of a variable, such a field item. You might use this element to confirm what a user has said. The `expr` attribute should specify the name of the variable or input item of the value to retrieve. Here is an example:

```
<prompt>You entered <value expr="accountNumber" /></prompt>
```

Adding Conditions

The `<if>` element is used for conditional statements. It has two optional children elements: `<else>` and `<ifelse>`. The `<if>` element has one attribute, `cond`, where you can specify which condition must be met in order for the in-line code to execute. Here is an example:

```
<if cond="validLogin = true">
  <prompt>You have successfully logged in.</prompt>
</if>
```

The child element `<else>` allows you to execute code that does not meet the conditional statement of the `<if>` element, as in this example:

```
<if cond="validLogin = true">
        <prompt>You have successfully logged in.</prompt>
<else />
<prompt>You have not successfully logged in</prompt>
</if>
```

The `<elseif>` element allows you to have stacked multiple conditional statements, which are evaluated to determine which in-line code to execute. Like the `<if>` element, it has one attribute: `cond`. The condition in the `cond` attribute must pass before the in-line code will execute.

```
<if cond="validLogin = true">
        <prompt>You have successfully logged in.</prompt>
<elseif cond="passwordValid = false " />
<prompt>The password you entered is invalid</prompt>
<elseif cond="userNameValid = false />
<prompt>The username you entered is invalid</prompt>
<else/>
<prompt>You have not successfully logged in</prompt>
</if>
```

Transitioning

You can use the `<goto>` element to transition to another form item or dialog in the current document, or transition to another document. To specify the item to go to, use either the `next` or `nextitem` attribute.

The `nextitem` attribute allows you to transition to another form item in the same document. The following example includes two field items: `<field name="pinNumber">` and `<field name="accountNumber">`. Instead of letting the FIA determine which field to visit next, the example uses the `<goto>` element to specify which field to navigate to next via the `nextitem` attribute.

```
<field name="accountNumber">
    <grammar src="PinDTMF.grxml#fourdigits"/>
    <prompt count=1>Please enter your account number</prompt>
    <prompt count=2>Using your Touch-Tone keypad, please
     enter your four-digit account number</prompt>
```

```
      <filled>
            <prompt>Got it!</prompt>
            <goto nextitem="pinNumber/>
      </filled>
</field>

<field name="pinNumber">
      <grammar src="PinDTMF.grxml#fourdigits"/>
      <prompt bargein="true" bargeintype="speech">Please enter your PIN</prompt>
      <filled>
            <prompt>Got it!</prompt>
      </filled>
</field>
```

The next attribute allows you to transition to either another dialog in the same document or to another document altogether. For example, you can use the <goto> element to move to the main menu after the account number and PIN are provided.

```
<filled namelist="accountNumber pinNumber" mode="all">
      <if cond="accountNumber == pinNumber">
            <goto next="#mainMenu" />
      <else />
            <clear namelist="accountNumber pinNumber" />
                  <throw event="nomatch" />
      </if>
</filled>
<menu id="mainMenu" scope="dialog" dtmf="true" accept="approximate">
```

Submitting Data to a Web Server

The <submit> element allows you to submit data to the web server. For example, you may want to submit the login data to the server to validate that the user submitted credentials. You can specify the list of variables that you want to submit via the namelist attribute. The namelist attribute is a space-separated field, allowing you to submit multiple variables by separating the names with a space. You can optionally specify the HTTP method to use—GET or POST—via the method attribute. If you do not specify a method, GET will be used by default.

For example, you might have a login process that checks if the submitted account number and PIN are equal, and want to do this on the server. You could use the <submit> element to transfer this data to an .aspx page to process the login, as in this example:

```
<filled namelist="accountNumber pinNumber" mode="all">
      <submit next="login.aspx" namelist="accountNumber pinNumber" method="post/>
</filled>
```

You can access the response in the login.aspx with the following code:

```
string accountNumber = Request.Params["accountNumber"] .ToString();
string pinNumber = Request.Rarams["pinNumber"].ToString();
```

Error Handling and Logging

All errors and events are handled by the <catch> element. The <catch> element allows you to perform actions after a certain event. It has three attributes: event, count, and cond. All of the attributes are optional. If you do not specify any attributes, all errors and events will be handled by the one <catch> element. The following example will play the prompt "An error or event has occurred" for every event or error.

```
<form id="login" scope="dialog">
    <field name="accountNumber" type="digits">
        <prompt>Please enter your account number</prompt>
    </field>
    <field name="accountPin" type="digits">
        <prompt>Please enter your PIN code</prompt>
    </field>
    <catch>
        <prompt>An error or event has occurred.</prompt>
    </catch>
</form>
```

This code works but it isn't very practical. Generally, you should catch only events that you can handle. For example, you might want to catch if the user's input did not match a grammar or if the user remained silent past the duration of the specified timeout. You can specify which event or events you wish to catch via the event attribute. You could use the following code to catch the nomatch and noinput events.

```
<form id="login">
    <field name="accountNumber" type="digits">
        <prompt>Please enter your account number</prompt>
    </field>
    <field name="accountPin" type="digits">
        <prompt>Please enter your PIN code</prompt>
    </field>
    <catch event="noinput nomatch">
        <prompt>You did not provide the correct expected input</prompt>
    </catch>
</form>
```

VoiceXML also includes several built-in events and errors, as listed in Table 5-2.

Table 5-2. *Built-in Events*

Built-in Events	Definition
cancel	User requested to cancel
connection.disconnect.hangup	Session disconnected due to a hang-up
connection.disconnect.transfer	Session disconnected due to a transfer
exit	User requested to exit application

Table 5-2. *Built-in Events*

Built-in Events	Definition
help	User requested help
noinput	User remained silent for duration of timeout
nomatch	Speech doesn't match any active grammars
maxspeechtimeout	User spoke longer than the duration of the timeout

When handling an event, you may want to reprompt users so that they can hear the question again. Consider the previous example, where the conversation might have sounded like this:

IVR: Please say your account number.

Caller: (*silent*)

IVR: You did not provide the correct expected input. *(catch event fires)*

Caller: 12345678

IVR: Please enter your PIN code.

You could replay the last prompt simply by adding the <reprompt> element, as in this example:

```
<catch event="noinput nomatch">
        <prompt>You did not provide the correct expected input</prompt>
        <reprompt />
</catch>
```

This would allow for the following dialog:

IVR: Please say your account number.

Caller: (*silent*)

IVR: You did not provide the correct expected input. *(catch event fires)*

IVR: Please say your account number.

Caller: 12345678

IVR: Please enter your PIN code.

Four shorthand <catch> elements provide a shorter way to writing the associated basic catch events: <error>, <help>, <noinput>, and <nomatch>. For example, instead of writing <catch event="noinput">, you can simply write <noinput>. These elements take the same two attributes as the <catch> element: cond and count.

You can use the <log> element to write log messages to the server. This element does not interact directly with the user. For example, you may want to log errors that have occurred for review:

```
<log>An error occurred from caller, <value expr=</log>
```

Finally, if there is nothing else the user can do in your application, you will want to use the `<disconnect>` element. This will automatically disconnect the user and throw a `connection.diconnect.hangup` event.

Putting It All Together

So far, this chapter covered individual pieces of a VoiceXML application. Now, let's consider how to put all the pieces together. This example uses the call flow shown in Figure 5-3.

Figure 5-3. *Sample form-filling dialog call flow*

As you can see from the call flow in Figure 5-3, the design is for a form-filling dialog, with three questions. Listing 5-1 shows the code for this application.

Listing 5-1. *Sample VoiceXML Application*

```
<var name="productName" />
<var name="productColor" />
<var name="productSize" />
```

```
<form id="Support" scope="dialog">
     <block>
          <prompt>Welcome to A B C Company Ordering System</prompt>
     </block>

     <field name="askProduct">
          <prompt>Would you like to order a Gadget,
Sprocket or Widget?
          </prompt>
          <grammar mode="voice" xml:lang="en-US"
version="1.0" root="productNames">
               <rule id="productNames" scope="public">
                 <one-of>
                   <item> gadget </item>
                   <item> sprocket </item>
                   <item> widget</item>
                 </one-of>
               </rule>
          </grammar>

          <filled>
            <assign name="document.productName" expr="askProduct"/>
          </filled>

     </field>

     <field name="askSize">
        <prompt>Do you want that in small, medium
or large?
        </prompt>
        <grammar mode="voice" xml:lang="en-US"
version="1.0" root="productSizes">
          <rule id="productSizes" scope="public">
            <one-of>
              <item> small </item>
              <item> medium </item>
              <item> large </item>
            </one-of>
          </rule>
        </grammar>

        <filled>
          <assign name="document.productSize" expr="askSize"/>
        </filled>

     </field>
```

```
    <field name="askColor">
        <prompt>Do you want that in red, white or
blue?
        </prompt>
        <grammar mode="voice" xml:lang="en-US"
version="1.0" root="productColors">
            <rule id="productColors" scope="public">
                <one-of>
                    <item> red </item>
                    <item> white </item>
                    <item> blue </item>
                </one-of>
            </rule>
        </grammar>

        <filled>
            <assign name="document.productColor" expr="askColor"/>
        </filled>

    </field>

    <filled mode="all">
        <goto next="#confirmOrder"/>
    </filled>

</form>

<form id="confirmOrder" scope="dialog">
    <block>
        <prompt>
            You ordered a
            <value expr="document.productSize"/><break/>
            <value expr="document.productColor"/><break/>
            <value expr="document.productName"/>
        </prompt>
    </block>
</form>

</vxml>
```

Let's review how we would go about building this application. First, we implement the simple greeting prompt, which uses the TTS engine to render the voice:

```
<prompt>Welcome to the A B C Company Ordering System</prompt>
```

Next, we declare variables to hold the data we are going to collect. We need one variable for each answer: product, color, and size. We declare the variables in the document scope so that the variables are accessible to any other form in the same document.

```
<var name="productName" />
<var name="productColor" />
<var name="productSize" />
```

Now we need to decide how we want to implement the questions we want to ask. Since we are asking a series of interdependent questions, the form-filling dialog approach would probably work best. So we need to create a `<field>` element for each question, create a prompt, and assign grammar for each field. We also need to assign the document-level variables using the `<filled>` element in each field. This example uses in-line grammar for the convenience of displaying the grammar; you probably will want to use an external `.grxml` file for your grammar.

```
<field name="askProduct">
    <prompt>Would you like to order a Gadget,
Sprocket or Widget?
    </prompt>
    <grammar mode="voice" xml:lang="en-US"
version="1.0" root="productNames">
        <rule id="productNames" scope="public">
            <one-of>
              <item> gadget </item>
              <item> sprocket </item>
              <item> widget</item>
            </one-of>
        </rule>
    </grammar>

    <filled>
        <assign name="document.productName" expr="askProduct"/>
    </filled>

</field>
```

In the preceding code, we are assigning the variable productName by using the document prefix because the variable is defined in the document scope.

Next, we need to add a form-level `<filled>` element, with a mode of all. This defines that this element will not be called until all of the fields have been filled.

```
<filled mode="all">
    <goto next="#confirmOrder"/>
</filled>
```

In the form-level `<filled>` element, we use the `<goto>` element to go to the confirmOrder form after all of the fields have been filled, which we specify with the mode attribute. In the confirmOrder form, we simply repeat what the user ordered using the document-level variables, which we assigned in the `<filled>` element for each field.

```
<form id="confirmOrder" scope="dialog">
  <block>
    <prompt>
      You ordered a
      <value expr="document.productSize"/><break/>
      <value expr="document.productColor"/><break/>
      <value expr="document.productName"/>
    </prompt>
  </block>
</form>
```

We use the `<break>` element to add pauses in between the different variable values.

Although the example in Listing 5-1 is a rather basic application, it is a good starting point for developing your own VoiceXML applications.

■Tip The VoiceXML Forum, which created VoiceXML, was formed by AT&T, IBM, Lucent, and Motorola in 2000. Microsoft, one of the founding members of the SALT Forum, recently joined the VoiceXML Forum. The VoiceXML Forum web site, `www.voicexml.org`, is a great resource for learning, getting certified, and reading about new improvements to the VoiceXML language.

Conclusion

As you have seen, VoiceXML is pretty flexible. You can create an entire IVR application simply by using the modified XML elements that make up VoiceXML. This simplicity creates a very powerful method in which you can create IVR applications.

VoiceXML and SALT are very similar, as they both rely on markup languages. If you would prefer not to use a markup language, you will be interested in the next chapter. It covers the third method of creating IVR applications—as Voice Response Workflow applications.

CHAPTER 6

■■■

Creating Voice Response Workflow Applications

The Voice Response Workflow project type allows you to develop an IVR application using a managed language such as Visual Basic .NET or C# and Windows Workflow Foundation (WF). If you do not have a strong preference for SALT or VoiceXML, you should choose to develop your IVR application using Voice Response Workflow.

With a Voice Response Workflow Application project, you can write purely in managed code and actually see the entire call flow. If you are familiar with .NET, you will find the Voice Response Workflow application development environment a friendly one. Even if you haven't worked with .NET before, Voice Response Workflow will save you time in development over SALT or VoiceXML.

Voice Response Workflow applications are still web applications in the sense that they run on IIS. All Voice Response Workflow applications have a `.speax` file, which is hosted on IIS. When a user establishes a call, it is directed to the URL of your application, such as `http://localhost/CallSample.speax`. This starts your workflow application.

In this chapter, you'll learn the details of creating Voice Response Workflow applications, beginning with an overview of the design environment.

Working with the Dialog Workflow Designer

In Visual Studio, you build your Voice Response Workflow application in the Dialog Workflow Designer, as shown in Figure 6-1. Even if you have never seen a Voice Response Workflow application before, you can easily understand what is going on just by viewing the workflow diagram.

In the Dialog Workflow Designer, you drag-and-drop activities to configure your workflow application. Figure 6-2 shows the activities available in the Speech Dialog Components toolbox.

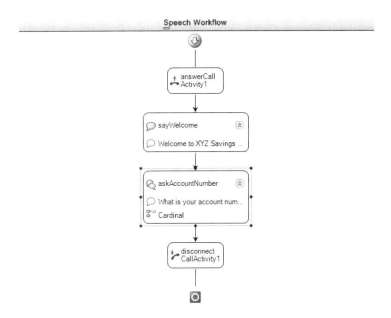

Figure 6-1. *Sample Voice Response Workflow application*

Figure 6-2. *Speech Dialog Components toolbox*

You can also add Windows WF activities to your Voice Response Workflow. Figure 6-3 shows the standard Windows Workflow toolbox.

■**Note** The Voice Response Workflow application type is built on top of WF. As mentioned in Chapter 1, you must have .NET Framework 3.0 and the Visual Studio Extensions for Windows Workflow Foundation installed.

Figure 6-3. *Windows Workflow toolbox*

You write managed code to interact with the designer objects in the *code-beside*. This is similar to the code-behind in an ASP.NET application. To access the code-beside, right-click in the Dialog Workflow Designer and choose View Code. Figure 6-4 shows the code-beside code that is automatically generated when you create a new Voice Response Workflow Application project.

The basic procedure for adding an activity to your workflow is to drag-and-drop the component from the Speech Dialog Components or Windows Workflow toolbox onto the designer surface and set its properties, either through the Properties window in the IDE or using code in the code-beside. This process is identical to developing an ASP.NET or a Windows Form application.

Of course, before you begin working on your Voice Response Workflow application, you need to create a project for it in Visual Studio.

```csharp
using System;
using System.ComponentModel;
using System.ComponentModel.Design;
using System.Collections;
using System.Diagnostics;
using System.Drawing;
using System.Workflow.ComponentModel.Compiler;
using System.Workflow.ComponentModel.Serialization;
using System.Workflow.ComponentModel;
using System.Workflow.ComponentModel.Design;
using System.Workflow.Runtime;
using System.Workflow.Activities;
using System.Workflow.Activities.Rules;
using Microsoft.SpeechServer.Dialog;

namespace VoiceResponseWorkflowApplication
{
    public sealed partial class Workflow1: SpeechSequ
    {
        public Workflow1()
        {
            InitializeComponent();
        }
```

Figure 6-4. *Workflow code-beside*

Creating a Voice Response Workflow Application Project

In Visual Studio, Voice Response Workflow Application projects are found under either the C# or Visual Basic .NET languages. To create a new Voice Response Workflow application, choose File ➤ New ➤ Project and choose Voice Response Workflow Application in the Templates list, as shown in Figure 6-5.

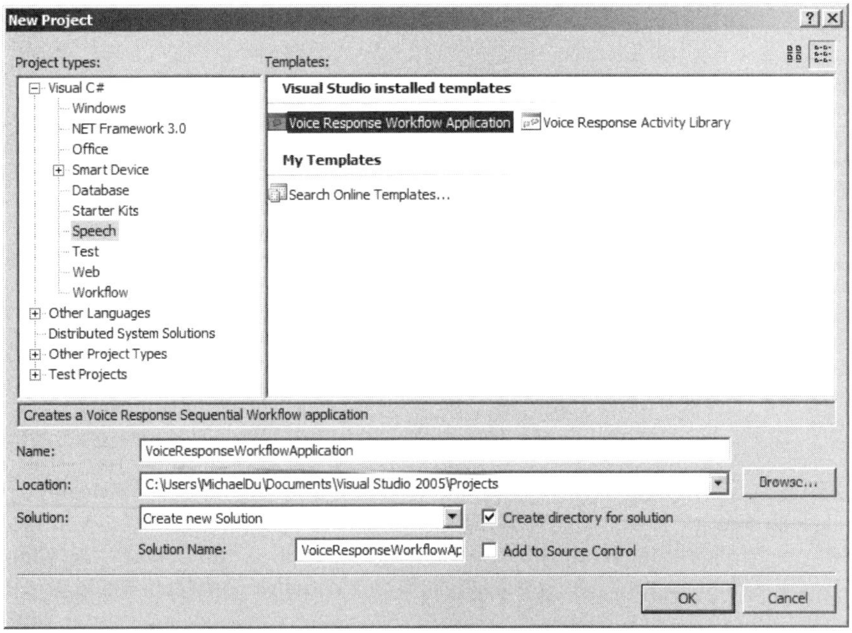

Figure 6-5. *Creating a new Voice Response Workflow Application project*

You will be prompted for which grammar, lexicon, and prompt files you would like to include automatically, as shown in Figure 6-6. If you choose to include a new prompt database, that prompt file will be added automatically in the Dialog Workflow Designer code. If you would like to use an existing prompt database, you can add that later, as described in the "Using a Prompt Database" section later in this chapter. It is probably a good idea to include the prompt project, lexicon, and standard grammar library. You can remove anything from the project you do not use.

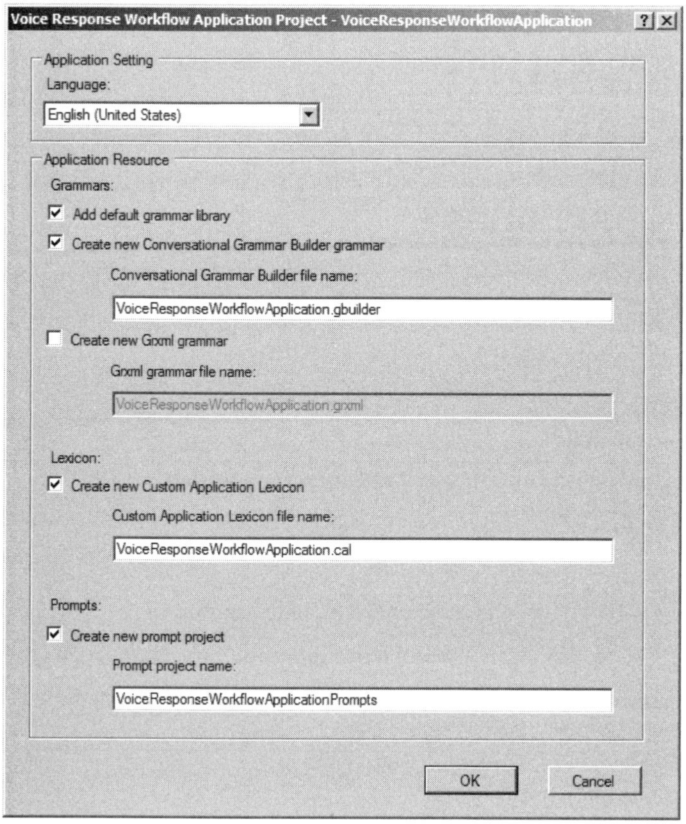

Figure 6-6. *Selecting application resources*

Your new project will open in the Dialog Workflow Designer, as shown in Figure 6-7, and you can begin adding and configuring workflow activities.

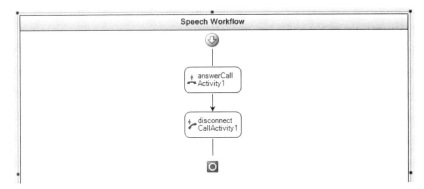

Figure 6-7. *A new Voice Response Workflow application in the Dialog Workflow Designer*

Controlling Call Connections

Six activities allow you to control call connectivity, as listed in Table 6-1. These are available from the Speech Dialog Components toolbox (see Figure 6-2).

Table 6-1. *Call Control Activities*

Activity	Description
AnswerCall	Initiates the incoming call and starts the workflow
DisconnectCall	Immediately disconnects the call
DeclineCall	Used to refuse incoming calls
BlindTransfer	Used to transfer to another extension or number
MakeCall	Used to place calls for outbound applications
DetectAnsweringMachine	Used for outbound calling applications to detect if an answering machine has picked up the line

When you create a new Voice Response Workflow application, the AnswerCall and DisconnectCall activities are automatically added to the workflow (see Figure 6-7). If your application will accept inbound calls, these activities are ready to go; the AnswerCall and DisconnectCall components do not need any configuration.

If your application will make outbound calls, you will need to replace the AnswerCall activity with a MakeCall activity. Here, we'll look at how to configure a simple outbound calling application with the MakeCall activity, as well as how to set up blind transfers with the BlindTransfer activity. Later in the chapter, in the "Creating Outbound Calling Applications" section, I'll describe how to build a more complex outbound calling application and also how to use the DetectAnsweringMachine activity.

Configuring Outbound Calls

For an outbound calling application, drag a MakeCall activity on to the designer. Specify the number you are calling via the `CalledParty` property, which can be either a telephone number or an SIP URI, and the number for your application via the `CallingParty` property. Obviously, if you hard-code the number to call, your application will be able to call only that number. Both of these properties are of type `Microsoft.SpeechServer.Dialog.PhoneNumberTelephonyAddress`. You can set them through either the code-beside or the Properties window in the IDE.

The following code demonstrates how to place a call using the Windows WF Code activity. Add a Code activity from the Windows Workflow toolbox to the workflow and set the `ExecuteCode` event to the method you want it to call when it executes—in this case, `Activity_ExecuteCode`.

```
Using Microsoft.SpeechServer.Dialog;
private void codeActivity_ExecuteCode(object sender, EventArgs e)
{
    PhoneNumberTelephonyAddress phoneToCall =
new.PhoneNumberTelephonyAddress();
    PhoneNumberTelephonyAddress phoneFrom =
new.PhoneNumberTelephonyAddress();

    phoneToCall.PhoneNumber = "5551212";
    phoneFrom.PhoneNumber = "5551313";

    this.makeCallActivity.CalledParty = phoneToCall;
    this.makeCallActivity.CallingParty = phoneFrom;
}
```

Later in this chapter, in the "Creating Outbound Calling Applications" section, I'll discuss how to use MSMQ to queue numbers to call and how to read them from the queue and dial those numbers.

Making Blind Transfers

For blind transfers, use the BlindTransfer control. Just set the `CalledParty` property to the phone number or SIP address you are trying to call, either through the Properties window or in the code-beside. A blind transfer doesn't require any other configuration.

You can use the Code activity from the Windows Workflow toolbox to set the properties in the code-beside. Place the Code activity before the BlindTransfer activity. Like the `CalledParty` property of the MakeCall component, the BlindTransfer `CalledParty` property is of type `Microsoft.SpeechServer.Dialog.PhoneNumberTelephonyAddress`.

```
Using Microsoft.SpeechServer.Dialog;
private void codeActivity_ExecuteCode(object sender, EventArgs e)
{
    PhoneNumberTelephonyAddress phoneToCall = new.PhoneNumberTelephonyAddress();
    phoneToCall.PhoneNumber = "5551212";
    this.blindTransferActivity.CalledParty = phoneToCall;
}
```

Playing Prompts and Getting User Input

The activities for playing prompts and collecting input from the user are summarized in Table 6-2. These are available from the Speech Dialog Components toolbox (see Figure 6-2).

Table 6-2. *Prompt and User-Input Activities*

Activity	Description
Statement	Plays a prompt to the user; it does not accept any input from the user
QuestionAnswer	Asks the user a question and collects a response from the user
GetAndConfirm	Gets an answer from the user and then confirms the response and allows the user to change the response
Menu	Speaks a list of options from a data source and asks the user to pick one
FormFillingDialog	Allows you to maintain a form-filling state
NavigableList	Allows you to specify a data source in which the user can navigate the rows by using commands such as Next, Previous, First, Last, Select, and Exit
GoTo	Allows your workflow to go to another activity, bypassing any activities in between
RecordAudio	Saves what the user says as an audio recording
RecordMessage	Saves what the user says as an audio recording, in the context of a messaging system

The activities have associated prompts. Table 6-3 lists the prompts and the activities that can use them.

Table 6-3. *Prompt Types*

Prompt	Description	Applies To
Main	The first prompt played after the control is selected. This prompt is required.	Statement, QuestionAnswer, GetAndConfirm, Menu, NavigableList
Help	The prompt played when the user triggers the Help command. The Help prompt should provide more detailed information to the user.	QuestionAnswer, GetAndConfirm, Menu, NavigableList
Repeat	The prompt played when the user triggers the Repeat command. The Repeat prompt should repeat the Main prompt.	QuestionAnswer, GetAndConfirm, Menu, NavigableList
Silence	The prompt played when the user remains silent for the duration of the InitialSilenceTimeout property.	QuestionAnswer, GetAndConfirm, Menu, NavigableList

Table 6-3. *Prompt Types*

Prompt	Description	Applies To
Escalated Silence	The prompt played when the `InitialSilenceTimeout` property setting expires more than once.	QuestionAnswer, GetAndConfirm, Menu, NavigableList
No Recognition	The prompt played when the user gives input that isn't recognized by the specified grammar.	QuestionAnswer, GetAndConfirm, Menu, NavigableList
Escalated No Recognition	The prompt played when the user gives input that isn't recognized by the specified grammar more than once.	QuestionAnswer, GetAndConfirm, Menu, NavigableList
Confirmation	The prompt played if the specified confidence threshold isn't met.	GetAndConfirm, Menu, NavigableList

The Main prompt is the only required prompt; all other prompts are optional. However, if you do not set the Silence and No Recognition prompts, when these events occur, the Main prompt will be repeated. Therefore, it is best practice to define at least the Silence and No Recognition prompts.

Each of these prompts can be set in code using the following syntax:

`[promptControlName].Prompts.[PromptType].[MethodToAdd]`

Table 6-4 lists the methods that allow you to control which prompt is spoken.

Table 6-4. *Prompt Type Methods*

Method	Description
`SetText`	Replaces all text in the `PromptBuilder` with the specified text
`AppendAudio`	Appends an audio to the prompt, by specifying the location of the file
`AppendBreak`	Appends a pause to the prompt
`AppendPromptBuilder`	Appends a `PromptBuilder` object to the prompt
`AppendSsml`	Appends an SSML file to the prompt by specifying the location of the file
`AppendSsmlMarkup`	Appends SSML markup to the prompt, by specifying a string containing markup
`AppendText`	Appends text to the prompt in the form of a string
`AppendTextWithHint`	Appends text to the prompt, along with a `Microsoft.SpeechServer.Synthesis.SayAs` enum
`AppendTextWithPronunciation`	Appends text to the prompt, along with a secondary string that contains pronunciation for the first string

For simplicity, most of the examples in this chapter use the AppendText method for setting the prompts. However, one example (in the "Creating Outbound Calling Applications" section) demonstrates probably the most useful method: AppendTextWithHint. The AppendTextWithHint method allows you to format a string of spoken text using formatting from Synthesis.SayAs enum. This has several options, including those for saying dates, telephone numbers, and acronyms. Here is an example of using the SpellOut option:

```
this.statementActivity.MainPrompt.AppendTextWithHint("ASP",
 Microsoft.SpeechServer.Synthesis.SayAs.SpellOut);
this.statementActivity.MainPrompt.AppendText("dot Net is great!");
```

With this setting, instead of the application saying "asp," it will pronounce each letter separately: "A" "S" "P."

Adding a Statement Activity

Typically, applications use the Statement activity for the greeting and whenever it's necessary to provide information without getting a response. This activity simply plays a prompt and does not accept any input from the user.

After you add the activity to the workflow, you need to specify the prompt. Double-click the [Edit Prompt] text to open the Statement Property Builder dialog box, as shown in Figure 6-8.

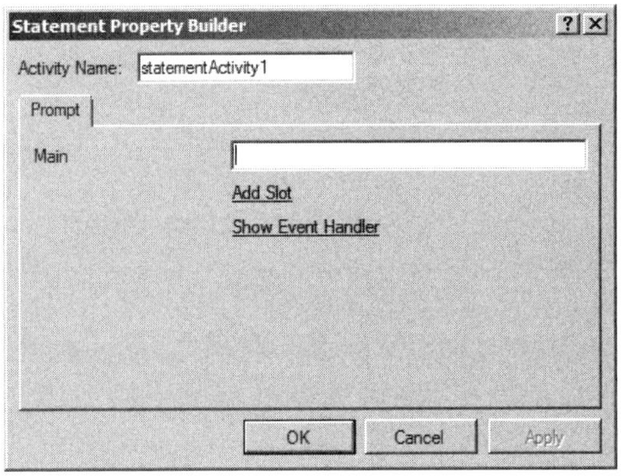

Figure 6-8. *Statement Property Builder dialog box*

For a Statement activity, you have two choices: a static prompt or a dynamic prompt. For a static prompt, such as the greeting, "Welcome to XYZ Savings and Loan," you type the prompt text directly in the Main text box.

For a dynamic prompt, such as a greeting based on the phone number of the caller, click the Show Event Handler link. If you have already specified an event handler, this link will take you to that point in the code-beside. Otherwise, it will add an event handler for the TurnStarting event, where you can set the prompt. Here is an example:

```
private void statementActivity_TurnStarting(object sender,
TurnStartingEventArgs e)
{
    statementActivity.MainPrompt.AppendText("Welcome to XYZ Savings and Loan");
}
```

Adding a QuestionAnswer Activity

A QuestionAnswer activity allows you to ask the user a question and collect the response. After you add this activity to your workflow, you need to specify the prompts and the grammar.

Adding Prompts

To add the prompts, double-click the [Edit Prompts] text in the designer. This will bring up the QuestionAnswer Property Builder dialog box, as shown in Figure 6-9.

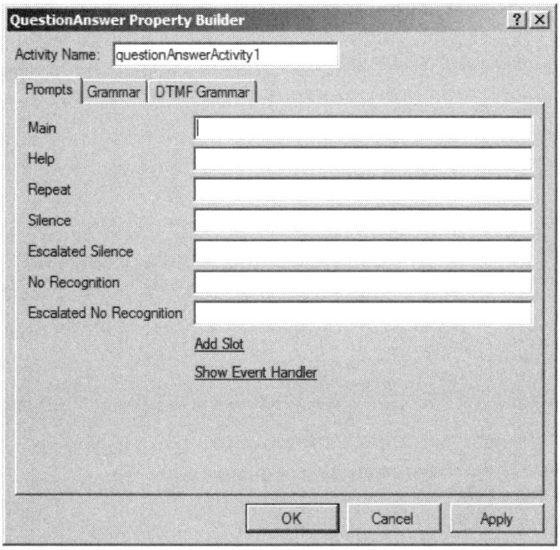

Figure 6-9. *QuestionAnswer Property Builder dialog box*

As with the Statement activity, you can add static prompts for each prompt type by typing them into the text boxes in the QuestionAnswer Property Builder dialog box. To create dynamic prompts, click the Show Event Handler link in the dialog box. This adds an event handler for the TurnStarting event.

The following sections discuss creating dynamic prompts for each of the QuestionAnswer prompt types. The examples add the prompt in the TurnStarting event and use the AppendText method to add the text in the form of a string.

Main Prompt

The Main prompt is the first prompt played after the control is selected. You can add a dynamic prompt to the TurnStarting event or the Executing event. Here is an example:

```
 private void questionAnswerActivity_TurnStarting(object sender,
TurnStartingEventArgs e)
{
     questionAnswerActivity.MainPrompt.ClearContent();
     questionAnswerActivity.MainPrompt.AppendText("Please say Balance,
Transactions or PIN");
}
```

Note that this example uses the `ClearContent` method as the first action before using the `AppendText` method. Without that method, if the application revisits the prompt for any reason, such as in a `NoRecognition` or `Silence` event, `AppendText` will append the same text again, which will result in a repeating prompt. Alternatively, you could use the `SetText` method, which will clear the prompt and set the text.

The code for each of the other prompts is added beneath the Main prompt code in the `TurnStarting` event.

Silence and Escalated Silence Prompts

The Silence prompt is played when the user remains silent for the duration of the `InitialSilenceTimeout` property setting. For example, you may want the prompt to play, "I could not hear you. Please say . . .," as in this example:

```
questionAnswerActivity.Prompts.SilencePrompt.AppendText("I
could not hear you. Please say Balance, Transactions or PIN.");
```

If the `InitialSilenceTimeout` expires more than once, the Escalated Silence prompt will play. (If the Escalated Silence prompt is not defined, the Silence prompt will play again.) You can use this type of prompt to play even more detailed information for the user, as in the following example.

```
questionAnswerActivity.Prompts.EscalatedSilencePrompt.AppendText("I still
could not hear you. If you would like to hear your account balance, say balance.
 To hear your most recent transactions, say transactions. To change your
PIN, say PIN.");
```

No Recognition and Escalated No Recognition Prompts

If the user gives input that isn't recognized by the specified grammar, the No Recognition prompt will play. You can use this prompt to give the users more detailed instructions about what they can say, as in this example:

```
questionAnswerActivity.Prompts.NoRecognitionPrompt.AppendText("
I did not understand what you said. Please say Balance, Transactions or
 PIN");
```

If the user gives unrecognized input again, the Escalated No Recognition prompt will play. You can use this prompt to tell the user you didn't understand and repeat more detailed instructions, as in this example:

```
questionAnswerActivity.Prompts.EscalatedNoRecognition.AppendText("I
still did not understand what you said. If you would like to hear your account
balance, say balance. To hear your most recent transactions, say transactions.
 To change your PIN, say PIN.");
```

Help and Repeat Prompts

The Help and Repeat prompts allow you to specify what is spoken to the user when the user triggers the Help command and Repeat command, respectively. Implementation of these commands is covered in the "Specifying Commands" section later in this chapter.

The Repeat prompt should repeat the Main prompt, like this:

```
questionAnswerActivity.RepeatPrompt.AppendText("Please say
Balance, Transactions or PIN");
```

The Help prompt should be used to provide more detailed information to the user. For example, in the main menu of your application, the Help prompt might clearly specify what each menu choice is and what it does.

```
questionAnswerActivity.HelpPrompt.AppendText(". If you would like to
hear your account balance, say balance. To hear your most recent transactions,
 say transactions. To change your PIN, say PIN.");
```

Using the examples in the previous sections, your final code for the QuestionAnswer control prompts should look like Listing 6-1.

Listing 6-1. *Sample QuestionAnswer Prompt Definition*

```
private void questionAnswerActivity_TurnStarting(object sender,
TurnStartingEventArgs e)
{
    questionAnswerActivity.MainPrompt.ClearContent();
    questionAnswerActivity.Prompts.SilencePrompt.ClearContent();
    questionAnswerActivity.Prompts.EscalatedSilencePrompt.ClearContent();
    questionAnswerActivity.Prompts.NoRecognitionPrompt.ClearContent();
    questionAnswerActivity.Prompts.EscalatedNoRecognitionPrompt.ClearContent();
    questionAnswerActivity.Prompts.HelpPrompt.ClearContent();
    questionAnswerActivity.Prompts.RepeatPrompt.ClearContent();

    questionAnswerActivity.MainPrompt.AppendText("Please say Balance, Transactions
 or PIN");
    questionAnswerActivity.Prompts.SilencePrompt.AppendText("I could not hear you.
 Please say Balance, Transactions or PIN");
    questionAnswerActivity.Prompts.EscalatedSilencePrompt.AppendText("I still
could not hear you. If you would like to hear your account balance, say balance.
To hear your most recent transactions, say transactions. To change your PIN,
say PIN.");
```

```
    questionAnswerActivity.Prompts.NoRecognitionPrompt.AppendText("I did not
understand what you said. Please say Balance, Transactions or PIN");
    questionAnswerActivity.Prompts.EscalatedNoRecognition.AppendText("I still did
 not understand what you said. If you would like to hear your account balance,
say balance. To hear your most recent transactions, say transactions.
To change your PIN, say PIN.");
    questionAnswerActivity.RepeatPrompt.AppendText("Please say
Balance, Transactions or PIN");
    questionAnswerActivity.HelpPrompt.AppendText(". If you would like to
hear your account balance, say balance. To hear your most recent transactions,
 say transactions. To change your PIN, say PIN.");

}
```

Specifying Grammar

For the QuestionAnswer activity, you can attach grammar by double-clicking the [Attach Grammar] link in the designer. This takes you to the Grammar tab of the QuestionAnswer Property Builder dialog box, as shown in Figure 6-10.

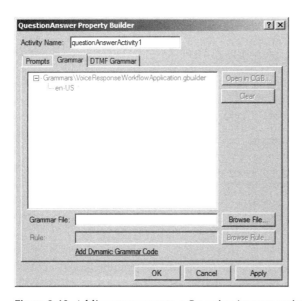

Figure 6-10. *Adding grammar to a QuestionAnswer activity*

You can specify a static grammar or create dynamic grammar in the code-beside. Static grammar must be created beforehand in either the Conversational Grammar Builder or the Grammar Editor, as described in Chapter 2. In the Grammar File field, enter the path to either a .grxml or .cfg file type, and the static grammar will be attached to your control.

To use dynamic grammar, click the Add Dynamic Grammar Code link. You can create grammar in managed code by using the base class, Microsoft.SpeechServer.Recognition. Grammar. This gives you a lot more flexibility in developing grammar, as you can use any available

.NET data sources to fill the grammar. Listing 6-2 shows an example of grammar created in managed code.

Listing 6-2. *Sample QuestionAnswer Grammar Definition*

```
using System;
using System.Collections.Generic;
using System.Text;
using Microsoft.SpeechServer.Dialog;
using Microsoft.SpeechServer.Recognition;
using Microsoft.SpeechServer.Recognition.SrgsGrammar;

namespace Samples
{
    internal class MenuGrammar : Grammar
    {
        public MenuGrammar()
            : base(CreateSrgsDocument())
        {}

        private static SrgsDocument CreateSrgsDocument()
        {
            SrgsDocument grammar = new SrgsDocument();
            grammar.Mode = SrgsGrammarMode.Voice;

            SrgsRule rule = new SrgsRule("MainMenu");
            SrgsOneOf choice = new SrgsOneOf();

            List<string> mainMenu = GetMainMenuData();
            for (int index = 0; index < mainMenu.Count; index++)
            {
                SrgsItem item = new SrgsItem(mainMenu[index].ToString());
                choice.Add(item);
            }

            rule.Add(choice);
            grammar.Rules.Add(rule);
            grammar.Root = rule;

            return grammar;
        }
        private static List<string> GetMainMenuData()
        {
            List<string> data = new List<string>();
            data.Add("Balance");
            data.Add("Transactions");
            data.Add("PIN");
```

```
        return data;
    }


    }
}
```

The first part of the code in Listing 6-2 to consider is the constructor:

```
public MenuGrammar():base(CreateSrgsDocument())
```

The base constructor parameter needs either an SRGS document or the URI of an SRGS document that contains the grammar you want to use. This example returns an SRGS document from the method `CreateSrgsDocument()`.

You start by setting up the structure of your grammar, which should be the same structure as if you created the grammar using the Grammar Editor. The same steps apply to dynamically creating the grammar as with creating the grammar using the Grammar Editor. You create the document, create the rule, and then define the rule, as explained in Chapter 3.

You first create the document:

```
SrgsDocument grammar = new SrgsDocument();
```

Next, set the mode. This can be either `DTMF` or `Voice`, depending on which type of application your grammar will support. The example uses `Voice` mode.

```
grammar.Mode = SrgsGrammarMode.Voice; or grammar.Mode = SrgsGrammarMode.DTMF;
```

Now you need to create the rules. The example has one rule, named `MainMenu`.

```
SrgsRule rule = new SrgsRule("MainMenu ");
```

For comparison purposes, here is what it would look if you were writing this grammar using the Grammar Editor with the XML-formatted grammar (GRXML):

```
<grammar xmlns="http://www.w3.org/2001/06/grammar" xml:lang="en-US" mode="voice">
<rule id="MainMenu">

</rule>
</grammar>
```

So, you have declared a rule, but it doesn't have any functionality. You want your rule to be a list of possible answers, so you need to create a list and then add items to it. To create a new list, use this line:

```
SrgsOneOf choice = new SrgsOneOf();
```

This is equivalent to the following GRXML:

```
<rule id="MainMenu">
    <one-of>
    </one-of>
</rule>
```

Next, you need to create the items that belong to the <one-of> list. This example uses a generic list with three options. Here is how you can create a new item, and then add that item to the <one-of> list.

```
SrgsItem item = new SrgsItem(mainMenu[index].ToString());
choice.Add(item);
```

■Tip This example could easily be converted to use a database instead of a static collection of grammar. In this case, you could modify the GetMainMenuData method and, using ADO.NET, connect and perform queries on your database to populate a generic list.

This is equivalent to the following GRXML:

```
<rule id="MainMenu" scope="public">
    <one-of>
            <item>PIN</item>
            <item>Transactions</item>
            <item>Balance</item>
    </one-of>
</rule>
```

After you have all the options added to the <one-of> list element, you need to add this list to the rule, and then add the rule to document:

```
rule.Add(choice);
grammar.Rules.Add(rule);
```

Once your grammar is created, you can assign the grammar to the QuestionAnswer activity:

```
MenuGrammar mainMenuGrammar = new MenuGrammar();
questionAnswerActivity1.Grammars.Add(mainMenuGrammar);
```

Accessing QuestionAnswer Results

Now that you have the greeting (Statement activity) and the main menu (QuestionAnswer activity), you need to access the results of the main menu. Of interest are three properties that return the confidence value, text, and semantic value. The text property will return the exact phrase the user said that triggered recognition. The semantic value returns the SML-formatted results. For example, the built-in grammar library Library.grxml has the rule Confirmation_YesNo. If you were using this rule, and the user gave a response of "Yep," the first line of the following code would return "Yep," and the second line of code would return "Yes."

```
string textResults = this.questionAnswerActivity1.RecognitionResult.Text;
string semanticResults = this.questionAnswerActivity1.RecognitionResult.Semantics.
Value.ToString();
```

For the QuestionAnswer example, you need to add an IfElse activity from the Windows Workflow toolbox onto the designer, and then add three branches: one for each of the main menu options. You then need to set a Declarative Rule Condition for each branch, which you can do via the IDE. For example, the "Balance Inquiry" branch expression might look like the following:

```
this.mainMenu.RecognitionResult.Semantics.Value.ToString() == "Balance"
```

Your application now has a greeting, main menu, and an IfElse activity to determine what to do next based on the response of the user. The workflow should look like Figure 6-11. (The activities were renamed via the Properties window in the IDE.)

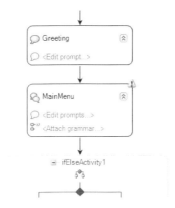

Figure 6-11. *Sample workflow*

Up to this point, you've seen how to access the results of relatively simple grammars. But what if you have grammar that contains several keywords that sound similar? For example, an airline reservation system may ask the user "Where would you like to go?" The Speech Recognizer Engine might get responses like "Las Vegas" and "Los Angeles" or "New York" and Newark" confused, depending on how clearly the user is speaking and the level of background noise. To address such issues, you can retrieve a list of possible alternatives that the Speech Recognizer Engine composed based on your grammar, along with individual confidence scores. Then you could prompt users to confirm their answer, like this:

IVR: Where would you like to go?

User: Las Vegas

IVR: Did you say Los Angeles or Las Vegas?

User: Las Vegas

By default, the Speech Recognizer Engine returns a single result with the highest confidence score. To get alternatives, you use SpeechRecognizer.MaxAlternates to tell the Speech Recognizer Engine how many alternatives you would like. You can do this by overriding the Initialize method of the Voice Response Workflow application. For the example of two alternatives, you would add the following line of code:

```
this.SpeechRecognizer.MaxAlternates = 2;
```

In the application itself, you need to add two QuestionAnswer activities: one to prompt the user "Where do you want to go?" and the second to act as the confirmation prompt. In the second QuestionAnswer activity, you would add the following code:

```
private void qaConfirmation_TurnStarting(object sender,
TurnStartingEventArgs e)
{
        qaConfirmation.MainPrompt.ClearContent();
        if (this.qaMainPrompt.RecognitionResult.Alternates.Count > 1)
        {
            qaConfirmation.MainPrompt.AppendText("Did you say {0} or {1}",
                qaMainPrompt.RecognitionResult.Alternates[0].Text,
                qaMainPrompt.RecognitionResult.Alternates[1].Text);
        }
        else
        {
            qaConfirmation.MainPrompt.AppendText("Did you say {0}",
                this.qaMainPrompt.RecognitionResult.Text);
        }
}
```

Now we'll look at the remaining activities. The procedure for adding them is basically the same as for adding the QuestionAnswer activity, so I won't detail all the steps again. Most of these examples use C# code in the code-beside.

Adding a GetAndConfirm Activity

The GetAndConfirm activity allows you to ask the user a question and specify a Confirmation prompt. If the user's response is less than the specified confidence threshold, the Confirmation prompt will play and give users a chance to change their answer. Consider the following dialog:

IVR: What size pizza would you like?

User: Large

IVR: Did you say small?

User: No, large

IVR: OK, a large pizza

The first step is to create the grammar for the different sizes: small, medium, and large. You can create this grammar by using the Grammar Editor as described in Chapter 2. This example shows you how to set the grammar and prompts through the use of C# code in the code-beside. Next, you need to create a grammar class that consumes the grammar.

```
internal class GCGrammar : Grammar
{
    public GCGrammar()
        : base(CreateSrgsDocument())
    {
    }
    private static SrgsDocument CreateSrgsDocument()
    {
        SrgsDocument grammar = new SrgsDocument(@"C:\Project \Grammars\
Library.grxml");
        grammar.Root = grammar.Rules["Size"];
        return grammar;
    }
}
```

Then you need to set up the Main prompt and the Confirmation prompt. You can set up the Main prompt in the TurnStarting event and the Confirmation prompt in the ConfirmationTurnStarting event, as follows:

```
private void getAndConfirmActivity_TurnStarting(object sender,
TurnStartingEventArgs e)
{
        this.getAndConfirmActivity.MainPrompt.ClearContent();
        this.getAndConfirmActivity.MainPrompt.AppendText("What size pizza
would you like, Small, Medium or Large?");
        this.getAndConfirmActivity.Grammars.Add(new GCGrammar());
}
private void getAndConfirmActivity_ConfirmationTurnStarting(object sender,
TurnStartingEventArgs e)
{
        this.getAndConfirmActivity.ConfirmationMainPrompt.ClearContent();
        this.getAndConfirmActivity.ConfirmationMainPrompt.AppendText("I heard
you say {0} is this correct?",
this.getAndConfirmActivity.RecognitionResult.
Semantics.Value.ToString());
}
```

Adding a Menu Activity

The Menu activity is a data-bound activity that allows you to speak a list of options from a data source and ask the user to pick one. This activity has the same prompt types as the QuestionAnswer activity plus a Confirmation prompt, which is played only if the specified confidence threshold isn't met.

The data-bound activities do not need grammar specified, as they build the grammar automatically based on the data provided to them. For example, the user can barge in and say "That one" or simply say the name of the item. If the user says "That one," the selected option for the menu will be the last bookmarked item. After an item has been selected, the Confirmation prompt will play if the confidence value is below the specified threshold. Consider the following dialog:

IVR: Please select one from the following:

IVR: Transaction 1001

IVR: Transaction 1002

IVR: Transaction 1003

User: That one

The code for this dialog would look like the following:

```
private string[] _choicesList = new string[] { "Transaction 1001",
"Transaction 1002", "Transaction 1003", "Transaction 1004", "Transaction 1005" };

private void menuActivity_TurnStarting(object sender, TurnStartingEventArgs e)
{
        menuActivity.DataSource = _choicesList;
        menuActivity.DataBind();

        menuActivity.MainPrompt.ClearContent();

        foreach (string option in _choicesList)
        {
            menuActivity.MainPrompt.AppendBookmark(option);
            menuActivity.MainPrompt.AppendText(String.Format(option));
        }

}
private void menuActivity_ConfirmationTurnStarting(object sender,
TurnStartingEventArgs e)
{
        menuActivity.ConfirmationMainPrompt.ClearContent();
        menuActivity.ConfirmationMainPrompt.AppendText("I heard {0}, is this
correct?", menuActivity.SelectedOption);
}
```

Adding a NavigableList Activity

The NavigableList activity is the other data-bound control. As with the Menu activity, its grammar is built automatically, and it has a Confirmation prompt in addition to the other prompt types.

A NavigableList activity allows you to specify a data source and let the user navigate its rows by using commands such as Next, Previous, First, Last, Select, and Exit. The grammar for these commands is built in automatically. You can leave these commands as they are, or you can create custom grammar for them and reference the grammar through the NavigableList Property Builder dialog box, as shown in Figure 6-12.

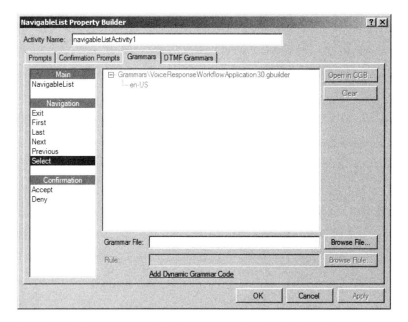

Figure 6-12. *Changing the default grammar for a NavigableList activity*

Now let's consider the following code for the NavigableList:

```
private string[] _choicesList = new string[] { "one", "two", "three", "four",
"five" };

private void navigableListActivity_Executing(object sender,
 ActivityExecutionStatusChangedEventArgs e)
{
    this.navigableListActivity.DataSource = _choicesList;
    this.navigableListActivity.DataBind();
}
private void navigableListActivity_TurnStarting(object sender,
SelectionTurnStartingEventArgs e)
{
    this.navigableListActivity.MainPrompt.ClearContent();
     this.navigableListActivity.MainPrompt.AppendText(this.navigableListActivity.
Items[this.navigableListActivity.CurrentItem.Value].ToString());
}
private void navigableListActivity_ConfirmationTurnStarting(object sender,
TurnStartingEventArgs e)
{
    this.navigableListActivity.ConfirmationMainPrompt.AppendText(
"Did you say {0}?",this.navigableListActivity.Items[this.navigableListActivity.
CurrentItem.Value].ToString());
}
```

You must set the data source and do the binding in the `Executing` event handler. If you do the data binding in the `TurnStarting` event, the data binding will occur every time the control is loaded. This will reset the state, and you will not be able to navigate correctly.

The most important line of code in this example is the setting of the Main prompt, using the `CurrentItem.Value` property:

```
navigableListActivity.MainPrompt.AppendText(navigableListActivity.Items
[navigableListActivity.CurrentItem.Value].ToString());
```

The `CurrentItem.Value` property contains the index of the record that is currently being read to the user. Once the user has said "Select," the Confirmation prompt will play if the confidence value is below the specified value.

A more common scenario would be to pull data from a database to bind to the control. For example, suppose you want to retrieve the records from the table shown in Figure 6-13 into a dataset and bind it to the NavigableList activity.

ID	TransactionType	TransactionDate	TransactionAm...	TransactionPayee
0	Debit	1/1/2007 12:00:...	100.5100	ATM
1	Debit	1/17/2007 12:0...	155.4500	ABC AutoLoans
2	Debit	1/21/2007 12:0...	55.5500	ABC Telephone
▶*	*NULL*	*NULL*	*NULL*	*NULL*	*NULL*

Figure 6-13. *Sample table used with a NavigableList activity*

The goal is to allow the user to use the default grammars to move between the rows of the table—in this case, records of transactions—and select one. After the user selects a record, your application will read the rest of the details of that row to the user. In the `Executing` event of the NavigableList, you can set the `DataSource` to the dataset, similar to the previous example. However, you also need to use the `DataMember` and `DataField` properties of the NavigableList. The `DataMember` should reference the table name (`Transactions` in this example) and the `DataField` should reference the column (`ID` in this example). The following code accomplishes this.

```
private void navigableListActivity1_Executing(object sender,
 ActivityExecutionStatusChangedEventArgs e)
{
.... this.navigableListActivity.DataSource = _choicesDataSet;
.... this.navigableListActivity.DataMember = _choicesDataSet.Tables[0].ToString();
.... this.navigableListActivity.DataField = _choicesDataSet.Tables[0].Columns[1].
ToString();
.... this.navigableListActivity.DataBind();
}
```

In the `TurnStarting` event, you need to specify what your prompt is going to say. In this case, you want to say something like, "Transaction number 1," where the transaction number is the `ID` column of your table. You also need a Confirmation prompt, which you create in the `ConfirmationTurnStarting` event.

```
private void navigableListActivity_TurnStarting(object sender,
SelectionTurnStartingEventArgs e)
{
.... this.navigableListActivity.MainPrompt.ClearContent();
      this.navigableListActivity.MainPrompt.AppendText("Transaction Number {0}",
this.navigableListActivity.
Items[this.navigableListActivity.CurrentItem.Value].ToString());

}
private void navigableListActivity_ConfirmationTurnStarting(object sender,
TurnStartingEventArgs e)
{
.... this.navigableListActivity.ConfirmationMainPrompt.ClearContent();
.... this.navigableListActivity.ConfirmationMainPrompt.AppendText("Did you
select Transaction Number {0}?", this.navigableListActivity.
Items[this.navigableListActivity.CurrentItem.Value].ToString());
}
```

The configuration of the NavigableList is complete. Now you need to add a Statement activity directly after the NavigableList in the workflow. The Statement activity's prompt will read the details of the selected row. This would say something like, "Debit on 1/1/2007 in the amount of $100.51," where "Debit," "1/1/2007," and "100.51" are columns from the selected row. The code would look like this:

```
private void statementActivity_TurnStarting(object sender, TurnStartingEventArgs e)
{
    this.statementActivity.MainPrompt.ClearContent();
    this.statementActivity.MainPrompt.AppendText("{0} on {1} in the amount of {2}",
    _choicesDataSet.Tables[0].Rows[this.navigableListActivity.
CurrentItem.Value][1].ToString(),
_choicesDataSet.Tables[0].Rows[this.navigableListActivity.
CurrentItem.Value][2].ToString(),
_choicesDataSet.Tables[0].Rows[this.navigableListActivity
.CurrentItem.Value][3].ToString());
}
```

Adding a FormFillingDialog

The FormFillingDialog activity allows you to ask users for input and then prompt them for any input that they did not provide. As explained in Chapters 2 and 3, this is called mixed-initiative dialog. The FormFillingDialog activity is just a container activity, in which you place QuestionAnswer activities.

For example, suppose you want to build an ordering system that asks users a series of questions:

- How many gadgets would you like to order?

- What size gadget would you like?

- What color gadget would you like?

- So you want *number, size, color* gadgets?

To accomplish this, you first need to create the grammar that can handle mixed initiative using the Grammar Editor, as described in Chapter 2. Next, add a FormFillingDialog activity to the workflow and add four QuestionAnswer activities to the FormFillingDialog, as shown in Figure 6-14.

Figure 6-14. *Adding a FormFillingDialog with QuestionAnswer activities*

In the code-beside, you need to declare three SemanticItems, initialize the objects, and add them to Answers collection for each QuestionAnswer activity.

```
private SemanticItem<string> _siSize;
private SemanticItem<string> _siColor;
private SemanticItem<string> _siQuantity;

protected override void Initialize(IServiceProvider provider)
{
        base.Initialize(provider);

        _siSize = new SemanticItem<string>(this, "Size");
        _siColor = new SemanticItem<string>(this, "Color");
        _siQuantity = new SemanticItem<string>(this, "Quantity");
```

```
        askSize.Answers.Add(_siSize);
        askColor.Answers.Add(_siColor);
        askQuantity.Answers.Add(_siQuantity);

        confirmOrder.Confirms.Add(_siSize);
        confirmOrder.Confirms.Add(_siColor);
        confirmOrder.Confirms.Add(_siQuantity);
}
```

Next, you need to create a grammar class to consume your mixed-initiative grammar.

```
internal class GadgetGrammar : Grammar
{
    public event EventHandler<SemanticUpdateEventArgs<string>> SizeRecognized;
    public event EventHandler<SemanticUpdateEventArgs<string>> ColorRecognized;
    public event EventHandler<SemanticUpdateEventArgs<string>>
QuantityRecognized;

    public GadgetGrammar()
        : base(CreateSrgsDocument())
    {
        base.Recognized += GadgetGrammar_Recognized;
    }
    private static SrgsDocument CreateSrgsDocument()
    {
        SrgsDocument grammar = new SrgsDocument(@"C:\ Projects\GadgetApplication
\Grammars\Library.grxml");
        grammar.Root = grammar.Rules["Gadget"];
        return grammar;
    }
    private void GadgetGrammar_Recognized(object sender, RecognizedEventArgs e)
    {
            if (e.Result.Semantics.ContainsKey("Size"))
            {
                SemanticValue size = e.Result.Semantics["Size"];
                SizeRecognized(this, new SemanticUpdateEventArgs<string>(
size.Value.ToString(), size.Confidence, e.Result.Text));
            }
            if (e.Result.Semantics.ContainsKey("Color"))
            {
                SemanticValue color = e.Result.Semantics["Color"];
                ColorRecognized(this, new SemanticUpdateEventArgs<string>
(color.Value.ToString(), color.Confidence, e.Result.Text));
            }
```

```
                if (e.Result.Semantics.ContainsKey("Quantity"))
                {
                    SemanticValue quantity = e.Result.Semantics["Quantity"];
                    QuantityRecognized(this, new SemanticUpdateEventArgs<string>
(quantity.Value.ToString(), quantity.Confidence, e.Result.Text));
                }


        }
    }
```

This grammar class contains event handlers for each of the SemanticItem objects. When a SemanticItem is updated, the GadgetGrammar_Recognized method is called, which sets the value for the SemanticItem objects. In your workflow, you need to reference these events. In the TurnStarting event of your first question, reference all the object events.

```
private void askGeneral_TurnStarting(object sender,
TurnStartingEventArgs e)
{
            this.askGeneral.Grammars.Clear();
            GadgetGrammar gadgetGrammar = new GadgetGrammar();

            gadgetGrammar.SizeRecognized += this._siSize.Update;
            gadgetGrammar.ColorRecognized += this._siColor.Update;
            gadgetGrammar.QuantityRecognized += this._siQuantity.Update;
            this.askGeneral.Grammars.Add(gadgetGrammar);
}
```

This allows the user to answer all the questions in one spoken phrase, such as, "I would like four large red gadgets." The application will then skip the questions for answers already provided. This is done by associating the SemanticItem with a QuestionAnswer activity. If the user were to say something like, "I want two gadgets," the application would ask the color and size questions.

```
private void askColor_TurnStarting(object sender,
TurnStartingEventArgs e)
{
            this.askColor.Grammars.Clear();
            ColorGrammar colorGrammar = new ColorGrammar();
            colorGrammar.ColorRecognized += this._siColor.Update;
            this.askColor.Grammars.Add(colorGrammar);
}
private void askSize_TurnStarting(object sender,
TurnStartingEventArgs e)
{
            this.askSize.Grammars.Clear();
            SizeGrammar sizeGrammar = new SizeGrammar();
            sizeGrammar.SizeRecognized += this._siSize.Update;
            this.askSize.Grammars.Add(sizeGrammar);
}
```

```
private void askQuantity_TurnStarting(object sender,
TurnStartingEventArgs e)
{
        this.askQuantity.Grammars.Clear();
        QuantityGrammar quantityGrammar = new QuantityGrammar();
        quantityGrammar.QuantityRecognized += this._siQuantity.Update;
        this.askQuantity.Grammars.Add(quantityGrammar);
}
```

The QuestionAnswer activity's Confirmation prompt makes sure the order is correct. You need to create a grammar class with event handling, so that you can deny or accept the confirmation based on the user's response. For this, you can use the Confirmation_YesNo rule from the built-in grammar file, Library.grxml.

```
internal class ConfirmationGrammar : Grammar
{
    public EventHandler<SemanticUpdateEventArgs<bool>> Yes;
    public EventHandler<SemanticUpdateEventArgs<bool>> No;

    public ConfirmationGrammar()
        : base(CreateSrgsDocument())
    {
        base.Recognized += ConfirmationGrammar_Recognized;
    }
    private static SrgsDocument CreateSrgsDocument()
    {
        SrgsDocument grammar = new SrgsDocument
(@"C:\Projects\GadgetApplication\Grammars\Library.grxml");
        grammar.Root = grammar.Rules["Confirmation_YesNo"];
        return grammar;
    }
    void ConfirmationGrammar_Recognized(object sender, RecognizedEventArgs e)
    {
        if (e.Result.Semantics.Value.ToString() == "Yes")
        {
            if (Yes != null)
            {
                Yes(this, new SemanticUpdateEventArgs<bool>(
true, e.Result.Confidence, e.Result.Text));
            }
        }
        else
        {
```

```
                    if (No != null)
                    {
                        No(this, new SemanticUpdateEventArgs<bool>
(true, e.Result.Confidence, e.Result.Text));
                    }
                }
            }
    }
```

The confirmation QuestionAnswer activity's TurnStarting event should look like the following:

```
private void confirmOrder_TurnStarting(object sender,
TurnStartingEventArgs e)
{
    this.questionAnswerActivity4.MainPrompt.ClearContent();
    this.questionAnswerActivity4.MainPrompt.AppendText("So you want {0}
{1} {2} gadgets?",new object[]{this._siSize.Value.ToString(),
this._siTopping.Value.ToString(), this._siMethod.Value.ToString()});

    this.questionAnswerActivity4.Grammars.Clear();
    ConfirmationGrammar grammar = new ConfirmationGrammar();
    this.questionAnswerActivity4.Grammars.Add(grammar);
    grammar.Yes += this.questionAnswerActivity4.Accept;
    grammar.No += this.questionAnswerActivity4.Deny;
}
```

If the user says "No," the Deny method will clear all of the SemanticItem objects, causing the application to reprompt the user for all of the information. If the user says "Yes," the application exits the FormFillingDialog activity and continues the workflow.

Recording User Input

If you need to record what a user says, such as in a voice confirmation or a voicemail system, you can use either the RecordMessage or the RecordAudio activities. The RecordAudio activity simply records the user and stores the recording. The RecordMessage activity records the user but then allows the user to listen and revise the recording.

Adding a RecordAudio Activity

The RecordAudio activity will prompt the users and record their response in the specified format. You can add either static prompts or dynamic prompts. To add static prompts, double-click the [Edit Prompts] link to open the RecordAudio Property Builder dialog box, as shown in Figure 6-15.

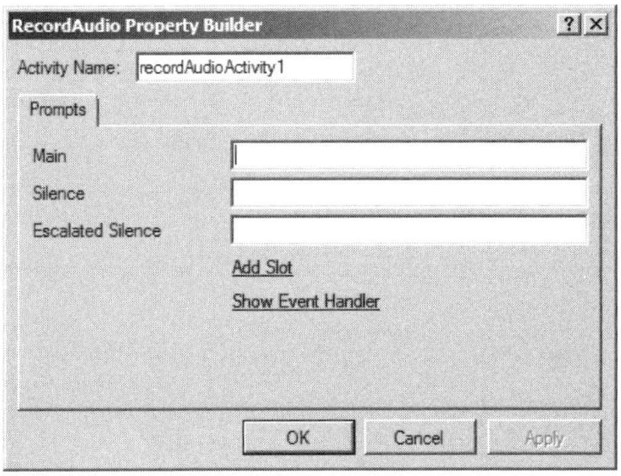

Figure 6-15. *RecordAudio Property Builder dialog box*

You can specify several properties for RecordAudio. One is `PlayBeep`, which sounds a beep after the prompt, to signal users that they should start speaking.

```
this.recordAudioActivity.PlayBeep = true;
```

Most users expect to hear a beep before recording starts, so it's a good idea to set this property.

RecordAudio has two timeout properties: `EndSilenceTimeout` and `InitialSilenceTimeout`. `InitialSilenceTimeout` defines how long the user can remain silent before the Silence prompt is played. `EndSilenceTimeout` specifies how long the user can pause before the recording is considered complete.

Setting the `TerminationDigits` property allows the users to enter DTMF input to specify that they are finished recording. This can be any digit on the telephone keypad, but the # key is the most common. Setting this property is useful, as it allows users to indicate when they are finished, rather than relying on the `EndSilenceTimeout` property.

```
this.recordAudioActivity.TerminationDigits =
 Microsoft.SpeechServer.RecordTerminationDigits.Hash;
```

Adding a RecordMessage Activity

The RecordMessage activity simply extends the RecordAudio activity. It explicitly asks users to confirm their message and allows them to continue recording, start over, or replay their recording.

After you add a RecordMessage activity to the workflow, right-click the activity and choose Property Builder. As shown in Figure 6-16, the RecordMessage Property Builder dialog box has tabs for two prompt categories: Recording Prompts and Action Prompts.

The call flow for a RecordMessage activity first plays the Main prompt on the Recording Prompts tab, before the user has had a chance to record a message. After the user has recorded a message, the RecordMessage activity then plays the Main prompt on the Action Prompts tab, shown in Figure 6-17.

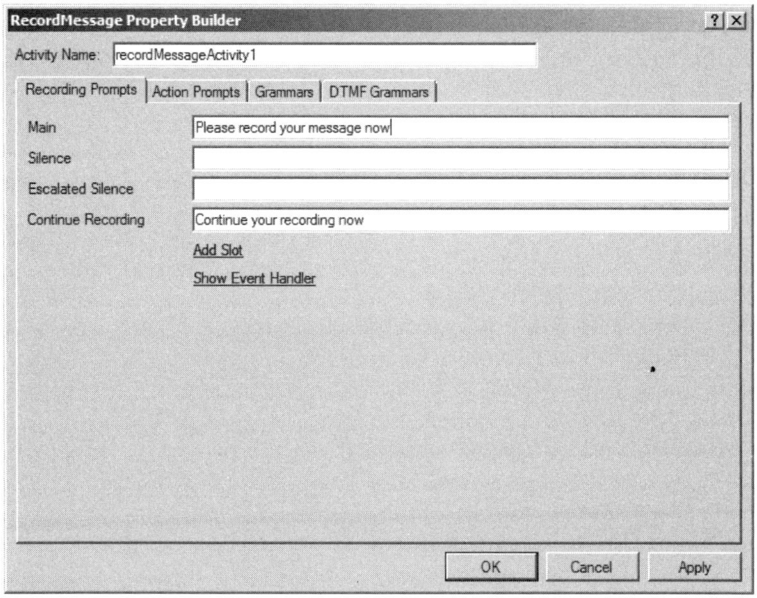

Figure 6-16. *Recording Prompts tab of RecordMessage Property Builder dialog box*

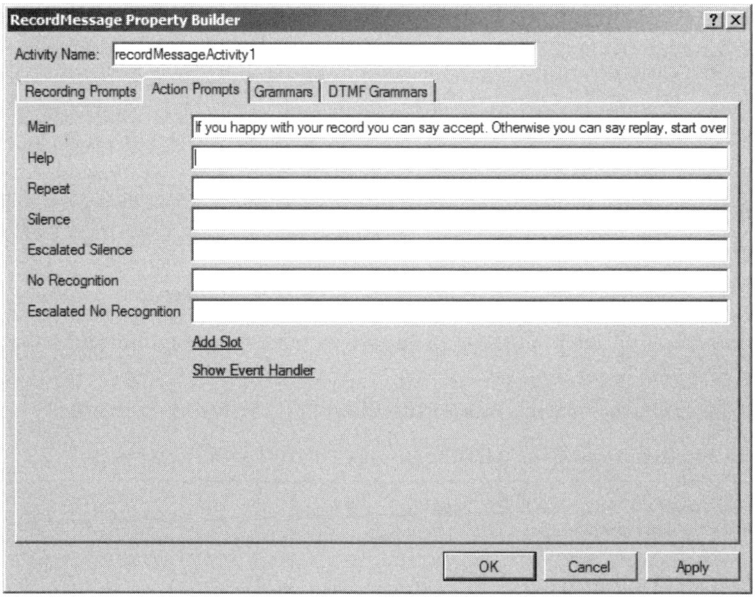

Figure 6-17. *Action Prompts tab of the RecordMessage Property Builder dialog box*

The RecordMessage activity has built-in grammars for navigation. However, you can also define your own custom grammars for each of the navigational commands via the Grammars tab, as shown in Figure 6-18.

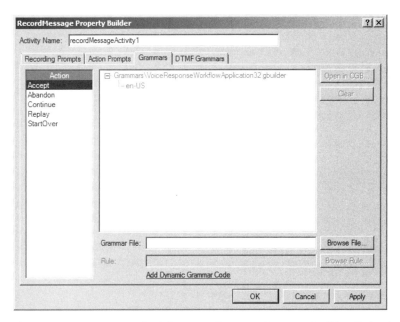

Figure 6-18. *Grammars tab of the RecordMessage Property Builder dialog box*

The actions listed on the Grammars tab are performed automatically based on which one is activated by the user via the grammar. Table 6-5 shows what occurs when each action is activated.

Table 6-5. *RecordMessage Actions*

Action	Description
Accept	Saves the recording and moves on to the next activity in the workflow
Abandon	Quits the activity and moves on to the next activity in the workflow
Continue	Plays the Continue Recording prompt and allows the user to continue recording a message
Replay	Allows the user to hear the message and then hear the main action prompt again
StartOver	Plays the main prompt again, allowing the user to re-record the message

Going to a Target Activity

The GoTo activity allows you to move to a different activity, ignoring the workflow. For example, if you prompt the user for a yes or no answer and make a decision using the IfElse activity, the If branch might continue the application, while the Else branch might use the GoTo activity to specify a previous activity, allowing users to correct their answers to earlier prompts.

After you add the GoTo activity to your workflow, you can set which activity it should target by double-clicking the [Select Target Activity] link and selecting the activity from the GoTo Property Builder dialog box, shown in Figure 6-19.

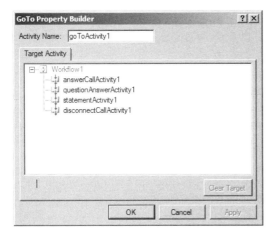

Figure 6-19. *GoTo Property Builder dialog box*

Using a Prompt Database

When you first create a new Voice Response Workflow application project, you can choose to include a new prompt database. If you already have a prompt database that you want to use, you can use the `PromptDatabase` property of the workflow itself and set it to the URI of the prompt database. Here is an example:

```
this.PromptDatabase = new System.Uri("Prompts\\Prompts.prompts",
System.UriKind.Relative);
```

The workflow will then use the prompt database you specified.

If certain prompts will use different databases, you can use the `AddPromptDatabase` method for those prompts. For example, if you have a QuestionAnswer activity, you can have the Main prompt use a different prompt database than the other prompts, like this:

```
questionAnswerActivity.MainPrompt.AddPromptDatabase(new
  System.Uri("Prompts\\Prompts.prompts", System.UriKind.Relative););
```

Specifying Commands

For each workflow, you can add commands that the user can say to interact with the application. You can use the HelpCommand and RepeatCommand activities in the Speech Dialog Components toolbox to add Help and Repeat commands. The Command activity allows you to develop your own custom commands.

To start working with commands, you need to switch the designer view from sequential workflow display to the command display, by clicking the View Commands icon at the bottom of the Dialog Workflow Designer, as shown in Figure 6-20. This takes you to the Command Handler view.

Figure 6-20. *Click the View Commands icon to switch Command Handler view.*

Adding Help and Repeat Commands

Earlier in this chapter, you saw how you can assign Help and Repeat prompts to some activities, such as the QuestionAnswer activity. These prompts are spoken only after you've added the corresponding commands to your workflow. Figure 6-21 shows an example of adding a HelpCommand activity to the Command Handler view of the workflow.

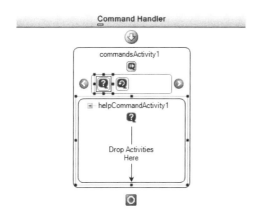

Figure 6-21. *Adding a Help command*

After you add the Help or Repeat command, you need to assign grammar for the commands. This way, when a user says "Help" or "Repeat," the application will automatically evaluate which activity is active and play the corresponding prompt. Here is an example of setting up the Help and Repeat prompts for two QuestionAnswer activities:

```
private void PickANumber_TurnStarting(object sender,
 TurnStartingEventArgs e)
{
    PickANumber.Prompts.MainPrompt.SetText("Pick a
number");
    PickANumber.Prompts.HelpPrompt.SetText("Say a
number between one and ten");
    PickANumber.Prompts.RepeatPrompt.SetText("I
said, Pick a number");
}

private void PickAColor_TurnStarting(object sender,
 TurnStartingEventArgs e)
```

```
{
     PickAColor.Prompts.MainPrompt.SetText("Say a
color");
     PickAColor.Prompts.HelpPrompt.SetText("Say
either red, white or blue");
     PickAColor.Prompts.RepeatPrompt.SetText("I
said, Pick a color");
}
```

In this example, one activity asks the user to pick a number, and the other asks the user to pick a color. If the user says "Help" while the PickANumber activity is active, the user will hear "Say a number between one and ten." If a user says "Help" while the PickAColor activity is active, the user will hear "Say either red, white, or blue."

You can also add activities to the Help and Repeat commands directly. For example, you might add a Statement activity to the Help command, which says, "Let me help you." Activities added directly to the command do not evaluate which activity in the parent workflow is currently active. So if you added a Statement activity to the Help command in the previous example, when a user says "Help" while either the PickANumber or PickAColor activity is active, it will first say "Let me help you," and then play the Help prompt defined on the activity, "Say a number between one and ten." or "Say either red, white or blue."

Adding Custom Commands

The Command activity can be used to specify custom commands. Command activities are similar to Help and Repeat commands, except they do not automatically evaluate which activity is currently active.

For example, you might want to allow the users to say "Operator" at any point in the application and be transferred to a live agent. For this example, you just need to add a Command activity to the Command Handler view and set the active grammar that will recognize the phrase "Operator." When the grammar is activated by the user, the Operator command will perform the actions defined. Figure 6-22 shows an example of adding an Operator command that performs a blind transfer to a live agent.

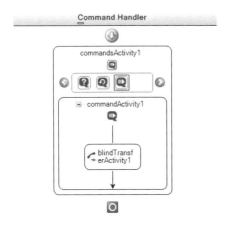

Figure 6-22. *Adding a custom command*

Handling Errors and Events

You can add handlers for application-level speech events and for specific exceptions. The workflow designer provides a separate view for speech events and fault handlers.

Handling Speech Events

Speech events are application-level events that you can define to decide whether or not the caller is being unresponsive. The Speech Dialog Components toolbox has three items for handling speech events:

- *ConsecutiveNoRecognitionsSpeechEvent*: Allows you to define how many no recognition error events are allowed to take place before the event is fired.

- *ConsecutiveSilencesSpeechEvent*: Allows you to define how many silence error events are allowed to take place before the event is fired.

- *ConsecutiveNoInputsSpeechEvent*: Allows you to define how many of both no recognition and silence error events are allowed to take place before the event is fired.

To handle any of these events, you first need to switch to the Speech Events view by double-clicking the View Speech Events icon at the bottom of the designer, as shown in Figure 6-23.

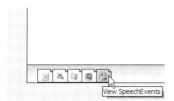

Figure 6-23. *Click the View Speech Events icon to switch to Speech Events view.*

For example, you might not want to allow more than four error events to be fired. After this many consecutive errors, the user simply doesn't understand how to work the application and is taking up valuable application resources. At this point, you can either let the user know that you are disconnecting him or transfer him to a live agent.

First, drag the events you are going to handle onto the designer. Then configure the actions you are going to perform for each event via the Properties window. Set the `MaximumNoInputs` property for each event, as shown in Figure 6-24.

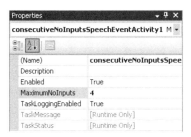

Figure 6-24. *Setting speech event properties*

Creating Fault Handlers

The fault handlers are a part of Windows WF. The fault handlers allow you to perform actions based on a specific exception. To view or add fault handlers, double-click the View Fault Handlers icon at the bottom of the designer, as shown in Figure 6-25.

Figure 6-25. *Click the View Fault Handlers icon to switch to Fault Handlers view.*

When you create a new Voice Response Workflow application, two predefined fault handlers are added automatically: `HandleGeneralFault` and `HandleCallDisconnect`. Typically, these two handlers are all you need. If you need to catch more detailed information about an exception, you can edit the `HandleGeneralFault`, which simply logs each exception and then detaches the debugger.

That being said, you may wish to catch other exceptions, such as a problem with the Speech Recognizer Engine itself. To add a fault handler, drag a Fault Handler activity from the Windows Workflow toolbox onto the Fault Handlers view of the workflow. Next, configure which exception this handler should catch via the `FaultType` property in the Properties window. When you set this property, you will be prompted with a list of current references. For example, for a problem with the Speech Recognizer Engine, you would choose `Microsoft.SpeechServer.Recognition`, then `SrgsRecognitionEngineException`, as shown in Figure 6-26.

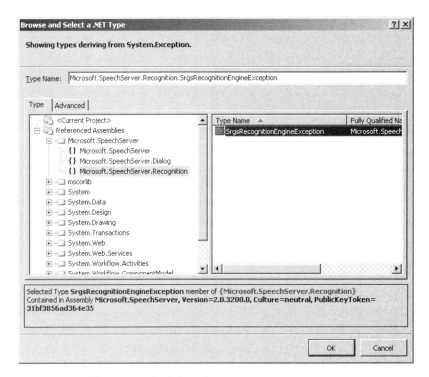

Figure 6-26. *Adding a new fault handler*

Adding Interpreters

The interpreter activities allow you to run SALT or VoiceXML pages inside a Voice Response Workflow application. This can be useful when migrating complex pages to a Voice Response Workflow application.

To use an interpreter, simply drag the corresponding activity—SaltInterpreter or VoiceXmlInterpreter—from the Speech Dialog Components toolbox onto your workflow design. Figure 6-27 shows an example of a SALT interpreter added to the workflow, along with its properties. The StartPage property is required. Until it's set, you'll see an exclamation point on the interpreter activity in the workflow, as in Figure 6-27.

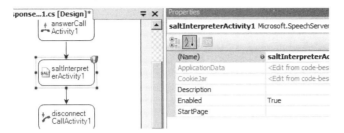

Figure 6-27. *Adding a SaltInterpreter activity*

You can set the `StartPage` property through the Properties window or in the code-beside, as in the following example. The property should reference the URL for either your SALT or VoiceXML page, depending on the interpreter control you are using.

```
this.saltInterpreterActivity.StartPage = "http://localhost/SpeechWebApplication";
```

This is all you need to do to run a SALT or VoiceXML page from your workflow. It's very simple, yet very useful!

Creating Custom Activities

For your Voice Response Workflow applications, you can create custom activities that you can reuse later. You can create three types of custom activities to add to your workflows:

- *Voice Response Seequential Workflow*: Allows you to create a custom workflow and then call it from another workflow.

- *Voice Response Sequence Activity*: Allows you to develop a standard workflow component using standard speech activities.

- *Voice Response Composite Activity*: Allows you to develop more complex activities and gives you direct access to the Speech Recognizer Engine and Speech Synthesis Engine objects.

You can add Sequence and Composite activities directly to your workflow project, or you can create a separate project for them. To add them to your current project, choose to add a new file, and then select either Voice Response Sequence Activity or Voice Response Composite Activity.

Creating a separate project will allow you to reuse this component in any other speech application. It also allows you to distribute the custom activity to other people. To create a custom activity in its own assembly, choose the Voice Response Activity Library project type from the Add New Project dialog box, as shown in Figure 6-28. Then add the corresponding file type to the project.

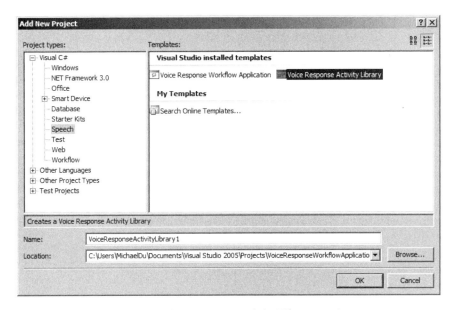

Figure 6-28. *Creating a new Voice Response Activity Library project*

Adding a Sequential Workflow Activity

Creating a Sequential Workflow activity is probably the easiest method to use. To add a Sequential Workflow activity, right-click your project in the Solution Explorer and choose Add New Item ➤ Sequential Workflow. Develop the activity in the same way as a Voice Response Workflow application. You can access all the functions of the standard activities.

Then add an InvokeWorkflow activity (located in the Speech Dialog Components toolbox) to your main workflow to call the sequential workflow.

Adding a Voice Response Sequence Activity

Suppose that you wanted to have an activity for logging in to an application. You could create a Sequence activity using standard speech activities, and also add the custom activity to your toolbox.

The first step is to add a new Voice Response Sequence Activity file to the project. Select File ➤ New and choose Voice Response Sequence Activity from the Add New Item dialog box, as shown in Figure 6-29.

The Dialog Workflow Designer starts without any activities added. It doesn't need the AnswerCall or DisconnectCall activity, as these are handled in the main workflow. In the example of creating a login component, you can simply add three QuestionAnswer activities with the following prompts:

- Is the number you are calling from tied to the account you are calling about?

- Please enter your 10-digit telephone number

- Please enter your 4-digit PIN

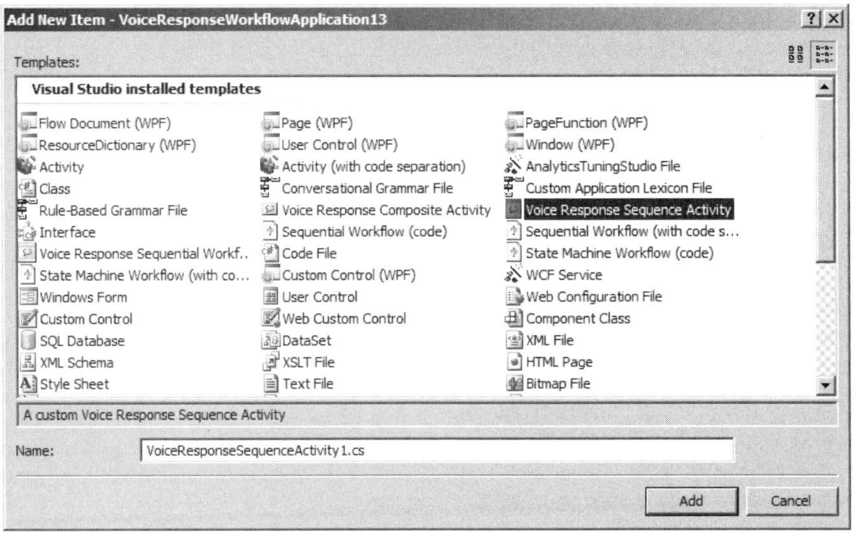

Figure 6-29. *Adding a Voice Response Sequence Activity file*

You can add an IfElse activity to check if the user said "Yes" or "No" to the first question. If she said "Yes," you can skip the telephone number prompt, as you already have that number. If she said "No," you need to ask for the telephone number. In the Sequence activity code, you need to add a string property named `CallingParty`, along with a backing field named `_callingParty`.

```
private string _callingParty;
public string CallingParty
{
    get
    {
        return _callingParty;
    }
    set
    {
        _callingParty = value;
    }
}
```

Your component will be added to the toolbox, as shown in Figure 6-30. Drag it onto your workflow.

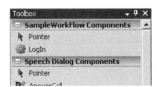

Figure 6-30. *A custom Sequence activity added to the toolbox*

In the main workflow, override the `Initialize` method and add code so that it looks like the following. This will pass the Automatic Number Identification (ANI) information to your Sequence activity, which will determine whether or not to ask for the user's telephone number.

```
protected override void Initialize(IServiceProvider provider)
{
    base.Initialize(provider);
    this.LogIn.CallingParty = TelephonySession.CallInfo.CallingParty.Uri.User;
}
```

In the designer, you'll notice that the workflow shows only the one block and the name of the instance of the Sequence activity; it doesn't actually show the components of the activity, as shown in Figure 6-31.

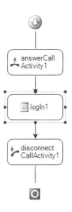

Figure 6-31. *Custom Sequence activity with compiler attribute*

If you want it to display the components of the Sequence activity, remove the following compiler attribute from the Sequence activity:

```
[Designer(typeof(System.Workflow.ComponentModel.Design.ActivityDesigner))]
```

Figure 6-32 shows the workflow after removing this line of code. With the custom Sequence activity displayed in the parent workflow, you can view the details of the component as well as add breakpoints to those components, so that you can debug the activity while you are still in the parent workflow.

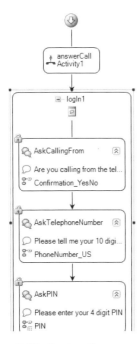

Figure 6-32. *Custom Sequence activity displayed in the designer*

Adding a Voice Response Composite Activity

If you need a component with functionally that no other current activity can provide, you can create a custom Composite activity. For example, perhaps you want to always append the text "Thank You" to the specified prompt. The Composite activity allows you to access the base Speech Recognizer Engine and Speech Synthesis Engine objects, along with standard functions.

To get started, add a new Voice Response Composite Activity file to your project, as shown in Figure 6-33.

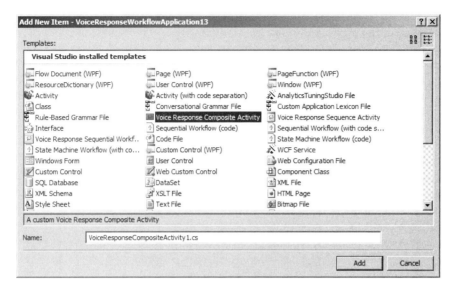

Figure 6-33. *Adding a new Voice Response Composite Activity file*

When you create a new Composite activity, the class is predefined for you, as follows:

```
public partial class VoiceResponseCompositeActivity1: SpeechCompositeActivity
{
    public VoiceResponseCompositeActivity1()
    {
        InitializeComponent();
    }

     protected override void ExecuteCore(
ActivityExecutionContext context)
        {
            // Add Core API calls here.
            // base.ExecuteCore(context);
        }
}
```

For the example of appending the text "Thank You" to prompts, you would use the following code:

```
public delegate void TurnStartingEventHandler(
object sender, TurnStartingEventArgs e);

public partial class CustomStatementActivity:
SpeechCompositeActivity
{
    public event EventHandler<TurnStartingEventArgs> TurnStarting;
```

```csharp
        private static InstanceDependencyProperty
MainPromptProperty = InstanceDependencyProperty.Register
("MainPrompt", typeof(PromptBuilder),
typeof(CustomStatementActivity));

        [BrowsableAttribute(false)]
        public PromptBuilder MainPrompt
        {
            get
            {
                return (PromptBuilder)
GetValue(MainPromptProperty);
            }
            private set
            {
                SetValue(MainPromptProperty, value);
            }
        }

        protected virtual void OnTurnStarting()
        {
            TurnStartingEventArgs args = new TurnStartingEventArgs(Workflow.History,
 Microsoft.SpeechServer.PromptType.Main);

            TurnStarting(this, args);
        }

        public CustomStatementActivity()
        {
            InitializeComponent();
            MainPrompt = new PromptBuilder();
        }

        protected override void
ExecuteCore(ActivityExecutionContext context)
        {
            Workflow.Synthesizer.SpeakCompleted += new EventHandler<SpeakCompleted
EventArgs>(Synthesizer_SpeakCompleted);
            OnTurnStarting();

            MainPrompt.AppendText("Thank You");
            Workflow.Synthesizer.SpeakAsync(MainPrompt);
        }
```

```
            private void Synthesizer_SpeakCompleted(object sender,
 SpeakCompletedEventArgs e)
            {
                Workflow.Synthesizer.SpeakCompleted -=
Synthesizer_SpeakCompleted;

                Close(e.Error);
            }
}
```

The first step is to create the properties. Instead of using standard backing fields, you need to create properties using InstanceDependencyProperty, in order to support runtime behaviors in the designer. For example, the MainPrompt property of the custom activity would look like the following:

```
private static InstanceDependencyProperty MainPromptProperty =
InstanceDependencyProperty.Register("MainPrompt",
typeof(PromptBuilder), typeof(CustomStatementActivity));

[BrowsableAttribute(false)]
public PromptBuilder MainPrompt
{
    get
    {
        return (PromptBuilder)GetValue(MainPromptProperty);
    }
    private set
    {
       SetValue(MainPromptProperty, value)
      }
}
```

The reason for adding the compiler attribute [BrowsableAttribute(false)] on the property is so that the property cannot be set via the Properties window in the IDE; it must be set in the code-beside.

Next, in the constructor, you set the MainPrompt to a new instance of the PromptBuilder:

```
public CustomStatementActivity()
{
    InitializeComponent();
    MainPrompt = new PromptBuilder();
}
```

In the ExecuteCore is the method that is called when the workflow encounters the custom activity. This is where you can set the event handler for the SpeakCompleted event, and append the text "Thank You" to the MainPrompt, along with speaking the MainPrompt.

```
protected override void ExecuteCore(ActivityExecutionContext context)
{
          Workflow.Synthesizer.SpeakCompleted += new EventHandler<SpeakCompleted
EventArgs>(Synthesizer_SpeakCompleted);

          MainPrompt.AppendText("Thank You");
          Workflow.Synthesizer.SpeakAsync(MainPrompt);
}
```

Now your custom activity is actually functional, but currently the Main prompt must be set outside the activity itself. Add an event for TurnStarting, so that in the workflow, you can set the Main prompt in the TurnStarting event, just as you would for a normal Statement activity. Add the following event, delegate, and method to your class:

```
public delegate void TurnStartingEventHandler(object sender,
TurnStartingEventArgs e);

public event EventHandler<TurnStartingEventArgs> TurnStarting;

protected virtual void OnTurnStarting()
{
          TurnStartingEventArgs args = new TurnStartingEventArgs(Workflow.History,
Microsoft.SpeechServer.PromptType.Main);

          TurnStarting(this, args);
}
```

In the ExecuteCore method, you need to call the OnTurnStarting method before the SpeakAsync call. This allows the Main prompt to be edited before the prompt is spoken.

Creating Outbound Calling Applications

Earlier in this chapter, you saw how the MakeCall activity can be used to place simple outbound calls. Here, I will show you how you can to create a more sophisticated outbound calling application. This application will read calls from MSMQ, determine if an answering machine has picked up, and then leave a message or speak to called party.

Placing Calls in a Queue

Chapter 1 explained how to set up MSMQ on the server; this must be done before the sample application described in this section will run. Once you have the queue set up, you need to create an application that places calls into MSMQ. For example, you might have an application that reads records from a database and places that information in MSMQ, which your application can call at a later time. Here is an example of code for adding information to a queue in MSMQ:

```
MessageQueue queue = null;
string path = ".\\private$\\CallCustomer";
if (MessageQueue.Exists(path))
{
    queue = new MessageQueue(path);
}
else
{
    queue = MessageQueue.Create(path);
}

Message message = new Message();
StringBuilder contents = new StringBuilder();

contents.Append("CustomerPhone=");
contents.Append(customerPhone);
contents.Append("&CustomerName=");
contents.Append(customerName);
contents.Append("AccountNumber=");
contents.Append(accountNumber);

message.Body = contents.ToString();
message.Priority = MessagePriority.Highest;
message.Label = "Call " + customerPhone;

queue.Send(message);
queue.Close();
```

Now that you have calls in MSMQ, let's look at how you can retrieve the information from the queue and then place calls to the corresponding telephone numbers.

Designing the Outbound Call Activities

In your workflow, you need to remove the AcceptCall activity and replace it with a MakeCall activity. What if your application encounters a voicemail system or answering machine? To handle that, add the DetectAnsweringMachine activity after the MakeCall activity.

In your queuing application, you have three parameters: `CustomerNumber`, `CustomerName`, and `AccountId`. Because all applications, including Voice Response Workflow applications, are technically web applications, you get these parameters via the query string. The first step is to collect these parameters, so you need to add a Code activity before your MakeCall activity. This will collect the parameters and store them. The code for your Code activity should look like the following:

```
private string _customerPhone;
private string _customerName;
private string _accountNumber;

private void CodeActivity(object sender, EventArgs e)
{
    _customerPhone =
Uri.UnescapeDataString(QueryString["CustomerPhone"]);
    _customerName =
Uri.UnescapeDataString(QueryString["CustomerName"]);
    _accountNumber =
Uri.UnescapeDataString(QueryString["CustomerName"]);

    this.CallCustomer.CallingParty = "5551212"; //Number we are calling from
    this.CallCustomer.CalledParty = _customerPhone; //Number to call
}
```

Now that you have enough information to call the user, you can set up your
DetectAnsweringMachine activity. First, create the detection grammar. The idea is that answering
systems and humans typically answer the phone differently. A human may answer the phone
saying, "Hello?" while an answering machine would probably say something like "You've
reached the Jones resident, please leave a message." For the DetectAnsweringMachine activity
to work correctly, your grammar needs to return the value ANSWERING_MACHINE_RESPONSE or
LIVE_PERSON_RESPONSE. Your detection grammar might look like Figure 6-34.

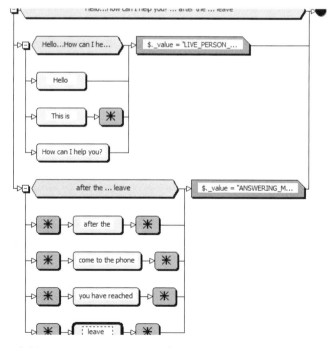

Figure 6-34. *Detection grammar in the Grammar Editor*

This grammar assumes a human has answered the phone if any of the following phrases are heard:

- Hello

- This is . . .

- How can I help you?

It also assumes that an answering machine has answered if it hears the following phrases:

- . . . after the . . .

- . . . come to the phone . . .

- . . . you have reached . . .

- . . . leave . . .

This type of grammar takes some creativity to build, and the sample used in Figure 6-34 is by no means complete. Such a grammar should really be built up over time, and adjusted occasionally for accuracy.

In the constructor of your workflow after the initialization, you need to add the following code:

```
public Workflow1()
{
    InitializeComponent();
     this.detectAnsweringMachine.Grammar =
new Grammar(new Uri(@"C:\Detection.grxml"), "DetectionRule");
}
```

In the TurnStarting event of the DetectAnsweringMachine activity, you need to set what you want the application to say if it encounters an answering machine. The Message property is played only if the application has detected an answering machine.

```
private void detectAnsweringMachine_TurnStarting(object sender,
TurnStartingEventArgs e)
{
     this.detectAnsweringMachine.Message.SetText("This
message is for {0}", _customerName);
}
```

You can then have a Statement activity with a prompt that will always play, whether a human or answering machine answers the call.

```
private void SpeakToCustomer_TurnStarting(object sender, TurnStartingEventArgs e)
{
    this.SpeakToCustomer.MainPrompt.ClearContent();
    this.SpeakToCustomer.MainPrompt.AppendText("Hello {0},
We are calling about your account, {1}. Please give us a call at ");
    this.SpeakToCustomer.MainPrompt.AppendTextWithHint(
"5551212", SayAs.Telephone);
}
```

Alternatively, you might want to have completely different prompts for human-answered calls and answering machines. You could create an instance of the `DetectionResult` class and use the IfElse activity to determine which was detected: `DetectionResult.LivePerson` or `DetectionResult.AnsweringMachine`. This would allow you to have QuestionAnswer activities for human-answered calls and Statement activities for automatically answered calls (at least until automated systems can start answering questions).

Conclusion

This chapter covered how to create Voice Response Workflow applications using speech dialog and Windows WF activities. Developers familiar with creating .NET applications will feel very comfortable in the Voice Response Workflow development environment.

The next chapter covers creating Unified Messaging and Unified Communications applications. With these types of applications, you can use Unified Messaging features such as those found in Microsoft Exchange 2007.

CHAPTER 7

■■■

Creating Unified Communications and Messaging Applications

The idea of *unified communications* (UC) is that all your real-time communications are accessible and provided via a single entity. This includes instant messaging, telephone calls, and even video conferencing. Microsoft has recently released an array of new products to provide these features, including OCS 2007, Office Communicator 2007, Office Live Meeting, and RoundTable.

Microsoft OCS 2007 is really at the forefront of unified communications, as it allows users to transform their instant messaging client, such as Office Communicator, into a soft phone. This means that users can access their office telephone calls and instant messaging messages from anywhere they have client connectivity.

The idea of *unified messaging* (UM) is that all your non-real-time messages are stored in a single location. This includes e-mail messages, voicemail messages, and faxes. The main Microsoft product that supports UM is Exchange 2007.

So where does Speech Server fit in? Speech Server plays a supportive role in both UC and UM, as you will learn in this chapter. But before we dive into creating a UM application that ties into Exchange, let's explore one of the interesting UM features of Exchange 2007.

Using Exchange 2007 Auto Attendants

Microsoft Exchange UM supports e-mail, voicemail, and faxes via an e-mail client such as Microsoft Outlook. Of particular interest to speech application developers is Exchange 2007's new auto attendant feature.

Auto attendants can direct callers to a specific area or person, similar to a Speech Server application. The difference is that Exchange auto attendants are not programmable; they are only configurable. So if you need anything outside the scope of the Exchange auto attendant, you will need to create a Speech Server application.

It's easy to let users access your Speech Server application via an Exchange 2007 auto attendant. You just need to define that as an action when you configure your auto attendant, as described in the "Defining Custom Actions" section later in this chapter.

Note Before you get started setting up an Exchange 2007 auto attendant, you need to create a UM Dial Plan and a UM IP Gateway. For details, see `http://technet.microsoft.com/en-us/library/bb125151.aspx` and `http://technet.microsoft.com/en-us/library/bb123526.aspx`, respectively.

Adding an Auto Attendant

Exchange's UM features are available through the Exchange Management Console. Beneath the Organization Configuration node, you'll find the Unified Messaging node. To add an auto attendant, select the Unified Messaging node, and then select the UM Auto Attendants tab. Then right-click in the right pane and choose New UM Auto Attendant, as shown in Figure 7-1.

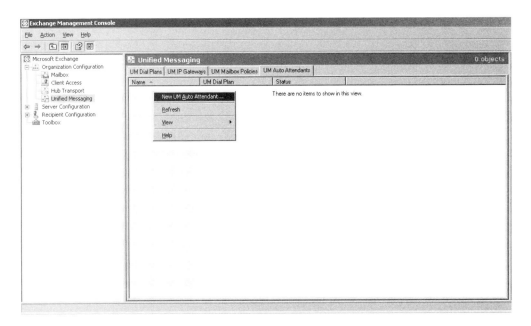

Figure 7-1. *Choosing to add a new UM auto attendant*

Exchange will prompt you for the name, dial plan, and extension number that users will call to get the auto attendant, as shown in Figure 7-2. The name needs to be unique to distinguish it from any other auto attendants.

If you select the Create Auto Attendant As Enabled check box, the auto attendant will be enabled immediately after you create it. Select the Create Auto Attendant As Speech-Enabled check box if you want the application to use speech recognition.

After you click New, your new auto attendant will be listed on the UM Auto Attendants tab in the Exchange Management Console, as shown in Figure 7-3.

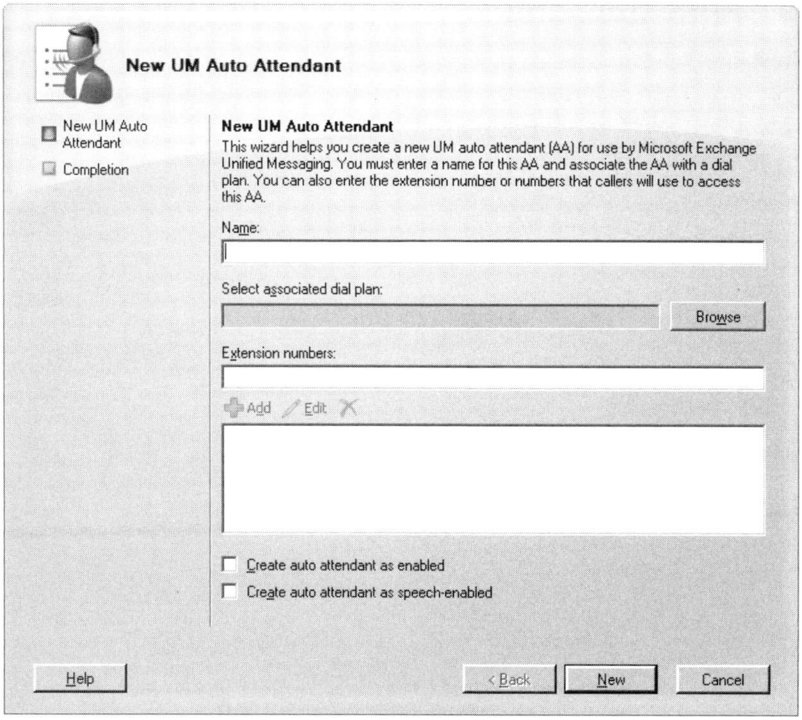

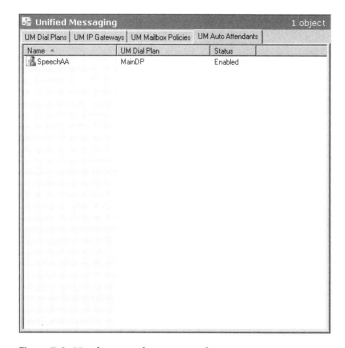

Figure 7-2. *Creating a new UM auto attendant*

Figure 7-3. *Newly created auto attendant*

Configuring an Auto Attendant

Next, you need to configure your auto attendant. Right-click its name on the UM Auto Attendants tab and choose Properties. The Properties dialog box contains General, Greetings, Times, Features, and Key Mapping tabs for setting up your auto attendant, as shown in Figure 7-4.

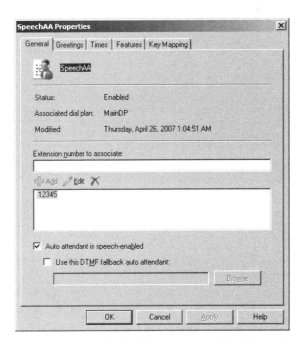

Figure 7-4. *General tab of the Auto Attendant Properties dialog box*

Setting Up a DTMF Fallback

On the General tab of the Properties dialog box, you can set up a DTMF fallback auto attendant. If you specified that your new auto attendant should be speech-enabled, it will accept only speech recognition. After three no recognition or silence events, the auto attendant will say, "Sorry, I couldn't help. Please call back later," and then hang up. Typically, this isn't what you want to happen. So you can provide a DTMF fallback by creating another new auto attendant that is not speech-enabled and specify that auto attendant on the General tab of your speech-enabled auto attendant.

Creating the Greeting and Main Menu Prompts

On the Greetings tab of the Properties dialog box, you set up the greeting and main menu prompts, as shown in Figure 7-5. For each prompt, you can specify a .wav file that contains your recorded custom message.

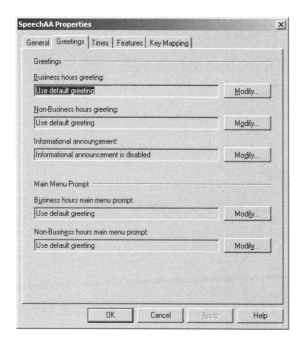

Figure 7-5. *Greetings tab of the Auto Attendant Properties dialog box*

You can specify both business hours and non-business hours prompts. These are played based on the schedule you set up on the Times tab, as described in the next section. If you are going to service calls 24/7, you need to specify only business hours prompts.

The default business hours greeting is "Welcome to the Microsoft Exchange Auto Attendant," so you will probably want to use a custom greeting. Click the Modify button and specify the location of the .wav file you want to play.

For the main menu prompts, the defaults are generated based on the key mappings you set up, as explained in the "Defining Custom Actions" section later in this chapter. Alternatively, you can specify prerecorded .wav files by clicking the Modify button.

Setting Hours of Operation

For your auto attendant, you can set your business hours and have different functionality based on those hours. You can set your hours on the Times tab of the Properties dialog box. The Business Hours drop-down list includes standard business times, as well as an option to add your own custom schedule, as shown in Figure 7-6. In the area below the hours list, you can specify business holidays.

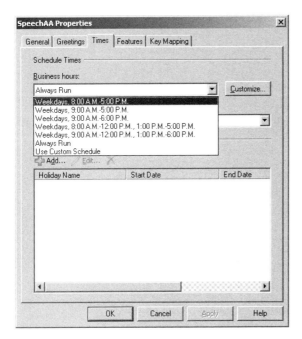

Figure 7-6. *Times tab of the Auto Attendant Properties dialog box*

Configuring Features

On the Features tab of the Properties dialog box, you can configure specific features for your auto attendant, as shown in Figure 7-7.

Most of the features are self-explanatory based on their names. One that may not be obvious is the Matched Name Selection Method option. This option determines how a user can find a user. You can inherit from the dial plan or select a different field, such as department, title, last name, or first name.

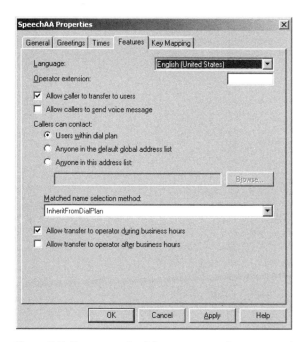

Figure 7-7. *Features tab of the Auto Attendant Properties dialog box*

Defining Custom Actions

On the Key Mapping tab of the Properties dialog box, you can define custom actions that a user can perform, such as pressing 1 for the Sales department. As shown in Figure 7-8, you can specify both business hours and non-business hours key mappings. These hours are determined by the hours you entered on the Times tab, as described earlier.

To set up each menu item, you need to add it to the Key Mapping tab. Click the Add button to open the Key Mapping Entry dialog box, as shown in Figure 7-9.

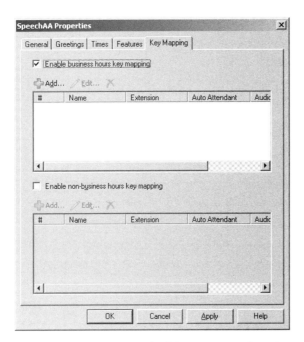

Figure 7-8. *Key Mapping tab of the Auto Attendant Properties dialog box*

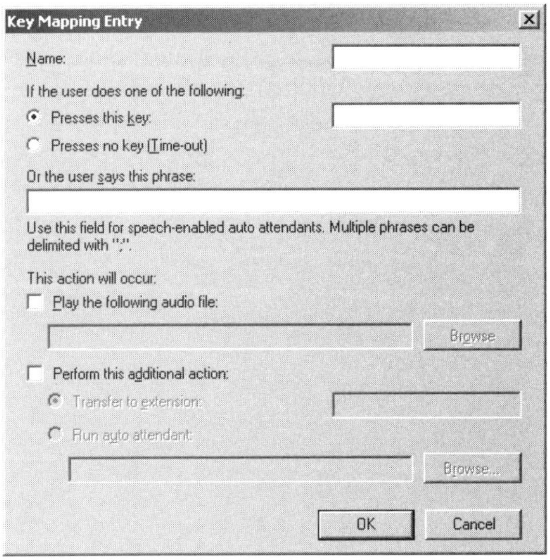

Figure 7-9. *Adding a new key mapping entry*

In the Name field, enter a unique and pronounceable name, because this text will be rendered using the TTS engine, and then select when the action should take place: upon a key press or a timeout. For example, you might name your key mapping entry Sales, select the Presses This Key option, and assign it 1. This would automatically produce "For Sales, press 1."

If the auto attendant is speech-enabled, you can specify a spoken text phrase to be recognized. This is the equivalent to grammar in Speech Server applications. So you could also add the phrase Sales in the Or the User Says This Phrase text box, which would then automatically render the prompt, "For Sales, press 1 or say Sales."

Next, you need to define the action that will occur when the user either says or presses the key you specified. You have three options:

- Play an audio file

- Transfer to an extension

- Run another auto attendant

If you have a Speech Server application that you want users to access via your Exchange 2007 auto attendant, you set that up here. Select the Perform This Additional Action option, choose Transfer to Extension, and enter the extension of that application in the text box next to the field.

Now that we've reviewed the Exchange UM auto attendant capabilities, let's see how to build a UM application with Speech Server.

Building a UM Speech Application

Exchange 2007 provides a few different web services that allow you to access a lot of the same functionality as any other Exchange client, such as Outlook. Here, I'll show you how you can access this API to build a UM speech application. This speech application will allow users to access their calendar, and it will read the appointments and meetings they have for the specified days. This involves creating a class that accesses the Exchange web service and collects information based on a given date, and then building the application. We'll use a Voice Response Workflow application in this example.

Accessing an Exchange Web Service

The first step is to create a new Voice Response Workflow Application project in Visual Studio. See Chapter 6 for details on creating a Voice Response Workflow application.

Next, add a web reference to the Exchange web service:

```
https://<ExchangeServer>/EWS/Exchange.asmx.
```

Then add a reference in code, in this form:

```
Using UMSpeechApplication.com.domain.exchange2k7;
```

This is the default reference name after you have added a web reference, where *UMSpeechApplication* refers to your application's namespace, *domain* refers to your domain name, and *exchange2k7* refers to your server name. Alternatively, you can assign a different web reference name when you add a web reference.

Now we need to create a class to house the data for our calendar events. We will populate this object for each instance of a calendar event and add it to a generic list collection. The class can be as simple as the one shown in Listing 7-1.

Listing 7-1. *CalendarObject Class*

```
public class CalendarObject
{
    private string _location;
    private string _subject;
    private bool _isMeeting;
    private DateTime _startDate;
    private DateTime _endDate;

    public CalendarObject()
    {
    }

    public string Location
    {
        get
        {
            return _location;
        }
        set
        {
            _location = value;
        }
    }
    public string Subject
    {
        get
        {
            return _subject;
        }
        set
        {
            _subject = value;
        }
    }
    public bool IsMeeting
    {
        get
        {
            return _isMeeting;
        }
        set
        {
            _isMeeting = value;
        }
    }
```

```
    public DateTime StartDate
    {
        get
        {
            return _startDate;
        }
        set
        {
            _startDate = value;
        }
    }
    public DateTime EndDate
    {
        get
        {
            return _endDate;
        }
        set
        {
            _endDate = value;
        }
    }
}
```

Next, we need to create a method to get the results from the web service. We want to be able to pass in a date and a return a generic list of `CalendarObject` objects. Returning a generic list collection makes it pretty simple to use this with a data-bound activity, such as the NavigableList activity.

```
 public static List<CalendarObject> GetCalendarData(DateTime
lookupDate)
```

We'll look at the `GetCalendarData` method code in sections. The first step is to create an `ExchangeServiceBinding`, followed by providing credentials for logging in to the Exchange server. The credentials determine what information you can view. For example, if you pass in credentials for Jason, and you want to get Mike's calendar, Jason must have rights to view Mike's calendar in order for the service to return any calendar data for Mike.

```
        ExchangeServiceBinding exchangeServer = new ExchangeServiceBinding();
        ICredentials creds = new NetworkCredential("jason", "password01");
        exchangeServer.Credentials = creds;
        exchangeServer.Url = @"https://exchange2k7 /EWS/Exchange.asmx";
```

The next piece of code is where we create a request and provide information about our request. Exchange provides different request classes depending on your request. In our example, we want to request availability of a user. We first create an instance of `GetUserAvailabilityType`, followed by an instance of the `EmailAddress` object and specify the e-mail address for which we want to get calendar events. In this example, we want calendar events only for `mike@domain.com`.

```
            GetUserAvailabilityRequestType request = new
GetUserAvailabilityRequestType();

            MailboxData[] mailboxes = new MailboxData[1];
            mailboxes[0] = new MailboxData();

            EmailAddress emailAddress = new EmailAddress();
            emailAddress.Address = "mike@domain.com";
            emailAddress.Name = String.Empty;
            mailboxes[0].Email = emailAddress;

            request.MailboxDataArray = mailboxes;
```

If we wanted to get calendar events for both Jason and Mike, we could easily create a new instance of the `EmailAddress` object for Jason and add it to the `MailBoxData` collection.

In the next piece of code, we need to specify the date range for which we want to search for calendar events. We do this by creating a new instance of the `FreeBusyViewOptionsType` and setting the `TimeWindow` property to the duration specified by the `GetCalendarData` parameter, `lookupDate`.

```
            Duration duration = new Duration();
            duration.StartTime = lookupDate;
            duration.EndTime = lookupDate.AddDays(1);

            FreeBusyViewOptionsType viewOptions = new FreeBusyViewOptionsType();
            viewOptions.TimeWindow = duration;
```

Using our instance of the `FreeBusyViewOptionsType` class, `viewOptions`, we need to set the `RequestedView` to `Detailed`, which will return the most detailed information. Other options are more limited, such as returning only header information.

```
            viewOptions.RequestedView = FreeBusyViewType.Detailed;
            viewOptions.RequestedViewSpecified = true;
            request.FreeBusyViewOptions = viewOptions;
```

Lastly for our request, we need to set the time zone information, including when daylight saving time starts and ends for our location. Typically, you set this to your server's time zone.

```
            request.TimeZone = new SerializableTimeZone();
            request.TimeZone.Bias = 480;
            request.TimeZone.StandardTime = new SerializableTimeZoneTime();
            request.TimeZone.StandardTime.Bias = 0;
            request.TimeZone.StandardTime.DayOfWeek =
DayOfWeekType.Sunday.ToString();
            request.TimeZone.StandardTime.DayOrder = 1;
            request.TimeZone.StandardTime.Month = 11;
            request.TimeZone.StandardTime.Time = "02:00:00";
            request.TimeZone.DaylightTime = new SerializableTimeZoneTime();
            request.TimeZone.DaylightTime.Bias = -60;
            request.TimeZone.DaylightTime.DayOfWeek =
```

```
DayOfWeekType.Sunday.ToString();
            request.TimeZone.DaylightTime.DayOrder = 2;
            request.TimeZone.DaylightTime.Month = 3;
            request.TimeZone.DaylightTime.Time = "02:00:00";
```

Now that we have the request built, we need to get the response. We do that by providing the request object, which contains all of our search parameters, to the GetUserAvailability method of our ExchangeServiceBinding object, exchangeServer. This will return an instance of the GetUserAvailabilityResponseType class. Similar to the request, an Exchange response has different response classes. The one you use depends on what information you are requesting. In our example, we are requesting calendar information, so we need to use the GetUserAvailabilityResponseType class.

```
GetUserAvailabilityResponseType response =
exchangeServer.GetUserAvailability(request);
```

Next, we create a nested foreach loop. The first loop represents different users. In our example, we are looking up information for only one user, so this loop will run only once. If our request contained multiple users, this loop would run once per user.

The nested loop runs once per calendar event it finds, based on the date parameter we provided in the request. This loop contains the five main fields we are looking for:

- Location

- Subject

- Start Date and Time

- End Date and Time

- IsMeeting

The fields correlate to the calendar item you see when creating an appointment in Outlook, as shown in Figure 7-10.

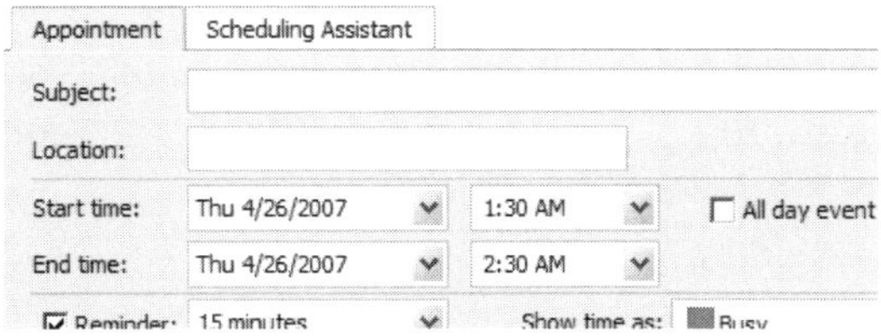

Figure 7-10. *Outlook appointment fields*

The IsMeeting field specifies if this calendar event is a meeting or an appointment. The difference is that a meeting typically involves other attendees, while an appointment usually refers to a calendar event for only the user.

Listing 7-2 shows the complete GetCalendarData method.

Listing 7-2. *GetCalendarData Method*

```
public static List<CalendarObject> GetCalendarData(DateTime
lookupDate)
  {
            ExchangeServiceBinding exchangeServer = new ExchangeServiceBinding();
            ICredentials creds = new NetworkCredential("jason", "password01");
            exchangeServer.Credentials = creds;
            exchangeServer.Url = @"https://exchange2k7 /EWS/Exchange.asmx";
            GetUserAvailabilityRequestType request = new
GetUserAvailabilityRequestType();

            MailboxData[] mailboxes = new MailboxData[1];
            mailboxes[0] = new MailboxData();

            EmailAddress emailAddress = new EmailAddress();
            emailAddress.Address = "mike@domain.com";
            emailAddress.Name = String.Empty;
            mailboxes[0].Email = emailAddress;

            request.MailboxDataArray = mailboxes;
            request.TimeZone = new SerializableTimeZone();
            request.TimeZone.Bias = 480;
            request.TimeZone.StandardTime = new SerializableTimeZoneTime();
            request.TimeZone.StandardTime.Bias = 0;
            request.TimeZone.StandardTime.DayOfWeek =
DayOfWeekType.Sunday.ToString();
            request.TimeZone.StandardTime.DayOrder = 1;
            request.TimeZone.StandardTime.Month = 11;
            request.TimeZone.StandardTime.Time = "02:00:00";
            request.TimeZone.DaylightTime = new SerializableTimeZoneTime();
            request.TimeZone.DaylightTime.Bias = -60;
            request.TimeZone.DaylightTime.DayOfWeek =
DayOfWeekType.Sunday.ToString();
            request.TimeZone.DaylightTime.DayOrder = 2;
            request.TimeZone.DaylightTime.Month = 3;
            request.TimeZone.DaylightTime.Time = "02:00:00";

            Duration duration = new Duration();
            duration.StartTime = lookupDate;
            duration.EndTime = lookupDate.AddDays(1);

            FreeBusyViewOptionsType viewOptions = new FreeBusyViewOptionsType();
            viewOptions.TimeWindow = duration;
```

```
            viewOptions.RequestedView = FreeBusyViewType.Detailed;
            viewOptions.RequestedViewSpecified = true;


            request.FreeBusyViewOptions = viewOptions;

            GetUserAvailabilityResponseType response =
exchangeServer.GetUserAvailability(request);

            foreach (FreeBusyResponseType responseType in
response.FreeBusyResponseArray)
            {
                if (responseType.FreeBusyView.CalendarEventArray.Length > 0)
                {
                    foreach (CalendarEvent calendar in
responseType.FreeBusyView.CalendarEventArray)
                    {
                        CalendarObject calendarObject = new CalendarObject();

                        calendarObject.Location =
calendar.CalendarEventDetails.Location;
                        calendarObject.Subject =
calendar.CalendarEventDetails.Subject;
                        calendarObject.StartDate = calendar.StartTime;
                        calendarObject.EndDate = calendar.EndTime;
                        calendarObject.IsMeeting =
calendar.CalendarEventDetails.IsMeeting;

                        calendarObjects.Add(calendarObject);
                    }
                }
            }

            return calendarObjects;
        }
    }
```

Creating the Application Workflow

Now that we have a class that is able to connect to Exchange via a web service, we can start working on the actual Voice Response Workflow application. Figure 7-11 shows how the workflow is laid out.

Figure 7-11. *Sample application workflow*

We start with one QuestionAnswer activity, which will ask the user, "For what date would you like to hear calendar events?" For the grammar, we can use the Date rule from the built-in grammar library, Library.grxml. This entire activity can be configured via the IDE.

The other three activities—Code, NavigableList, and Statement—need to be configured via the code-beside, using the code shown in Listing 7-3.

Listing 7-3. *Code, NavigableList, and Statement Activity Configuration*

```
private List<CalendarObject>_calendarObjects;
        private void getCalendarEvents_ExecuteCode(object sender, EventArgs e)
        {
            _calendarObjects = ExchangeCalendar.GetCalendarData(new
DateTime(2007, 12, 25));

            calendarEvents.DataSource = _calendarObjects;
            calendarEvents.DataField = "Subject";

            calendarEvents.DataBind();
        }
```

```
        private void calendarEvents_TurnStarting(object sender,
SelectionTurnStartingEventArgs e)
        {

            calendarEvents.MainPrompt.SetText("Calendar Event: {0}",
this.calendarEvents.Items[this.calendarEvents.CurrentItem.Value]);


        }

        private void calendarEvents_ConfirmationTurnStarting(object
sender, TurnStartingEventArgs e)
        {
            calendarEvents.ConfirmationMainPrompt.SetText("You
Selected {0} is that correct?",
this.calendarEvents.Items[this.calendarEvents.CurrentItem.Value]);
        }

        private void sayEventDetails_TurnStarting(object sender,
TurnStartingEventArgs e)
        {
            bool isMeeting = calendarObjects[this.calendarEvents.
CurrentItem.Value].IsMeeting;

            string eventType = "meeting";
            if (isMeeting == false)
            {
                eventType = "appointment";
            }

            sayEventDetails.MainPrompt.SetText(" {0} is a {1}
scheduled to start on {2} at {3} and to end on {4} at {5},
located at {6}",
                _calendarObjects[this.calendarEvents.CurrentItem.Value].Subject,
                eventType,
                _calendarObjects[this.calendarEvents.CurrentItem.Value].StartDate.
ToLongDateString(),
                _calendarObjects[this.calendarEvents.CurrentItem.Value].StartDate.
ToShortTimeString(),
                _calendarObjects[this.calendarEvents.CurrentItem.Value].EndDate.
ToLongDateString(),
                _calendarObjects[this.calendarEvents.CurrentItem.Value].EndDate.
ToShortTimeString(),
                _calendarObjects[this.calendarEvents.CurrentItem.Value].Location);

        }
```

After we get the date through the QuestionAnswer activity, we pass that date to our previously created class, which uses that date to query the Exchange web service. After we have the generic list, we data-bind that list to a NavigableList activity, and finally read the details based on which event the user selected using a Statement activity.

So how would this application sound? First, let's consider a sample Outlook Calendar with three calendar events, as shown in Figure 7-12.

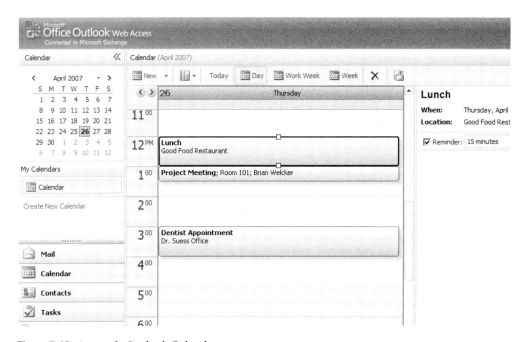

Figure 7-12. *A sample Outlook Calendar*

Using the example in Figure 7-12, the call flow might go like this:

IVR: For what date would you like to hear calendar events?

User: April 26, 2007

IVR: Lunch

User: Next

IVR: Project Meeting

User: Select

IVR: Project Meeting is a meeting scheduled to start on April 26 at 1:00 p.m. and to end on April 26 at 1:15 p.m., located in Room 101

Conclusion

This chapter described how to configure Exchange 2007 auto attendants and how to integrate Speech Server into the auto attendant functionality. It also covered how to use Exchange 2007 web services in conjunction with Speech Server to create a UM application.

In the next chapter, you will learn how to handle logging and reporting for your Speech Server applications.

CHAPTER 8

■■■

Speech Application Analysis and Tuning

The Analytics and Tuning Studio is new to OCS 2007 Speech Server. It provides reports and tools to help you analyze your applications so that you can improve the experience for your users, as described in this chapter. However, before you can generate any reports or use the analysis tools, you need to configure logging options and specify which log files you want to analyze, so we'll look at how to do that first.

Setting Up Your Log Files

The Analytics and Tuning Studio uses information from the event trace logs for its reports and grammar evaluations. So, your first steps are to configure the trace logging options and import your log files into a database.

Configuring Trace Log Options

The Trace Logging options determine what information is logged to the log files. You configure these options through the Administrator Console (opened by selecting Start ➤ Programs ➤ Microsoft Office Communications Server 2007 Speech Server).

In the Administrator Console, right-click your server and choose Properties. In the Properties dialog box, choose the Trace Logging tab, as shown in Figure 8-1.

Make sure that trace logging is enabled and that you have selected the correct storage directory, as Speech Server will automatically create the directory if it does not exist. These logs are stored in the Logs directory of your Speech Server installation.

Depending on your call volume, you may want to adjust how often you create a log file. If your call volume is high, you should create a log file more often. If you have lower call volume, you should create a log file less frequently.

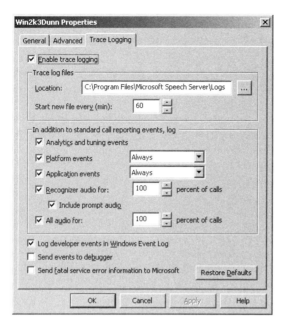

Figure 8-1. *Trace logging properties*

Turn on logging for the events you want to track:

- *Analytics and tuning events*: These events pertain to items such as out-of-grammar phrases spoken by the user. If you do not enable this option, you will not be able to use the Grammar Tuning Advisor or the Validation Re-recognition tool.

- *Platform events*: These events pertain to anything that happens on the server itself, such as a network connection failure or Speech Recognizer Engine failure.

- *Application events*: These are the events that happen in your applications, such as no recognition and silence events.

The Audio options allow you to audit a percentage of calls, including what the application is saying to the user (the Include Prompt Audio option) and what the user has said to the application. I recommend at least 10% for each; set this higher if you have the disk space. This will allow you to listen to entire calls and determine if you should make changes to certain prompts.

Importing Log Files

To run Analytics and Tuning Studio reports, you first need to import your event trace log files (.etl files) into a Microsoft SQL Server database. To do this, run the MssLogToDatabase tool, which is located in the SDK directory of your Speech Server installation.

Several command-line tools are available for working with log files, as shown in Table 8-1. All of these tools are available in the SDK directory, and their syntax is well documented in the tools themselves.

Table 8-1. *Log File Tools*

Tool	Use
MssLogToDatabase	Used to import .etl log files into a SQL Server database
MssDataPurge	Used to purge data from a database
MssDataFilter	Used to extract data from .etl log files for a specific application
MssContentExtract	Used to extract audio recording from log files
MssLogToText	Used to convert .etl log files to .txt files

Starting the Analytics and Tuning Studio

Once you have imported your data into your SQL Server database, you can either create a new Analytics and Tuning Studio project in Visual Studio or simply add a new Analytics and Tuning Studio file to your IVR application project, as shown in Figure 8-2.

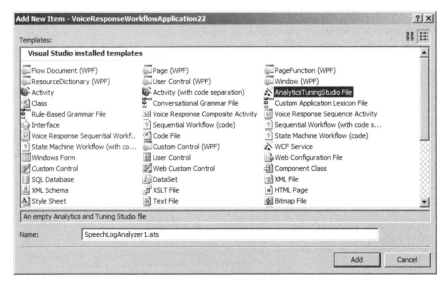

Figure 8-2. *Adding a new Analytics and Tuning Studio file*

When you first open the Analytics and Tuning Studio, you will be prompted for basic information about your database, such as the server name and database name, as shown in Figure 8-3.

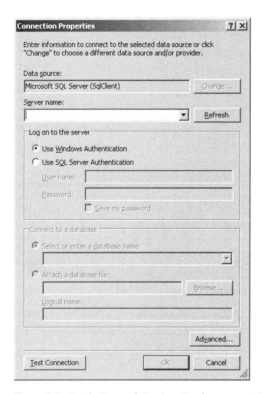

Figure 8-3. *Analytics and Tuning Studio connection setup*

Generating Reports

Analytics and Tuning Studio generates reports, called views, that provide easy-to-read information about your applications. The available reports are listed in the Tuning Views pane on the left side of the Analytics and Tuning Studio window, organized in Report Views, List Views, and Details Views folders, as shown in Figure 8-4. For each report, you can filter the data you wish to view via the View Filters options beneath the list of views.

▪Tip If you are using SQL Server with Reporting Services, you can customize a built-in report by editing its `.rdl` file in SQL Server Reporting Services.

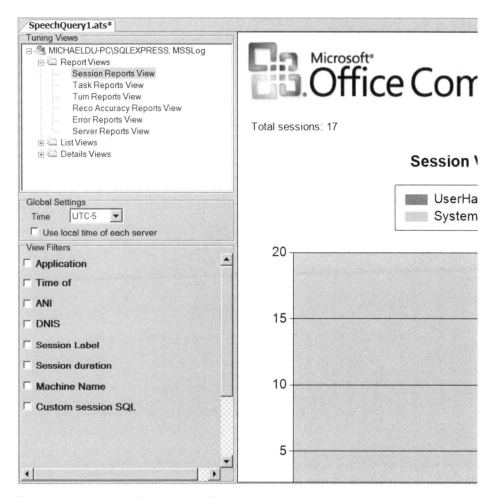

Figure 8-4. *Analytics and Tuning Studio Reports*

Session Reports

Three main reports are available for sessions: Session Reports, Session List, and Session Details. Each one goes progressively deeper into the logged sessions.

Session Reports View

The Session Reports view provides a high-level overview in a graph and pie chart. This information is pretty basic. It includes number of sessions, average length of sessions, and how the application disconnected. Figure 8-5 shows an example of this type of report.

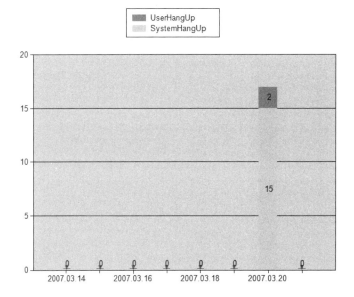

Figure 8-5. *Session Reports view*

In the Session Reports view, you should be looking for the number of user hang-ups compared to system hang-ups. If you have a high number of user hang-ups compared to system hang-ups, this might indicate something is wrong with your application, as users typically shouldn't be hanging up before your application has finished. You should then drill down a little more using the Session List view to investigate the problem.

Session List View

The Session List view shows a list of every logged session, along with errors and turns that occurred. Figure 8-6 shows an example.

Application	Version	Time	ANI	DNIS	Tasks	Turn Count	Errors	Duration	Ended	Answer Latency
http://loc...	1.0.0.0	3/20/2007 12:40:03 PM	5559876	5554321	Workflow1:Unset	1		00:00:07	SystemHangUp	00:04.618
http://loc...	1.0.0.0	3/20/2007 12:40:17 PM	5559876	5554321	Workflow1:Unset	4		00:00:23	SystemHangUp	00:00.156
http://loc...	1.0.0.0	3/20/2007 12:40:48 PM	5559088	5554321	Workflow1:Unset	1		00:00:02	UserHangUp	00:00.109
http://loc...	1.0.0.0	3/20/2007 12:40:56 PM	5559988	5554321	Workflow1:Unset	3		00:00:10	SystemHangUp	00:00.124
http://loc...	1.0.0.0	3/20/2007 12:41:12 PM	5559977	5554321	Workflow1:Unset	1		00:00:03	SystemHangUp	00:00.109
http://loc...	1.0.0.0	3/20/2007 12:41:22 PM	5551134	5554321	Workflow1:Unset	2		00:00:07	SystemHangUp	00:00.125
http://loc...	1.0.0.0	3/20/2007 12:41:35 PM	5558906	5554321	Workflow1:Unset	1		00:00:01	SystemHangUp	00:00.125
http://loc...	1.0.0.0	3/20/2007 12:41:40 PM	5558906	5554321	Workflow1:Unset	1		00:00:04	SystemHangUp	00:00.125
http://loc...	1.0.0.0	3/20/2007 12:41:46 PM	5558906	5554321	Workflow1:Unset	2		00:00:16	SystemHangUp	00:00.156
http://loc...	1.0.0.0	3/20/2007 12:42:09 PM	5559754	5554321	Workflow1:Unset	1		00:00:05	SystemHangUp	00:00.266
http://loc...	1.0.0.0	3/20/2007 12:42:16 PM	5559754	5554321	Workflow1:Unset	1		00:00:08	SystemHangUp	00:00.172
http://loc...	1.0.0.0	3/20/2007 12:42:28 PM	5554545	5554321	Workflow1:Unset	1		00:00:01	UserHangUp	00:00.124
http://loc...	1.0.0.0	3/20/2007 12:42:35 PM	5558965	5554321	Workflow1:Unset	1		00:00:03	SystemHangUp	00:00.141
http://loc...	1.0.0.0	3/20/2007 12:42:41 PM	5558965	5554321	Workflow1:Unset	3		00:00:13	SystemHangUp	00:00.172
http://loc...	1.0.0.0	3/20/2007 12:43:02 PM	5556678	5554321	Workflow1:Unset	1		00:00:04	SystemHangUp	00:00.609
http://loc...	1.0.0.0	3/20/2007 12:43:07 PM	5556678	5554321	Workflow1:Unset	1		00:00:06	SystemHangUp	00:00.093
http://loc...	1.0.0.0	3/20/2007 12:43:20 PM	5553489	5554321	Workflow1:Unset	2		00:00:12	SystemHangUp	00:00.094

Figure 8-6. *Session List view*

A *turn* represents each prompt the user heard. Typically, a high number of turns would suggest either a large number of errors have occurred or that your application has too many prompts. When users have problems giving the correct input, they have a higher turn count, as they are prompted every time they give an incorrect response.

If you notice a high number of errors and turns for users who hung up, you probably should change the prompts where the problems occurred. You can see these details in the Session Details view.

Session Details View

The Session Details view shows every session and allows you to expand a specific session to see more details, such as the individual turns for each session and the different ending statuses for each turn. Figure 8-7 shows an example.

You can either filter to a specific session or view all sessions at once. It is probably a good idea to start by looking at the sessions that users hung up on and that contain a large number of turns and errors.

Session	Session Duration	Ending Status	ANI	Timestamp
Session:	00:00:07	SystemHangUp	5559876	3/20/2007 12:40:03 PM
Task: Workflow1	00:00:07	Unset		3/20/2007 12:40:07 PM
Turn: AskNumber	Pick a Number	one	Answer	3/20/2007 12:40:07 PM
Turn: AskNumber	Pick a Number	one	Answer	3/20/2007 12:40:07 PM
Prompt: Main	<speak version...	0		3/20/2007 12:40:08 PM
Reco: Speech	[1 (0.91)]	one		3/20/2007 12:40:12 PM
Reco: Speech	[1 (0.99)]	one		3/20/2007 12:40:14 PM
SessionDisconnectEvent	System Hang-up			3/20/2007 12:40:14 PM
Session:	00:00:23	SystemHangUp	5559876	3/20/2007 12:40:17 PM
Task: Workflow1	00:00:23	Unset		3/20/2007 12:40:17 PM
Turn: AskNumber	Pick a Number	(Rejected)	Rejected	3/20/2007 12:40:17 PM
Turn: AskNumber	Pick a Number	two	Answer	3/20/2007 12:40:17 PM
Prompt: Main	<speak version...	0		3/20/2007 12:40:17 PM
Reco: Speech	[2 (0.00)]	two		3/20/2007 12:40:21 PM
Reco: Speech	[2 (0.98)]	two		3/20/2007 12:40:22 PM
Turn: AskNumber	Pick a Number	(Rejected)	Rejected	3/20/2007 12:40:22 PM
Turn: AskNumber	Pick a Number	two	Answer	3/20/2007 12:40:22 PM
Prompt: NoRecognition	<speak version...	0	01:00.000	3/20/2007 12:40:22 PM
Reco: Speech	[2 (0.00)]	two		3/20/2007 12:40:28 PM
Reco: Speech	[2 (0.98)]	two		3/20/2007 12:40:30 PM
Turn: AskNumber	Pick a Number	(Rejected)	Rejected	3/20/2007 12:40:30 PM
Turn: AskNumber	Pick a Number	two	Answer	3/20/2007 12:40:30 PM
Prompt: EscalatedNoRec...	<speak version...	0	01:00.000	3/20/2007 12:40:30 PM
Reco: Speech	[2 (0.00)]	two		3/20/2007 12:40:36 PM
Reco: Speech	[2 (0.98)]	two		3/20/2007 12:40:37 PM
Turn: AskNumber	Pick a Number	four	Answer	3/20/2007 12:40:37 PM
Turn: AskNumber	Pick a Number	four	Answer	3/20/2007 12:40:37 PM
Prompt: EscalatedNoRec...	<speak version...	0	01:00.000	3/20/2007 12:40:37 PM
Reco: Speech	[4 (0.89)]	four		3/20/2007 12:40:40 PM
Reco: Speech	[4 (0.99)]	four		3/20/2007 12:40:41 PM
SessionDisconnectEvent	System Hang-up			3/20/2007 12:40:41 PM
Session:	00:00:02	UserHangUp	5559088	3/20/2007 12:40:48 PM
Task: Workflow1	00:00:02	Unset		3/20/2007 12:40:48 PM
Turn: AskNumber	Pick a Number	(None)	None	3/20/2007 12:40:48 PM

Figure 8-7. *Session Details view*

Turn Reports

The turn reports display more information about a specific turn or all logged turns. You can right-click a specific turn in the Session Details view or pick the report from the Tuning Views list to view all turns.

Turn Reports View

The Turn Reports view provides a high-level overview of the logged turns in your application, as shown in Figure 8-8. This offers a quick way to see the number of silence, normal speech recognition, and error events. If you have a large percentage of silence events, this might suggest that your prompt isn't clear enough for your users and you should probably rephrase the question.

Total turns: 48

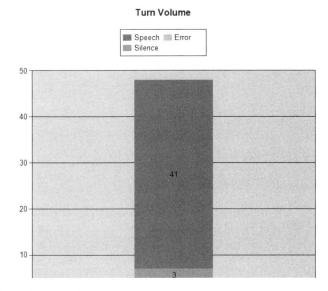

Figure 8-8. *Turn Reports view*

Turn List View

The Turn List view displays all turns and gives basic information, such as confidence value, recognized text, and prompt type. Figure 8-9 shows an example.

Name	Turn Type	Prompt Text	Recognized Text	Confidence	Response Type	Prompt Type	Prompt Completion	Mode
AskNumber	Ask	Pick a Number	one	0.915	Answer	Main	Complete	Speech
AskNumber	Ask	Pick a Number	one	0.990	Answer	Main	Complete	Speech
AskNumber	Ask	Pick a Number	two	0.001	Rejected	Main	Complete	Speech
AskNumber	Ask	Pick a Number	two	0.978	Answer	Main	Complete	Speech
AskNumber	Ask	Pick a Number	two	0.001	Rejected	NoRecognition	Complete	Speech
AskNumber	Ask	Pick a Number	two	0.978	Answer	NoRecognition	Complete	Speech
AskNumber	Ask	Pick a Number	two	0.001	Rejected	EscalatedNoRec...	Complete	Speech
AskNumber	Ask	Pick a Number	two	0.978	Answer	EscalatedNoRec...	Complete	Speech
AskNumber	Ask	Pick a Number	four	0.892	Answer	EscalatedNoRec...	Complete	Speech
AskNumber	Ask	Pick a Number	four	0.992	Answer	EscalatedNoRec...	Complete	Speech
AskNumber	Ask	Pick a Number		0.000	None	Main	Complete	Error
AskNumber	Ask	Pick a Number		0.000	InitialSilenceTime...	Main	Complete	Silence
AskNumber	Ask	Pick a Number		0.000	None	Silence	Complete	Error
AskNumber	Ask	Pick a Number	one	0.933	Answer	NoRecognition	Complete	Speech
AskNumber	Ask	Pick a Number	one	0.990	Answer	NoRecognition	Complete	Speech
AskNumber	Ask	Pick a Number	seven	0.953	Answer	Main	Complete	Speech
AskNumber	Ask	Pick a Number	seven	0.987	Answer	Main	Complete	Speech
AskNumber	Ask	Pick a Number		0.000	InitialSilenceTime...	Main	Complete	Silence
AskNumber	Ask	Pick a Number	four	0.894	Answer	Silence	Complete	Speech
AskNumber	Ask	Pick a Number	four	0.992	Answer	Silence	Complete	Speech
AskNumber	Ask	Pick a Number	four	0.992	Answer	Main	Complete	Speech
AskNumber	Ask	Pick a Number	two	0.959	Answer	Main	Complete	Speech
AskNumber	Ask	Pick a Number	two	0.978	Answer	Main	Complete	Speech
AskNumber	Ask	Pick a Number	seven	0.007	Rejected	Main	Complete	Speech
AskNumber	Ask	Pick a Number		0.000	InitialSilenceTime...	Main	Complete	Silence
AskNumber	Ask	Pick a Number	six	0.622	Answer	Silence	Complete	Speech
AskNumber	Ask	Pick a Number	six	0.932	Answer	Silence	Complete	Speech

Figure 8-9. *Turn List view*

In this report, check the Confidence and Prompt Type columns to identify problem areas. For example, if you see a lot of EscalatedNoRecognition types in the Prompt Type column or low values in the Confidence column, you should take a closer look at the grammar or the wording of the prompt itself.

Turn Details View

To see details of particular turn in the Turn List view report, double-click it. To view details of all the logged turns, select the Turn Details view from the Tuning Views list. The Turn Details view shows each logged turn and allows you to identify individual turns and hear the actual recording of the call. Figure 8-10 shows an example of the full report.

Turn	Prompt Text	Reco Audio/Text	Response Type	Timestamp
Turn: AskNumber	Pick a Number	one	Answer	3/20/2007 12:40:07 PM
Turn: AskNumber	Pick a Number	one	Answer	3/20/2007 12:40:07 PM
Prompt: Main	<speak version="1.0" xmlns="htt...	0		3/20/2007 12:40:08 PM
Reco: Speech	[1 (0.91)]	one		3/20/2007 12:40:12 PM
Reco: Speech	[1 (0.99)]	one		3/20/2007 12:40:14 PM
Turn: AskNumber	Pick a Number	(Rejected)	Rejected	3/20/2007 12:40:17 PM
Turn: AskNumber	Pick a Number	two	Answer	3/20/2007 12:40:17 PM
Prompt: Main	<speak version="1.0" xmlns="htt...	0		3/20/2007 12:40:17 PM
Reco: Speech	[2 (0.00)]	two		3/20/2007 12:40:21 PM
Reco: Speech	[2 (0.98)]	two		3/20/2007 12:40:22 PM
Turn: AskNumber	Pick a Number	(Rejected)	Rejected	3/20/2007 12:40:22 PM
Turn: AskNumber	Pick a Number	two	Answer	3/20/2007 12:40:22 PM
Prompt: NoRecognition	<speak version="1.0" xmlns="htt...	0	01:00.000	3/20/2007 12:40:22 PM
Reco: Speech	[2 (0.00)]	two		3/20/2007 12:40:28 PM
Reco: Speech	[2 (0.98)]	two		3/20/2007 12:40:30 PM
Turn: AskNumber	Pick a Number	(Rejected)	Rejected	3/20/2007 12:40:30 PM
Turn: AskNumber	Pick a Number	two	Answer	3/20/2007 12:40:30 PM
Prompt: EscalatedNoRecognition	<speak version="1.0" xmlns="htt...	0	01:00.000	3/20/2007 12:40:30 PM
Reco: Speech	[2 (0.00)]	two		3/20/2007 12:40:36 PM
Reco: Speech	[2 (0.98)]	two		3/20/2007 12:40:37 PM
Turn: AskNumber	Pick a Number	four	Answer	3/20/2007 12:40:37 PM
Turn: AskNumber	Pick a Number	four	Answer	3/20/2007 12:40:37 PM
Prompt: EscalatedNoRecognition	<speak version="1.0" xmlns="htt...	0	01:00.000	3/20/2007 12:40:37 PM
Reco: Speech	[4 (0.89)]	four		3/20/2007 12:40:40 PM
Reco: Speech	[4 (0.99)]	four		3/20/2007 12:40:41 PM
Turn: AskNumber	Pick a Number	(None)	None	3/20/2007 12:40:48 PM
Prompt: Main	<speak version="1.0" xmlns="htt...	0		3/20/2007 12:40:48 PM
SessionDisconnectEvent	User Hang-up			3/20/2007 12:40:50 PM
Turn: AskNumber	Pick a Number	(InitialSilenceTimeou...	InitialSilenceTime...	3/20/2007 12:40:56 PM
Prompt: Main	<speak version="1.0" xmlns="htt...	0		3/20/2007 12:40:56 PM
Reco: Speech		InitialSilenceTimeout...		3/20/2007 12:41:00 PM
Turn: AskNumber	Pick a Number	(None)	None	3/20/2007 12:41:00 PM
Prompt: Silence	<speak version="1.0" xmlns="htt...	0		3/20/2007 12:41:00 PM
Turn: AskNumber	Pick a Number	one	Answer	3/20/2007 12:41:03 PM

Figure 8-10. *Turn Details view*

Using Analytics and Tuning Studio Tools

The Analytics and Tuning Studio includes a couple of tools for evaluating your application's prompts and grammar:

- *Grammar Tuning Advisor*: Indicates any out-of-grammar errors and in what frequency they occurred.

- *Validation Re-recognition*: Allows you to specify a new grammar and run it against saved recordings of actual users to see how many of the out-of-grammar errors detected by the Grammar Tuning Advisor will be matched by your new grammar.

You can access these tools from the Analytics and Tuning Studio toolbar. Before you can run these tools, you'll need to import the application log files into a database using the MssLogToDatabase command-line tool, as described earlier in this chapter.

On the Analytics and Tuning Studio toolbar, shown in Figure 8-11, the Grammar Tuning Advisor icon is just to the right of the Re-Recognizer icon. To the right of the Grammar Tuning Advisor icon are icons for tools that allow you to play prompt audio, recognized audio, session audio, and export audio. To the left of the Re-recognizer icon are icons for navigational tools to interact with the reports. All of these tools are also available via the Analyzer menu in Visual Studio.

Figure 8-11. *Analytics and Tuning Studio toolbar*

The following sections use the example of running the tools for the PickANumber application, which is a Voice Response Workflow application. It has one QuestionAnswer activity that accepts a number from one to ten.

Grammar Tuning Advisor

The Grammar Tuning Advisor analyzes all logged audio and determines if there were any out-of-grammar errors and in what frequency they occurred. It does this by running the logged audio against a dictation grammar and the original grammar. The Grammar Tuning Advisor will recognize anything the user has said, even if it doesn't match the grammar that the application is using. This can help you determine if you need to add possible responses to the grammar.

When you first start the Grammar Tuning Advisor, you will be prompted for information about what you want it to evaluate, as shown in Figure 8-12. For example, you could evaluate a single turn, such as a specific QuestionAnswer activity. You can also specify any new grammars you want to use for the evaluation.

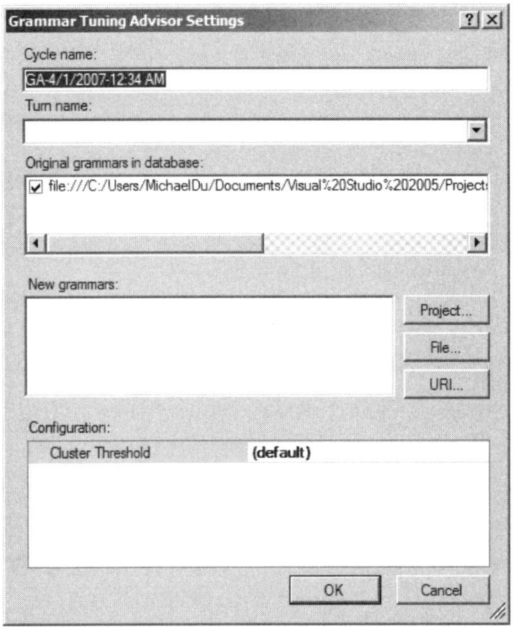

Figure 8-12. *Grammar Tuning Advisor Settings dialog box*

The sample PickANumber application currently accepts only numbers one through ten. The Grammar Tuning Advisor will let you know if the user gave other responses, such as eleven. Figure 8-13 shows the Grammar Tuning Advisor running against the PickANumber application logs.

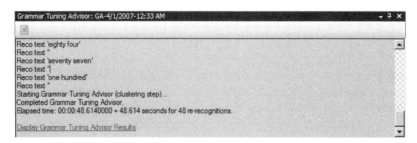

Figure 8-13. *Grammar Tuning Advisor running against the PickANumber application*

After the Grammar Tuning Advisor has completed running, you can view the result by clicking the Display Grammar Tuning Advisor Results link shown in the progress monitor. Figure 8-14 shows the results for this example. The results are grouped into clusters and use the wildcard character, *. In the example, the Grammar Tuning Advisor found that a user said "100." The results are broken up into results of * hundred, one *, and one hundred.

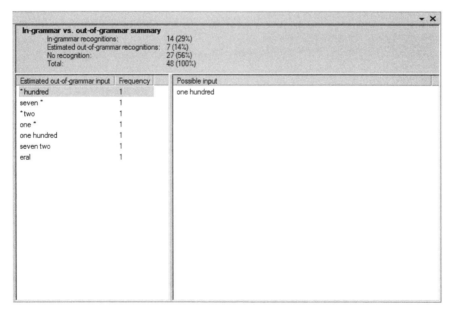

Figure 8-14. *Grammar Tuning Advisor results*

Based on the Grammar Tuning Advisor results, you might improve your application by making the prompt more specific to ensure users understand the question, or edit the grammar to handle the out-of-grammar responses. On the other hand, if the frequency of out-of-grammar responses is low, that might mean that just one user did not understand the question or the context of the question. This tool can tell you what users are saying, but you will need to decide what do with the results, if you do anything at all.

Validation Re-recognition

The Validation Re-recognition tool allows you to evaluate a new grammar, which you might have created based on the results of the Grammar Tuning Advisor, against saved recordings of actual users. You can see how many of those out-of-grammar errors will be matched by your new grammar, and then use this information to decide whether you should implement the grammar in your production environment.

When you first run the Validation Re-recognition tool, you will see the Validation Re-recognition Settings dialog box, as shown in Figure 8-15. You can run your results based on a specific turn or all turns in the application. You should also specify the new grammar you are considering implementing.

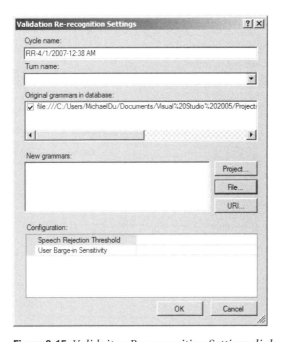

Figure 8-15. *Validaiton Re-recognition Settings dialog box*

In the Configuration section, you can set two settings:

- *Speech Rejection Threshold*: The Validation Re-recognition tool basically performs recognition as if this were a new call using stored audio from old calls. You can change the confidence value to use to reject recognition via the Speech Rejection Threshold setting. For example, if you want to reject recognition when the confidence value is less than 80%, enter .08 here.

- *User Barge-in Sensitivity*: This setting allows you to choose how sensitive the tool should be when determining if the user is barging in. You have three options: Low, Medium, or High.

As with the Grammar Tuning Advisor, while the Validation Re-recognition tool is running, you can see the responses that were not handled by your application's grammar, as shown in Figure 8-16.

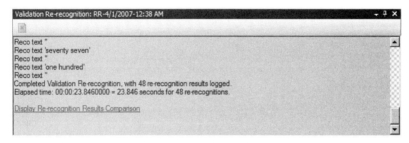

Figure 8-16. *Validation Re-recognition running against the PickANumber application*

Once it has completed running, you can view the results by clicking the Display Re-recognition Results Comparison link. Figure 8-17 shows an example of the results.

Original	Transcription	Original Semantics	RR-4/1/2007-12:38 AM	RR-4/1/2007-12:38 AM Semantics
seven		[7 (0.01)]	seventy seven	[77 (0.95)]
six		[6 (0.62)]	fifty	[50 (0.90)]
six		[6 (0.93)]		
two		[2 (0.66)]	twenty two	[22 (0.86)]
two		[2 (0.98)]		
four		[4 (0.82)]	forty four	[44 (0.94)]
four		[4 (0.99)]		
seven		[7 (0.86)]	seven	[7 (0.91)]
seven		[7 (0.99)]		
two		[2 (0.00)]		
two		[2 (0.98)]		
one		[1 (0.95)]	one	[1 (0.95)]
one		[1 (0.99)]		
seven		[7 (0.84)]	twenty seven	[27 (0.87)]
seven		[7 (0.99)]		
four		[4 (0.44)]	eighty four	[84 (0.74)]
four		[4 (0.99)]		
seven		[7 (0.01)]	seventy seven	[77 (0.91)]
seven		[7 (0.99)]		

Figure 8-17. *Validation Re-recognition results*

The Original column contains the original recognized text. In the first row of the example in Figure 8-17, the application recognized "seven" as the user's response. The Original Semantics column contains the original semantics results, and for the first row, it had only a 0.01 confidence value that the user said "seven". The RR columns shows that after re-recognition, the users actually said "seventy-seven," with a confidence value of 0.95. The reason for this is that the original grammar did not handle anything greater than 10, while the new grammar handles numbers up to 100.

Conclusion

This chapter covered the reports and tools of the Analytics and Tuning Studio. You can use these features to evaluate your application's prompts and grammar. This is a great way to indirectly get user feedback. Any time you first deploy an IVR application or make changes to an existing system, you should run the Analytics and Tuning Studio to see how your changes are affecting the users. The goal of an IVR application is to reduce the time the user spends using the application. If you simply deploy your application and never look back, you will never know if your application is doing what it is intended to do.

This concludes the Speech Server topics. The next chapter covers how to create desktop applications that have speech synthesis and speech recognition capabilities, using some of the same standards as Speech Server.

CHAPTER 9

■■■

Creating Speech Applications for Windows Vista

The new Speech Application Programming Interface, SAPI 5.3, has added support for some of the standards that OCS 2007 Speech Server supports. These include Speech Recognition Grammar Specification (SRGS) XML-formatted grammars (GRXML), covered in Chapter 2, and Speech Synthesis Markup Language (SSML), covered in Chapter 3. Using your knowledge of these standards, you can create Windows Vista applications that support speech synthesis and recognition, as you'll learn in this chapter. But before we look at using the Speech API, you should be aware of the speech-recognition features built into Windows Vista.

Windows Vista Speech-Recognition Features

Windows Vista is Microsoft's first operating system to include built-in speech recognition. With previous versions, like Windows XP, you needed to install speech recognition capabilities as a separate installation. This means that most applications running under Windows Vista support speech without accessing the Speech API directly. The speech recognizer actually reads the text of an application, such as text on a button or menu, and allows you to access those simply by saying their name. Windows Vista includes support for 13 languages:

- English (US and UK)

- French

- Chinese (Traditional and Simplified)

- Japanese

- Danish

- Dutch

- Finnish

- German

- Italian

- Korean

- Norwegian

- Portuguese

- Spanish

The language of the speech recognizer and voices depends on the language version of the operating system. For example, if you have the English version of Windows Vista, the application will not recognize speech in Chinese, nor be able to hear the Chinese voice (Lili).

If you are using Windows Vista Ultimate or Enterprise, you can install additional language packs and have access to other speech recognizers and voices, via Windows Update. Once you have the other language packs installed, you can choose which speech recognition and voice you want to use, via the Control Panel, as shown in Figure 9-1. To access these options choose Ease of Access ➤ Speech Recognition Options ➤ Advanced Speech Recognition Options.

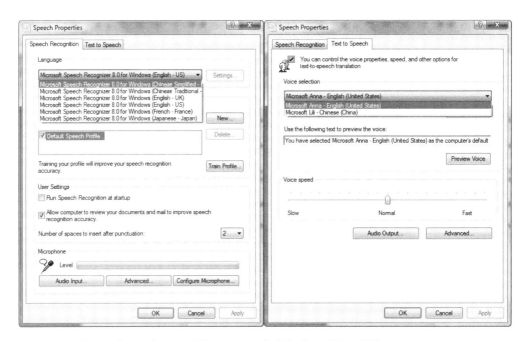

Figure 9-1. *Advanced speech recognition options in Windows Vista Ultimate*

No matter which version of Windows Vista you are using, you can start the Speech Recognition feature by selecting Start Menu ➤ Accessories ➤ Ease of Access ➤ Speech Recognition, as shown in Figure 9-2.

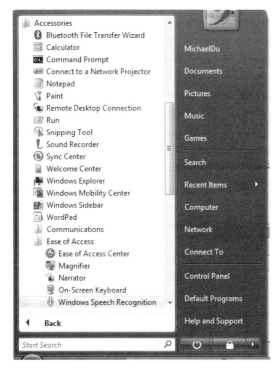

Figure 9-2. *Starting Speech Recognition*

Improved Voices

Windows Vista includes two new voices: Microsoft Anna and Microsoft Lili. Anna is the English voice, and Lili is the new Chinese voice. What makes these voices different is that they are based on real-life recordings, not algorithms, as was the case with the older voices like Microsoft Sam.

A good example of hearing that the voices are based on real recordings is to have Lili speak English. You will hear Lili speak English with a Chinese accent.

I will show you how to access both of these voices in your code using the Speech API in the "Selecting Voices" section later in this chapter.

Speech Toolbar

Windows Vista includes a new Speech toolbar, as shown in Figure 9-3. This toolbar not only allows quick access to turn off and on the recognizer, but also gives the user feedback, such as "That command isn't recognized" or "You said red." This is a great way to give users visual confirmation or indicate errors.

Figure 9-3. *Windows Vista Speech toolbar*

I will show you how you can access the Speech toolbar in your code in the "Accessing the Speech Toolbar" section later in this chapter.

Forms of Speech Recognition

Windows Vista supports two forms of speech recognition:

- *Command and control*: Basically, these are typically short phrases to perform a single action.

- *Dictation*: The ability to generate text with your voice. There is no limit on what you can say. You can type an entire document (or e-mail message) simply by using your voice. You can enter text into a control such as a text box by using your voice. This even works for your custom applications, without the application accessing the Speech API directly.

Command and control is probably the easiest form of speech recognition to use and implement. Vista has a few commands built in. To view these commands, right-click the Speech toolbar and choose Open Speech Reference Card. You'll see the common commands, as shown in Figure 9-4.

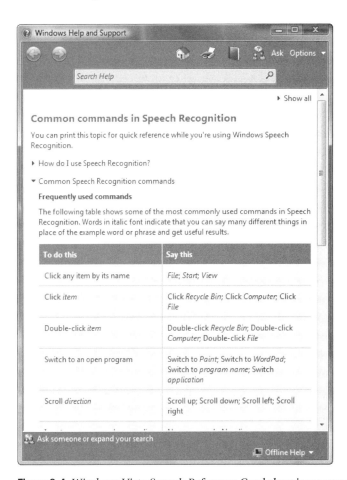

Figure 9-4. *Windows Vista Speech Reference Card showing common commands*

An interesting command is Mouse Grid, which allows users to control their mouse with their voice. When you say "Mouse Grid," a grid is displayed on the entire screen with a number assigned to each section, as shown in Figure 9-5. You can then say the number of the cell you want, which will place an even smaller grid on that cell. You can keep doing this until you have a cell on the area in which you want to click. At that point, you could say "Double-click cell x," where x is the number of the cell, and your mouse will move to that cell and double-click.

Figure 9-5 . *Windows Vista Mouse Grid command*

So how do these commands affect your application? Well let's consider a custom application that has two similarly named buttons: Submit Order and Submit Quote. When a user says "Submit" while your application has focus, Windows Vista will assign each button a number. The user can select the button he wants by saying the number assigned to the button. Alternatively, a user could say "Show Numbers," which would assign a number to every object on your form, as shown in Figure 9-6.

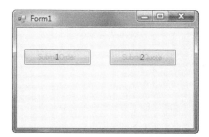

Figure 9-6. *Windows Vista Show Numbers command*

So why should you access the Speech API if Vista supports speech in your applications indirectly? Let's see what the new Speech API has to offer.

Using the Speech Synthesis API

Vista will support your application by reading the text of the menus, buttons, links, and so on. But what if you want to perform a different action, like click a certain button using a different phrase other than the displayed text? For that capability, you need to access the Speech API.

The `System.Speech` API is a part of .NET Framework 3.0 and works with SAPI 5.3. It has two main areas: speech synthesis and speech recognition. We'll look at speech synthesis here and cover speech recognition in the next section.

■**Note** While you can use the `System.Speech` API to target a different SAPI engine, like Windows XP SAPI 5.1, some features, such as support for the W3C SRGS and SSML standards, work only with SAPI 5.3. They are not supported in those other SAPI engines.

The `Speech.Synthesis` namespace provides the functionality that allows your application to speak to the user. In the `Speech.Synthesis` namespace, the main class to use is `SpeechSynthesizer`, as in the following code:

```
SpeechSynthesizer speechSynthesizer = new SpeechSynthesizer();

speechSynthesizer.SetOutputToDefaultAudioDevice();

speechSynthesizer.SelectVoice("Microsoft Anna");
speechSynthesizer.Speak ("Hello, I'm Microsoft Anna");

speechSynthesizer.SelectVoice("Microsoft Lili");
speechSynthesizer.SpeakAsync("and I'm Microsoft Lili.");
```

Selecting Voices

Earlier I mentioned the different voices that are available: Microsoft Anna and Microsoft Lili. You can select different voices by using the `SpeechSynthesizer` object's `SelectVoice` method or `SelectVoiceByHints` method.

The `SelectVoice` method is the easiest one to use:

```
speechSynthesizer.SelectVoice("Microsoft Anna");
```

■**Caution** Whichever voice you select, it must be installed locally. Otherwise you will encounter an `ArgumentException` exception. You can check to see if the voice is installed locally by using the `GetInstalledVoices` method, as described in this section.

The SelectVoiceByHint method allows you to select a voice by properties of the voice instead of by name. For example, you could select a voice based on gender, like this:

```
speechSynthesizer.SelectVoiceByHints(VoiceGender.Female);
```

This would choose the default female voice for the user. If your application were to support both English and Chinese, you could select the voice by culture, and use the appropriate voice at the appropriate time. For example, you could pass in just the culture information parameter to retrieve the default voice for that culture.

```
speechSynthesizer.SelectVoiceByHints(VoiceGender.NotSet,
 VoiceAge.NotSet,0, new System.Globalization.CultureInfo("zh-CN") );
```

The SpeechSynthesizer class also has the GetInstalledVoices method, which allows you to get a collection of the installed voices. You can use this method to see if a certain voice is installed.

```
foreach (InstalledVoice voice in speechSynthesizer.GetInstalledVoices())
{
    if (voice.VoiceInfo.Name == "Microsoft Anna")
    {
        speechSynthesizer.SelectVoice("Microsoft Anna");
        return;
    }
}
```

Specifying the Synthesizer Output Location

You will probably use the speech synthesizer primarily to play audio that the user can hear immediately. However, the speech synthesizer has a few methods that allow you to change the output location of the spoken text, such as outputting to a wave file, as listed in Table 9-1.

Table 9-1. *Synthesizer Output Methods*

Method	Description
SetOutputToNull	No output
SetOutputToDefaultAudioDevice	Plays synthesized speech over the user's speakers or headphones
SetOutputToWavFile	Saves the synthesized speech to a wave file

You can change the output type only before you start speaking. For example, you could speak text to the default audio device and then speak text to a wave file as follows:

```
SpeechSynthesizer speechSynthesizer = new SpeechSynthesizer();
speechSynthesizer.SetOutputToDefaultAudioDevice();
speechSynthesizer.Speak("Hello!");

speechSynthesizer.SetOutputToWaveFile(@"C:\hello.wav");
speechSynthesizer.Speak("Hello!");
```

Starting Speech

To get your application to actually start speaking, you need to decide which method you want to use: Speak or SpeakAsync. The Speak method is a blocking method, meaning nothing else in your application can occur while it is speaking. The SpeakAsync method is nonblocking and allows the user to interact with the rest of your application while it speaks. Consider the following form load event:

```
private void frmMain_Load(object sender, EventArgs e)
{
    SpeechSynthesizer speechSynthesizer = new SpeechSynthesizer();
    speechSynthesizer.Speak("Hello World!");
}
```

If you wanted the form to load completely while also speaking, you would use the SpeakAsync method instead.

```
private void frmMain_Load(object sender, EventArgs e)
{
    speechSynthesizer.SpeakAsync("Hello World!");
}
```

With the SpeakAsync method, you can get notified when the SpeakAsync event completes by creating a delegate and an event handler. Here is an example:

```
speechSynthesizer.SpeakCompleted += new
EventHandler<SpeakCompletedEventArgs>(
speechSynthesizer_SpeakCompleted);

private void speechSynthesizer_SpeakCompleted(object sender,
SpeakCompletedEventArgs e)
{
    //Do Completed Events
}
```

Building Prompts

Up to now, you've seen how to get the speech synthesizer to speak a simple string. But if you need more, you can use the PromptBuilder class to build larger, more complex phrases.

A good example of using the PromptBuilder is for a phrase that you need to build from multiple pieces of information, such as saying a simple string, followed by playing an audio recording, and then speaking a string with a hint. Here is an example:

```
PromptBuilder promptBuilder = new PromptBuilder();
promptBuilder.AppendText("Hello World.");
promptBuilder.AppendAudio(new Uri(@"C:\greeting.wav"),
"My name is Lili. My name is spelled");
promptBuilder.AppendTextWithHint("lili", SayAs.SpellOut);

speechSynthesizer.Speak(pb);
```

While you can create complex prompts in-line, SAPI 5.3 now supports SSML, which was covered in Chapter 3. The benefit of using SSML is that you can make changes to the prompts without recompiling, so it is great for static prompts. Consider the following SSML:

```
<speak version="1.0" xmlns="http://www.w3.org/2001/10/synthesis" xml:lang="en-US">

  <emphasis level="strong">Hello</emphasis> World!
  Take a deep breath <break strength="strong"/>

  <!--Rate-->
  Say it a little <prosody rate="x-slow">slower</prosody>

  <!--Volume-->
  Say it a little <prosody volume='x-loud'>louder</prosody>

</speak>
```

You can use the AppendSSML method of the PromptBuilder to reference this SSML file using either the physical or relative path of the file.

```
PromptBuilder promptBuilder = new PromptBuilder();
promptBuilder.AppendSsml (@"C:\example.ssml");
speechSynthesizer.Speak(pb);
```

Using the Speech Recognition API

The Speech.Recognition namespace contains the API you can use to add speech recognition to your application. Adding speech recognition involves three main steps: choose which recognizer to use, create the grammar, and decide what to do with the results.

Choosing a Recognizer

The Speech.Recognition API provides two ways to do speech recognition:

Shared recognizer. The shared recognizer should be your first choice when creating a custom speech recognition application because it relies on the shared process that Windows Vista uses for speech recognition. This gives you access to the Speech toolbar. The limitation is that you can't use any of the keywords that Vista uses, such as mousegrid, start, file, close, and so on, as these grammars are already active. The previous examples in this chapter use the shared recognizer.

In-process recognizer. The in-process recognizer allows you to maintain a separate state from the built-in recognizer that Vista uses. The advantages are that you can use any grammar you want, even keywords that Vista uses, and that the user doesn't need to start the recognizer via the Vista Speech toolbar. The disadvantage is the user cannot turn off speech recognition at the operating system level. Users might expect that if they turn off speech recognition in Vista, your application will also stop doing any speech recognition.

Whichever recognizer you choose, you first need to create an instance of the recognizer. Create a shared recognizer instance like this:

```
SpeechRecognizer sharedRecognizer = new SpeechRecognizer();
```

Or created an in-process recognizer instance like this:

```
SpeechRecognitionEngine inprocessRecognizer = new SpeechRecognitionEngine();
```

Creating Grammar

After you have created an instance of your speech recognizer, you need to decide which grammar to implement and how you want to implement it. SAPI 5.3 supports SRGS XML-formatted grammar and semantic interpretation. This means that you have many of the same grammar options as you have with Speech Server. Your choices are as follows:

- Use SRGS XML-formatted grammar

- Use the `GrammarBuilder`

- Create a custom grammar class

If your grammar is going to be static—meaning it's not going to change often—you can use the SRGS XML-formatted grammar. This is the equivalent of using the Grammar Editor in OCS 2007 Speech Server, as described in Chapter 2.

■**Tip** You can create your grammar using the Grammar Editor in Speech Server, as it produces SRGS XML-formatted grammar.

If your grammar is going to be dynamic—meaning you are going to build the values at runtime—you have two choices: use the `GrammarBuilder` or create a custom SRGS grammar class. If the grammar is small, you can use the `GrammarBuilder`. However, if the grammar is going to be large or unpredictable, such as reading values from a database, it's best to create a custom SRGS grammar class.

Using SRGS XML-Formatted Grammar

Let's consider the following XML-formatted grammar, which should look very familiar:

```
<grammar>
    <rule id="Rule1" scope="public">
        <one-of>
            <item>
                <one-of>
                    <item>purple</item>
                    <item>blue</item>
                </one-of>
                <tag>$._value = "blue"</tag>
```

```
                    </item>
                    <item>
                        <one-of>
                                <item>gray</item>
                                <item>white</item>
                        </one-of>
                         <tag>$._value = "white"</tag>
                </item>
                <item>
                      <one-of>
                              <item>maroon</item>
                              <item>red</item>
                        </one-of>
                        <tag>$._value = "red"</tag>
                </item>
            </one-of>
      </rule>
</grammar>
```

As I mentioned, this is the same type of grammar that is supported by OCS 2007 Speech Server. SAPI 5.3 fully supports SRGS XML-formatted grammar, including semantics interpretation. For example, the preceding example groups colors like white and gray. If the user says either one of these colors, the semantic results will return "white," as indicated by the script tag, `<tag>$._value = "white"</tag>`.

Once you have the grammar created, you can use the `LoadGrammar` method of your recognizer object.

```
SpeechRecognizer sharedRecognizer = new SpeechRecognizer();
Grammar grammar = new Grammar(@"C:\grammar.grxml", "colors");
sharedRecognizer.LoadGrammar(grammar);
```

You have two options to load grammar into your recognizer: `Load` or `LoadAsync`. The `LoadAsync` method loads the grammar asynchronously, allowing you to perform other events in your applications while it loads.

You can also unload your grammar with one of two methods: `UnloadGrammar` or `UnloadAllGrammars`. With `UnloadGrammar`, you must specify which grammar object to unload. `UnloadAllGrammars` unloads every grammar.

Using the GrammarBuilder

While SRGS XML-formatted grammar is great for static grammar, you may need to create in-line grammar during runtime. For that, you can use the `GrammarBuilder`, as in the following example.

```
Choices choices = new Choices();
choices.Add("red");
choices.Add("blue");
choices.Add("white");
```

```
GrammarBuilder grammarBuilder = new GrammarBuilder(choices);
Grammar grammar = new Grammar(grammarBuilder);
sharedRecognizer.LoadGrammar(grammarBuilder);
```

This example demonstrates how to create a simple keyword grammar using the Choices class. You can also create complex phrases. Consider the following code.

```
GrammarBuilder grammarBuilder = new GrammarBuilder();
grammarBuilder.Append("large");
grammarBuilder.Append("white");
grammarBuilder.Append("bird");

Grammar grammar = new Grammar(grammarBuilder);
sharedRecognizer.LoadGrammar(grammar);
```

At first glance, you might assume that this is looking for "large," "white," or "bird" separately, but that isn't the case. It is actually looking for the whole phrase "large white bird." If you simply said "large," it would not be accepted as a recognized phrase.

Using the GrammarBuilder and Choices classes, you can create a more complex grammar that accepts multiple keywords that make up a phrase, as in this example:

```
Choices sizes = new Choices();
sizes.Add("small");
sizes.Add("medium");
sizes.Add("large");

Choices colors = new Choices();
colors.Add("red");
colors.Add("white");
colors.Add("blue");

Choices animals = new Choices();
animals.Add("dog");
animals.Add("cat");
animals.Add("bird");

GrammarBuilder grammarBuilder = new GrammarBuilder();
grammarBuilder.Append(sizes);
grammarBuilder.Append(colors);
grammarBuilder.Append(animals);

Grammar grammar = new Grammar(grammarBuilder);
sharedRecognizer.LoadGrammar(grammarBuilder);
```

This code will accept a phrase made up of any word from each choice. So "small white dog" or "large red cat" would both be recognized.

Creating a Custom SRGS Grammar Class

You can also create a custom SRGS class. You might use this method if you need a more complex grammar, such as one created from a database. Consider the following class.

```
using System;
using System.Collections.Generic;
using System.Text;
using System.Speech.Recognition.SrgsGrammar;

class SrgsGrammar : SrgsDocument
{
    private static string[] _colors = new string[] {"red", "white", "blue"};

    public SrgsGrammar(): base(GrammarRule())
    {

    }

    private static SrgsRule GrammarRule()
    {
        //Create new rule
        SrgsRule rule = new SrgsRule("Color");
        //Create a oneof list
        SrgsOneOf choices = new SrgsOneOf();

        //Get items to add to oneof list
        foreach (string color in _colors)
        {
            SrgsItem grammarItem = new SrgsItem(color);
            choices.Add(grammarItem);
        }

        //Add list to rule
        rule.Add(choices);

        //Return rule
        return rule;
    }
}
```

Notice that it inherits from `Speech.Recognition.SrgsGrammar.SrgsDocument`, which calls the static method `GrammarRule` in the constructor: `public SrgsGrammar(): base(GrammarRule())`

The `GrammarRule` method creates a grammar rule based on the static string array `colors`: `private static string[] _colors = new string[] {"red", "white", "blue"}`. This could easily be changed to use a data reader instead, so that it could pull information from a database.

It is probably easiest to think of creating this type of grammar in almost the same fashion as you would a static SRGS grammar document. For example, the equivalent GRXML would look like the following:

```
<grammar>
<rule id="Colors" scope="public">
    <one-of>
            <item>red</item>
      <item>white</item>
            <item>blue</item>
    </one-of>
  </rule>
</grammar>
```

You first create a rule using the `<rule>` element and assign it a name. Next, you create a list by using the `<one-of>` element. Finally, add items to the list using the `<item>` element. Creating the grammar dynamically is very similar. You first create the rule and assign it a name:

```
SrgsRule rule = new SrgsRule("Colors");
```

Next, you define a list object:

```
SrgsOneOf choices = new SrgsOneOf();
```

Finally, you add an item to the list for each of the valid responses:

```
foreach (string color in _colors)
{
    SrgsItem grammarItem = new SrgsItem(color);
    choices.Add(grammarItem);
}
```

You can now load this grammar on your recognizer using the `LoadGrammar` method:

```
colorGrammar colors = new colorGrammar();
sharedRecognizer.LoadGrammar(colors);
```

Getting Recognizer Results

For both the shared recognizer and the in-process recognizer, you can get the results via handled events.

Handling Recognizer Events

Three main events help you get recognition results:

- `SpeechDetected`: Fires when the recognizer encounters any speech, whether or not it matches grammar.

- `SpeechRecognized`: Fires if the speech matches any active grammar.

- `SpeechRecognitionRejected`: Fires if the speech doesn't match any active grammars.

Let's look at how you can handle each of these events:

```
SpeechRecognizer sharedRecognizer = new SpeechRecognizer();

sharedRecognizer.SpeechDetected += new
EventHandler<SpeechDetectedEventArgs>(sharedRecognizer
_SpeechDetected);

sharedRecognizer.SpeechRecognitionRejected +=
new EventHandler<SpeechRecognitionRejectedEventArgs>(
sharedRecognizer_SpeechRecognitionRejected);

sharedRecognizer.SpeechRecognized += new EventHandler<SpeechRecognizedEventArgs>(
sharedRecognizer_SpeechRecognized);

private void sharedRecognizer_SpeechDetected(
object sender, SpeechDetectedEventArgs e)
{
    //Incoming Speech
}
private void sharedRecognizer_SpeechRecognitionRejected(
object sender, SpeechRecognitionRejectedEventArgs e)
{
     //Speech Not Recognized
}
private void sharedRecognizer_SpeechRecognized(
object sender, SpeechRecognizedEventArgs e)
{
    //Speech Recognized
}
```

Obtaining the Results

You can use the `RecognitionResult` object to obtain the actual results of the event handlers. Consider the following code,

```
RecognitionResult results = new RecognitionResult();

private void sharedRecognizer_SpeechRecognized(
object sender, SpeechRecognizedEventArgs e)
{
    results = e.Result;
}
```

This is a pretty straightforward method for getting the results. Let's assume that the recognizer has the following grammar:

```
<grammar>
    <rule id="Colors" scope="public">
            <one-of>
                    <item>red</item>
                    <item>white</item>
                    <item>blue</item>
            </one-of>
    </rule>
     <rule id="Sizes" scope="public">
             <one-of>
                    <item>small</item>
                    <item>medium</item>
                    <item>large</item>
             </one-of>
     </rule>
     <rule id="Animals" scope="public">
                <one-of>
                        <item>bird</item>
                        <item>cat</item>
                        <item>dog</item>
                </one-of>
     </rule>
     <rule id="Seen" scope="public">
            <ruleref uri="#Sizes" type="application/srgs+xml"/>
            <tag>$.Size = $$</tag>
            <ruleref uri="#Colors" type="application/srgs+xml"/>
            <tag>$.Color = $$</tag>
            <ruleref uri="#Animals" type="application/srgs+xml"/>
            <tag>$.Animal = $$</tag>
     </rule>
</grammar>
```

This grammar has four rules: the first three represent values of information you are seeking from the user. The Seen rule simply references each of those rules, and you place the value in a property of the SML results. So you can get the result of the phrase simply by using the Text property of the RecognitionResult object, which was set in your SpeechRecognized event. Here is an example:

```
string recognizedText = results.Text;
float confidenceValue  = results.Confidence;
```

Now because you created the grammar to assign a semantic property for each value, you can get individual recognition results along with individual confidence scores via the Semantics property. Here is an example:

```
string size = results.Semantics["Size"].Value.ToString();
float sizeConfidence = results.Semantics["Size"].Confidence;

string color = Results.Semantics["Color"].Value.ToString();
float colorConfidence = results.Semantics["Size"].Confidence;

string animal = Results.Semantics["Animal"].Value.ToString();
float animalConfidence = results.Semantics["Size"].Confidence;
```

Getting Alternative Results

How could you handle a grammar that accepted similar-sounding words, such as "to," "two," and "too"? Well, this is where alternates come in. The recognizers will give you a list of alternate words that might also match the grammar you specified.

To get the alternate results, you need to specify the maximum number of alternates you want to obtain. You could specify a maximum alternate count of four, for example, by setting the MaxAlternates property of the recognizer as follows:

```
sharedRecognizer.MaxAlternates = 4;
```

For example, suppose you had the following grammar.

```
<rule id="altWords" scope="public">
    <one-of>
      <item>to</item>
            <item>too</item>
      <item>two</item>
    </one-of>
  </rule>
</grammar>
```

Even though you have set MaxAlternates to 4, you will get a list of three, because there are only three items defined in the grammar. The alternates returned will always be a subset of the possible grammar.

Once you have set the MaxAlternates property, in your SpeechRecognized event handler, you can get the list of alternates from the e.Result.Alternates property.

```
private void sharedRecognizer_SpeechRecognized(
object sender, SpeechRecognizedEventArgs e)
{

    //Add Alternatives to List
    foreach (RecognizedPhrase rp in e.Result.Alternates)
    {
        Debug.WriteLine(rp.Text);
    }
}
```

Accessing the Speech Toolbar

If you are using the shared recognizer, `SpeechRecognizer`, you can send results to the Windows Vista Speech toolbar, allowing users to visually confirm what they said. You can also send messages when users say something your application doesn't recognize, as in this example:

```
private void sharedRecognizer_SpeechRecognitionRejected(object
 sender, SpeechRecognitionRejectedEventArgs e)
{
    SpeechUI.SendTextFeedback(e.Result, "Didn't
recognize what you said", false);

}
```

This would display the message "Didn't recognize what you said" in the Speech toolbar every time the `SpeechRecognitionReject` event fired.

You can add the recognized text to the `SpeechRecognized` event, so that the user can visually see what was recognized:

```
private void sharedRecognizer_SpeechRecognized(object
sender, SpeechRecognizedEventArgs e)
{
    SpeechUI.SendTextFeedback(e.Result, e.Result.Text, true);
}
```

The first parameter is the actual recognition results, and the second parameter is the text that you want to appear in the Speech toolbar itself—in this case, just the recognized text. The third parameter allows you to tell the Speech toolbar whether the recognition results were successful. The Speech toolbar plays a different sound to the user depending on whether or not the speech was recognized. In the `SpeechRecognized` event, set this parameter to `true`, and in the `SpeechRecognitionRejected` event, set it to `false`.

Conclusion

This chapter has covered the basics of creating a speech application for Windows Vista. As you have seen, this is very similar to creating a speech application for OCS 2007 Speech Server, as they both support the same W3C standards.

The Windows Vista built-in speech recognition and the new .NET 3.0 SAPI reflect the growing importance of speech recognition in general becoming a common part of our everyday lives. With the knowledge you've gained in this book, you can build IVR applications that work efficiently and give users good experiences.

Index

You Need the Companion eBook

Your purchase of this book entitles you to buy the companion PDF-version eBook for only $10. Take the weightless companion with you anywhere.

We believe this Apress title will prove so indispensable that you'll want to carry it with you everywhere, which is why we are offering the companion eBook (in PDF format) for $10 to customers who purchase this book now. Convenient and fully searchable, the PDF version of any content-rich, page-heavy Apress book makes a valuable addition to your programming library. You can easily find and copy code—or perform examples by quickly toggling between instructions and the application. Even simultaneously tackling a donut, diet soda, and complex code becomes simplified with hands-free eBooks!

Once you purchase your book, getting the $10 companion eBook is simple:

❶ Visit **www.apress.com/promo/tendollars/**.

❷ Complete a basic registration form to receive a randomly generated question about this title.

❸ Answer the question correctly in 60 seconds, and you will receive a promotional code to redeem for the $10.00 eBook.

THE EXPERT'S VOICE™

2855 TELEGRAPH AVENUE │ SUITE 600 │ BERKELEY, CA 94705

Offer valid through 9/25/07.